Socialists   ...list
Recession ...   F
K

Raphie De Santos, Michel Husson, Claudio Katz,
Ernest Mandel & others

Resistance Books

Socialist Resistance would be glad to have readers' opinions of this book, its design and translations, and any suggestions you may have for future publications or wider distribution.

Socialist Resistance books are available at special quantity discounts to educational and non-profit organisations, and to bookstores.

To contact us, please write to:

Resistance Books,
PO Box 1109,
London N4 2UU,
Britain

contact@socialistresistance.org
visit: www.socialistresistance.org

Published by *Socialist Resistance*, March 2009

Printed in Britain by Lightning Source

ISBN: 978-0-902869-84-4
EAN: 9780902869844

C O N T E N T S

Notes On The Contributors

Phil Hearse is a member of the Socialist Resistance editorial board and is a longstanding supporter of the Fourth International.

François Sabado is a member of the Executive Bureau of the Fourth International and of the National Leadership of the Revolutionary Communist League (LCR, French section of the Fourth International).

Andy Kilminster teaches Economics at Oxford Brookes University, is editor of `Debatte: Journal of Contemporary Central and Eastern Europe'* and a supporter of Socialist Resistance and the Fourth International.

Sean Thompson is a Marxist and ecosocialist. He is a member of the Green Party and a contributor to Socialist Resistance.

Raphie de Santos is a member of the Scottish Socialist Party and a supporter of the Fourth International. He has been a guest lecturer on derivatives and financial markets at Harvard and New York universities and the London School of Economics and has spoken at the annual Nobel Foundation conference in Stockholm.

Claudio Katz is an economist, and researcher. He is a Fellow at the International Institute for Research and Education, in Amsterdam, and a teacher at the University of Buenos Aires. Katz is involved in the Argentine network 'Economistas de Izquierda' (Economists of the Left).

Joel Geier is an associate editor of *International Socialist Review*, a bimonthly journal of revolutionary Marxism published by the International Socialist Organisation in the USA.

Michel Husson is an economist, in charge of employment at the Institut de recherches economiques et sociales (IRES) in Paris. He is member of the Fondation Copernic, a left-wing think tank, and of the Scientific Council of ATTAC. He has just published *Un pur capitalisme*, Éditions Page Deux, Lausanne.

François Chesnais is a member of the Scientific Council of ATTAC-France and the author of several books and numerous articles on economics.

John Bellamy Foster is an editor of Monthly Review. He is a professor in sociology at the University of Oregon. He is the author of numerous works on ecology and Marxism, including *Marx's Ecology* (2000) and *Ecology Against Capitalism*, 2002

Paul Le Blanc is the author of many books, including *A Short History of the U.S. Working Class* (Humanity Books, 1999) and *Black Liberation and the American Dream* (Humanity Books 2003), and is an internationally known and respected historian of the life and works of Rosa Luxemburg.

Ernest Mandel was a Marxist economist and political theorist, and a longstanding leader of the Fourth International. He died in 1995.

Alan Thornett was a leading activist in the car industry for many years and is a leading member of the ISG, British Section of the Fourth International, and sits on the Executive Committee of Respect.

6

Introduction: The Decline And Fall Of Neoliberal Globalisation

Phil Hearse

The new millennium was heralded in November 1999 by giant demonstrations outside the meeting of the World Trade Organisation in Seattle, which dramatised protests against the super-exploitation imposed on workers in the first and third worlds by neoliberal globalisation. In the eight years since then the real character of neoliberalism – of ultra-mobile capital, outsourcing, privatisation and vastly increasing inequality - has become very clear.

As the present economic crisis broke the UN announced that the number of people undernourished in the world had crossed the one billion mark. Two billion people – one third of the world's population - live on no more than a few dollars a day. A similar number have no access to proper sanitation or clean water. These figures in themselves would be enough to proclaim a huge crisis of human civilisation. But on top of that we have had since the start of the new century rampant imperialist militarism in Iraq and Afghanistan, responsible for hundreds of thousands of deaths and of course a tremendous worsening of the ecological crisis – so much so that many experts believe that within a few decades global warming will inflict huge damage on numerous countries.

As things stand it seems that average world temperatures will rise by between 2% and 4% in the next 50 years. The 2006 Stern report pointed out that with world temperatures on course to rise by two to three degrees in 50 years, rainfall could be catastrophically reduced in some of the world's poorest countries, while others grapple with floods from melting glaciers. The result could be the largest migration of refugees in history. As François Chesnais points out in his article in this volume, the climate crisis will combine with the crisis of capital.

Now, to add insult to injury in the world's woes comes the credit crunch itself the precursor of a giant economic slump, not just inevitable but actually underway. It is thus very timely the Socialist Resistance books should now be publishing this volume that attempts not to only to describe the present crisis, but also to understand its causes and debate socialist solutions.

Causes of the crisis

In the mainstream media and among right-wing politicians the truth of this slump is simply not being discussed. Thus the irresponsible lending of bankers is blamed and bankers pilloried – as was Lehman Brothers boss Richard Fuld in front of a Congressional sub-committee in October 2008. It seems that Fuld himself is likely to be prosecuted by US authorities.

Otherwise, the cause is put down to irresponsible consumption by a whole generation who have, allegedly, been partying and living comfortable well-pensioned lives for decades and who must now pay the price for their feck-lessness – and indeed pass that price on to generations to come. Of course the banks lent recklessly. But the elephant in the room is never addressed – the fact that the present slump was deeply embedded in the DNA of ne-oliberal globalisation at birth and is an inevitable consequence of central features of the neoliberal 'regime of accumulation'. How so?

The basic facts of the matter are blindingly simple to comprehend, unlike the thousands of column inches of mumbo-jumbo on the crisis that appear in the mainstream press. Neoliberal globalisation has an inbuilt tendency towards *deflation* (an accentuation of basic features of the capitalist sys-tem). As explained by Sean Thompson in his article in this volume, this has been caused by historic defeats of the international workers movement, fi-nancialisation and above all international outsourcing and relocation to sites of cheap labour. This has undermined union bargaining power, held down wage levels and repressed workers' purchasing power - contrary to numerous myths and often appearances. So the only way to ensure contin-uous economic growth and ever-greater capital accumulation was to pump endless credit into the system in the form of historically high levels of household and company debt. It is the enormous mountain of debt that has underpinned the lifestyles of the comfortable middle classes and indeed regularly employed workers.

The scale of this debt mountain is stupendous. In 1997 the debt held by in-dividuals in the UK was £570 billion. Ten years later it was £1,511.7 billion, an increase of 165%. In the same period personal debt in the United States grew from £5,547.1 billion to $14, 375 billion. In the UK personal debt had increased from 102% of personal income to 173% of personal income; in the US the figure went from 93% to 139%. These are staggering figures.

The worsening of the underlying relative decline in workers purchasing power has especially been the case since privatisation of the public utilities. Gas, electricity and water (together with oil) have become cash cows for multinational corporations and the banks who lend them money, hoovering up vast swathes of the disposable income of workers and the middle class. This together with high prices generally (especially in the UK) meant that even apparently affluent families have been unable to save money; their only real assets have been their houses, themselves financed by colossal borrowing; the collapse of the housing market is now doing away with even the illusion of affluence for millions.

That such huge levels of debt could be tolerated and its fragility not immediately obvious has been due to the enormous inflation of the value of assets, mainly housing. The millions borrowing on credit cards or directly from banks, borrowed (whether they realised it or not) against the guarantee of their house or apartment. There is growing evidence that this housing bubble was welcomed or even actively sponsored by governments, not least in the US and UK, precisely because of the 'wealth effect' that it created. But that wealth effect has now been shattered by the realisation that much of that debt is irrecoverable and that many of the banks' loans (put down in their balance sheets as 'assets') are worthless.

Neoliberal globalisation has been a system of smoke and mirrors where the basic instability and unsustainability of the whole system has been covered up by the credit bubble. Now the bubble has burst, the consequences will be terrible for countless millions.

Debt-fuelled growth boosts inequality
This turn of events really undermines the arguments of those who like ex-British Prime Minister John Major who says "we're all middle class now" or indeed people on the left who regard the whole of the working class in the North as a privileged layer on a world scale. When American workers are losing their jobs at a rate of half a million a month – in a country with a very limited welfare system – the realities of wealth and power in Western capitalism are about to be demonstrated with some force.

But the debt-fuelled engines of globalised neoliberalism did enable a certain level of consumption and comfort for most Western workers, that is for sure. Nonetheless it has been a system of deepening inequality for at least two decades as the share of wages and salaries in national economies has everywhere stagnated or declined and as the wealthy became fabulously wealthy and went into conspicuous consumption overdrive.

A section of the working class not in regular employment – especially, but not only, single mothers in part-time jobs and older industrial workers whose companies have closed and who will never work again - has been pushed out of any substantial share in consumption. These are the millions living in what the British call 'sink estates', housing projects with huge levels of unemployment, poverty, drug abuse and crime.

Even for the regularly employed workers the last two decades have not been a period of unalloyed hedonism. The brake on the share of wages in the national economy has meant that the idyll of the 1950s – the nuclear family with just one wage earner – has largely disappeared. In most families, especially those with children, a second job has been essential to maintain living standards.

Work has become longer and harder everywhere, as 'flexibility' and the target-driven regimes imposed from the teachings of the American human resource departments have worsened the experience of work and made many jobs virtually undoable, at least to the standards expected by employers. One small but topical example is the demand of the British Post Office that postal delivery workers maintain a regular four mph walking rate, literally impossible with heavy sacks, hills to climb, stairs to go up in apartment blocks and biting dogs to be evaded. If imposed it will result in postal workers delivering mail in their own time, which is really what happens in countless jobs – a reduction in the proportion of paid time for workers who take work home and who stay late. In the slump this will only get worse.

The consequence of the decline in the share of GDPs going to wages and salaries has of course been a tremendous over-accumulation of capital, especially in the financial sector. But much of this is now revealed as worthless, fictitious capital, and is being daily destroyed in the stock markets and by asset write-downs as this introduction is written.

The essence of neoliberal globalisation has been therefore a cheap labour regime. Contrary to those who thought that technological advance would produce a 'leisure' economy, modern capitalism is a structure for producing an ever greater number of commodities through the incorporation into international capital circuits of ever greater number of labourers on a world scale. The crazed demand for ever greater profits from multinational corporations and finance capital – which like a vast protection racket demands its cut from every sphere of economic activity – has spawned a huge increase in the production of commodities, industrial goods as well services. That's why China and other Asian countries have supplied huge amounts of cheap labour; indeed China really is the workshop of the world.

But this huge mountain of commodities is utterly irrational and unsustainable. Modern capitalism creates an avalanche of new 'needs' and new commodities and is ransacking the earth's resources to produce them. Out of the crisis, as described by John Bellamy Foster in his article here, the left has to articulate an alternative which breaks with the imperative towards ever greater numbers of commodities, and focuses instead on human need.

Consequences of the Slump

The consequences of the present crisis are difficult to predict in detail precisely because the duration of the slump cannot be foretold. But virtually every commentator from left and right agrees that this will last a long time. It is difficult to see how a new long wave of economic growth in capitalism can be generated. Billionaire former financial speculator George Soros says the crisis is the end of 60 years of capitalist expansion. If he is right, then capitalism faces a huge task of going through the slump and generating new engines of growth.

Some consequences are very easy for foresee however, and they are of frightening proportions. First, obviously, unemployment will mushroom putting huge strains on welfare systems, and in countries without substantial unemployment insurance, it will lead to immiseration with huge numbers losing their houses and a sharp rise in homelessness. We are about to see the return of the soup kitchen in advanced countries for the first time in 70 years.

Second government spending will be savagely hit with inevitable cutbacks across the board and big redundancies among public sector workers, especially in those countries like Britain where state finances have been mortgaged in the tens of billions of dollars spend to refloat the banks.

Pensions will be hit, with some pension funds just collapsing and many more losing some of their value. Many people are going to have a much poorer old age than they imagined – especially as most workers in their 50s now may unemployed will never work again.

Young people will be hit in myriad ways. As recently pointed out by Jenni Russell (Guardian 13 December 2008) the economic return of a university education – at least in Britain but probably in many other advanced countries – is now in question. It has been calculated that the overall economic gain for many in less prestigious universities in the UK could be as little as £20,000 over a lifetime – easily offset by the three years not working and not saving for a private pension, as many will now be forced to do. But many young people are just not going to find jobs, whether they went to university or not. Youth unemployment is going to skyrocket.

As poverty increases in the advanced countries, all the social problems associated with it – violence, crime, drug abuse and other anti-social behaviour – is going to sharply increase. If you want to see a model for it, go to some of the pit villages where the coalmines were closed down by Thatcher's Tory government in the 1980s – places like Grimethorpe, Hemsworth and South Kirby. These villages have never recovered, they are drab and poor; crime and drug abuse is rampant, and large numbers of young people just leave. The problem is that you can't leave a whole economy, except to emigrate. And then, where would you go to avoid a worldwide slump? There may seem to be some better options, but nowhere is safe from the monster at the door.

Even for many of those in work the future is going to become much more difficult; many low-paid workers are going to have to find a second or even a third job to make ends meet. Work regimes will become tougher in many firms when employers know there are thousands of unemployed out there willing to take jobs with lower pay and worse conditions.

If the crisis now seems most acute in Britain and the USA and other advanced countries, its effects on the third world are going to be tremendous. In the first place economic growth in China and India will slow down rapidly with hundreds of thousands losing their jobs. Debts levels in many third world countries are likely to rise, and Western governments will become even less committed to helping the poorer countries though international aid.

Many in the United States may be breathing a sigh of relief because of the election of Barrack Obama as president, which will do wonders for America's international image, but really the credit crunch and the slump, which started in the US after all, is going to be a hard knock against that country's dominant international position. As explained in the article by François Sabado, the period since the turn of the century has been a disaster for American capitalism; first the catastrophe in Iraq and of the Bush government in general, and now an economic collapse that has completely undermined neoliberalism's 'Washington Consensus'. The New *American* Century that the likes of Bush, Cheney, Wolfowitz and Rumsfeld thought they were creating is turning out to be anything but. Of course the United States remains the world's largest economy and easily most powerful country militarily. But its dominance is now visibly declining in a way that seemed improbable seven or eight years ago. Certainly the economic crisis – like its predecessors – will rearrange the international division of labour and with it the world political pecking order, but in ways that cannot yet be exactly foretold.

Ideological and political consequences: repoliticisation

The economic crisis combined with looming ecological disaster is the biggest ideological blow to capitalism since World War 2. Marx's theory of crisis has been utterly confirmed, especially the notion of the trend towards the over-accumulation of capital and thus towards a secular decline in the rate of profit. Francis Fukuyama's notion of the 'end of history' looks plain stupid now, and as Neil Clark points out in his recent article *Socialism's Comeback* (New Statesman 4 December), the same author's prediction of the end of socialism looks a bit stupid too. Not only in Latin America but also in many places in Europe the left appears to be on the up. But so far this is mainly small shoots, relatively small parties with some electoral purchase, although in Germany and the Netherlands left-wing parties (the Left Party and the Socialist Party respectively) are especially significant. Nor should we ignore the spectacular emergence of the New Anti-Capitalist Party in France, which has enormous potential to challenge the right-wing 'Socialist' party from the left.

The worker and student upsurge that broke out in Greece in December 2008 is a harbinger of things to come. It is absolutely impossible to have the degree of economic crisis now on the agenda, with such terrible social consequences, without enormous outbreaks of social discontent. This creates enormous opportunities for the left, but to really capitalise politically it is necessary to create the broadest unity of socialist and anti-capitalist forces that can stop the political fruits of economic slump falling into the hands of the right and even the ultra-right.

In the process of reinforcing the strength of the workers movement, and the political and ecological left, a giant battle of ideas is now opening up. A glance at the Blogosphere shows how this is true. Economic crisis is leading to a significant repoliticisation as normally apathetic and non-political people are forced to stare the crisis in the face. Many young people who never bothered with politics can now be brought into the ambit of the left and brought to see that the mindless celebrity culture of commodity society is empty and devoid of human values.

The ideologues of capitalism are on the defensive. But the Marxist explanation of the crisis has to be hammered home. Who caused this crisis? Why did it occur? What is it in capitalism that leads to the globalisation of poverty while a tiny elite become mega-wealthy? And what are possible alternatives? This book is a signal contribution to making those arguments.

The global justice movement greeted the new millennium by chanting, "another world is possible". Fortunately this is true. But only if we fight for it.

December 2008

Taking The Measure Of The Crisis

François Sabado

From the beginning of the "subprime" crisis of September 2007, we noted that this banking and financial crisis was the forerunner to a total economic crisis, that marked a historical turning point in the world economy and situation. Today, for all commentators, the historical bench mark for estimating the extent of the crisis is "the crisis of 1929", with differences... but it is of this breadth. In fact, this crisis of 2007-2008, is at the crossroads of several historical changes.

Generalized systemic crisis

A new depression of the recessionary long wave, which started at the end of the 1960s, has, combined with the world ecological crisis, reached the "historical limits" of the capitalist system. Immanuel Wallerstein is correct to locate this crisis at the crossroads of a systemic crisis and a historical phase of capitalist decline which started nearly forty years ago, but we cannot speak, as he does, of an "end of capitalism", because there is no "situation without exit for capitalism"... until its overthrow. This crisis is not a crisis of short cycle, an economic crisis, it is a structural crisis. It illustrates well the historical limits of the capitalist system. For the first time in history this system covers the whole planet: there is a world market of generalized commodity production and a world market in labour power. No sector of the economy escapes not only domination but integration into the capitalist system. And this extension/generalization of capitalism occurs in a world economy marked by a recessionary wave, which has lasted for nearly 40 years. It is a system where "production for production" runs up against the limits of the solvent demand of millions of employees, peasants, and workers, and where its logic of search for capitalist profit rather than the satisfaction of the social needs of the peoples leads to ever stronger crises of over accumulation of capital and overproduction of goods. The explosion of fictitious capital, of a financialisation of the world economy, a generalized debt can up to a certain point push the limits of the system, defer the reckoning, but sooner or later its major contradictions lead to crises.

They succeed each other, at increasingly close intervals. Six crises in fifteen years: the Mexican crisis in 1994, the Asian crisis in 1997, the Russian crisis in 1998, the Argentine crisis in 2001, the Internet bubble crisis in 2001, the subprime crisis in 2007... The current crisis is qualitatively more important because it is no longer the periphery but the centre of the capitalist system which is affected. More importantly, something new in history is the conjunction of an economic crisis with multiple dimensions like the food crisis, that of raw materials and a major ecological crisis in which global warming is one of the most serious dimensions. The ecological crisis will worsen because it combines with a capitalism in crisis. "Green capitalism" is the response of the dominant classes to this crisis. But the logic of the search for profit above all else combined with the capitalist mode of management and the destruction of the public services can only lead to new catastrophes as in New Orleans or in poorer countries. From this point of view, you do not have to be a catastrophist to envisage catastrophes...

I do not know if we are or are not at the end of the recessionary long wave that started at the beginning of the years 1970, but in any case we are in a systemic generalized crisis ... A crisis which will last. Because to exit from the recessionary wave factors exogenous to economic logic are needed, in general political factors, wars and/or revolutions... These big breaks are not yet on the agenda, immediately, this will last, will get worse and while waiting, the cost of capitalist domination is likely to be ever higher, with increasingly significant recurrent crises, situations of stagnation and economic and social degradation, ecological or human disasters, in particular for the poorest countries and people. The productivist choices of a capitalist economy in crisis, with recession, devalorization of capital, reduction of public budgets, will also worsen the world ecological crisis.

Exhaustion of the neoliberal model of accumulation

This historical change is expressed in the crisis and exhaustion of the global neoliberal model of accumulation, which has been exploded by the US economy. The origin of this crisis is the Washington consensus, a series of defeats and social setbacks of the 1980s and the early 1990s, a clear degradation of the overall relation of forces between the classes to the detriment of the world of labour. There has been a considerable fall in real wages and the share of wages in wealth produced, generalized deregulation, privatisations of the public services. Between 1980 and 2006 the share of wages went from 67% to 57% of wealth produced in the majority of the fifteen OECD countries. It thus lost 10 points and the share of profits increased by the same amount. According to the International Labour Organisation (ILO) in its 2008 "World of Work Report" "The largest decline in the share of wages in GDP took place in Latin America and the Caribbean (-13 points), followed by Asia and the Pacific (-10 points) and the Advanced Economies (-9 points)". It is an "exceptionally low level by historical standards", according to Alan Greenspan, former director of the US Federal Bank.

Profits thus increased considerably but they were not reinvested in production, they went where there were more "profits", namely the financial markets. This logical mechanism led to a durable fall in investment: in 2005, for the United States, Europe and Japan the rate of profit increased by 5.5% and the rate of investment by only 2%. This mass of profits not reinvested in production flooded the financial markets: in the USA, in 2005, financial investment increased by 21% and financial profits by 150%. In 2006, at the apogee of the financial markets, the transactions on these markets represented 50 times the amount of the gross domestic product (GDP) of all the countries of the world! Whereas world GDP rose to 45,000 billion dollars, transactions rose to the astronomical sum of 2,100,000 billion dollars. These differences between wages and profits as between profits and investments were thus filled by the explosion of finance, the luxury goods industry and the search for new markets in China and in the ex-eastern bloc countries. In the United States, generalized debt substituted for the fall in wages: household debt went from 62% of disposable income in 1975 to 127% in 2006. And the trade deficit - 700 billion in 2008 - was financed by the investments of Chinese capital or "sovereign" funds, which replaced the decline of US industry... of which a good part relocated to Asia.

This approach to the crisis is important because it does not counterpose a "financial capitalism" predatory on the economy to a healthy "entrepreneurial" capitalism. It is the internal logic of capitalism, which seeks maximum profit, punctures wages and leads financial capital (which, for decades, already amounts to the merger of industrial and banking capital) into ever more speculation.

This model is today exhausted. The billions of the Paulson Plan have contained the banking and financial crisis... but until when? We will know only in several months the breadth of "toxic" products throughout US and world banking structures, especially after the last modifications of the Paulson plan, which consist in leaving the "toxic" credits on the banking markets. The Stock Exchanges have broken down: down by 50% on the main markets, or 25,000 billion losses in stock exchange capitalization. The injection of thousands of billions into the banks and the fall in interest rates has not restarted the economic machine. The hypothesis of an acceleration of the fall of the British pound can lead to a situation where Great Britain cannot continue to borrow and thus refund its debt. The Icelandic bankruptcy is today the nightmare of the dominant classes in the world. The economic deceleration, recorded before the financial crisis, and maintaining the contraction of credit (the "credit crunch"), transforms the crisis into generalized economic recession: lower activity, lower consumption, restructuring, and dismissals. Unemployment is rising in all the advanced capitalist countries. The International Monetary Fund (IMF) envisages for 2009 world growth of around 3%, even less, which would pan out in the form of growth of 0% in the United States and in Europe and 6% in the rest of the world.

It estimates the number of unemployed at 25 million. In the United States nearly 1.2 million jobs have been destroyed since the beginning of the year, including 240,000 in October alone. The cars sector has broken down. General Motors and Ford require public funds to start again! Thousands of dismissals are envisaged at Renault, Volvo, Seat as well as among equipment suppliers and subcontractors.

We referred previously to the crisis of 1929: there are many common points in the extent of the current crisis but also great differences. The first is that, fortified by experience, states and the governments have intervened to contain it. The second – as we have already indicated, and we cannot measure all its consequences - is the interpenetration of the national economies in a globalized world capitalist economy. This internationalization amplifies the crisis. The global commodity economy has penetrated all the sectors of the economy, the rural world, the countries of the ex-third - world and, because of the restoration of capitalism, what was known as the "second world" (the ex-USSR and its "bloc", China, Indo-China). The shock waves of the crisis are global. But this "internationalization" can also absorb the shock and defer its effects. It is within this framework that a question arises: can capitalist development in China and the BRIC countries (Brazil, Russia, India and China) limit the effects of the world-wide crisis?

There are already the elements of a response. The growth of the BRIC countries cannot avoid the crisis. The theory of "decoupling" between the world recession and China has not been confirmed. Growth in China and Asia is also affected by the world recession: the dependence of Chinese exports on the capacity of absorption of the US and European markets weighs directly on their economic equilibrium. The forecasts for Chinese growth have gone from 11% to 7%. It is a significant reduction. In recent months more than 3,000 factories have been closed in the area of Canton. Will this growth, even reduced, be sufficient to absorb the shock of the world-wide crisis? That raises another question: will the Chinese domestic market have developed sufficiently to restart the world economic machine? That supposes a certain level of wages, a certain development of infrastructures and public services in China. Political questions which relate to the class struggle and the political struggle inside society and the ruling party (the CPC).

But beyond the questions on the place of China in its relationship with the world economy, the crisis in the United States and in the Euros zone has only begun. We are in its first phases. The bourgeois economists are themselves in panic. Pessimistic forecasts abound. The cumulative effects of the crisis are difficult to envisage. But in the coming months, activity will be increasingly reduced, credit conditions will harden, company bankruptcies will multiply, dismissals and unemployment will explode, and consumption will be reduced. This will be also the occasion for the great capitalist groups to restructure, intensify productivity, lay off employees and lower wages. That will have effects on world trade with greater competition. The transformation of the recession into deep depression is not excluded. We cannot envisage the rhythms, the comings and goings, but the prospect for the months ahead is crisis.

Decline of the United States?

The USA remains the dominant power in the world economy and politics. But a series of factors have degraded this position. The crisis at the very heart of the Empire, the evolution of the relationship between the USA and China, and the weakening of the dollar pose a central question: is US hegemony over the world called into question... Is the political cycle opened in the 1980s-1990s, around the fall of the Berlin wall, now being closed again? The victory of Obama is a historic event. It is necessary, from this point of view, to distinguish two things, the immense significance of the victory of Obama for African-Americans, for black people and more generally the poorest, for the whole world, and the policy which he will carry out, that of the capitalist class and the US political-military machine. The latter, as well as the leadership of the Democratic Party, chose Obama because the US position was so weakened that what was needed was not only a new face but a new team which in a certain way reflect the new relationship of forces and again takes the initiative. It is too early to measure all the consequences of Obama's coming to power, but this historical event - the election of a black president in the USA - can be understood only by recording the US retreat in the world. This retreat required a significant change - this is what explains the choice of Obama rather than that of Hillary Clinton within the Democratic Party. It is also the reason for the support of the main sectors of the dominant classes for Obama. The crisis did the rest... Because for millions of Americans, to vote Obama was also to sanction the Republican right and the Wall Street elite. What will Obama's policies be? He has spoken a lot about social security, a new tax policy, new environmental policies, and withdrawal of the troops from Iraq. On withdrawal, the timescales are being diluted over time. On the economic and social questions, it is probable, in the continuity of his support for the Paulson plan that he will make wage earners and the popular classes pay for the crisis.

But beyond the US elections, there is a decline of the US share in world GDP, a decline accentuated by the current crisis (let us recall that the IMF envisages zero growth for the United States, Japan and the Euro zone in 2009). A decline expressed by the inversion of flows of capital on a world scale: the latter now come from China, the emergent countries and their "sovereign" funds towards the United States.

The weakening of the US position is also reflected when we discuss the hypothesis of accompanying the dollar as currency of reference by other currencies, the euro or the yuan. At this stage the dollar is holding up well, supported by the value of the investments made in the USA. But the crisis is likely to weaken the position of the US currency. Because, beyond these monetary discussions, there are new relations of economic forces which are emerging in the world economy. The economic crisis will also lead to a new phase of competition, which will sharpen relations between the United States, Europe and Asia. Multipolar relations are restructuring the world. The US position is weakened, in particular from the economic point of view, but let us not forget that it remains decisive on the political-military plane. Even if the United States meets sizeable obstacles in Iraq and Afghanistan and their capacities of intervention in other parts of the world are weakened (as in Latin America or on the borders of Russia), they remain hegemonic at the military level.

And they will make use of it. The sharpening of economic competition, the fight for control of the oil resources or the production of raw materials, the strategic requirements in relation to China and Russia, and the control of Latin America in relation to Cuba and the "progressive regimes" (Venezuela, Bolivia, Ecuador) can lead them into new military interventions. The Georgian crisis is a good example of US military adventurism in a context of accentuation of inter-imperialist contradictions. The situation in Iran will be, from this point of view, decisive in the months to come.

"Return of the State"?
Behind this question, there is the discussion about the assumption of a change in bourgeois economic policies, of a certain break with neoliberal policies. The dominant classes will try to respond to the historical changes produced by the crisis. Their "model" and even more, the political and ideological representation of the model, do not function any more. But at this stage, it is necessary to distinguish discourse from facts. The discourse can be very "regulationist", but to our knowledge, none of the US or European government decisions call into question the hard core of neoliberal policies. The only initiative, which deserves to be stressed, is the renationalization of pensions in Argentina, even if it also helps the Argentine authorities to manage debt servicing. As for the nationalizations of the Banks, these are partial and temporary nationalizations, which only serve to socialize the losses.

We are very far from the political relations, which had dominated, for example, the situation in the post-war period. There are, indeed, a series of official interventions, in particular on the banking level, where the State comes to the aid of the capitalist economy, or in some way "socializes the losses" but there is no return of the state... because the State never left. There were changes in the modes and functions of the state but it always remained an instrument of neoliberal policies. All the theories of Negri and Hardt on the "disappearance of states in the Empire" are again invalidated by the facts. What is true is that neoliberal policies pushed back "the social state" notably to the benefit of "the penal State", but the hard cores of the state remained and the return of "the social State" is not on the agenda.

To our knowledge there is no Keynesian revival, in the sense where priority would be given to increasing demand through wage increases or a policy of defence and extension of the public services. On the contrary the pressure on wages, employment and public services will continue.

Therefore, no "New Deal", no recovery plan in Europe, no neo-Keynesian return! The dominant classes, beyond speeches or gesticulations, remain committed to their neoliberal policies. No significant measure to "re-regulate" either. It is true that the "New Deal", like the Keynesian changes, resulted from waves of struggle in the United States at the beginning of the 1930s, or in Europe. To exit from the capitalist crisis of the period, the Second World War was needed... thus enormous changes in socio-political relations... There will be no changes without broad social struggles. That relativizes all the discourse on this "return of the State".

On a more general political level, the crisis will accentuate class polarizations and could put on the agenda, for the dominant classes, authoritarian solutions, which will take immigrants in particular for their target. Another question about inter-state relations concerns Europe. We have heard and above all seen a number of gesticulations, in particular from Sarkozy, on the revival of political Europe. We have seen many European meetings, but not the equivalent of a Paulson plan on the scale of the European Union and above all a revived competition, for example between France and Germany, on the level of operations of banking reorganization and concentration. Each state apparatus takes care of its own interests.

New configuration for the labour movement and the social movements?
Here again it is too early to analyse all the consequences of the crisis on the labour movement. The dominant classes have just undergone a political and ideological defeat. That gives new space for anti-neoliberal and anti-capitalist ideas, but this is within an overall relation of forces, which re-

mains unfavourable to the world of labour. It is necessary, now, to follow in detail what will occur at the level of social struggles in the societies affected by the crisis, in the cars sector for example. But also more broadly in all the sectors of the world of labour. In general in the first months of the crisis, there is fear, paralysis, disorganization. But then the accumulated potential, the existence of a strong public sector can give points of support to resistance to neoliberal governments of the right or the left. The existence of partial struggles against dismissals in France, like the exceptional mobilization of youth in Italy show that in countries which have until now had combative social movement, there is social resistance. The two-month strike by the mechanics of Boeing in Seattle goes in the same direction.

We said that there was no change of course for the dominant classes but nor is there any change of orientation by social democracy and its allies. The crisis will involve upheavals throughout the left and the labour movement, and the gap between the elementary defence of the living and working conditions of millions of wage earners and the adaptation by the apparatuses of social democracy and its allies to the management of liberal capitalism will deepen. There may be some oscillations to the left but at this stage social democracy will maintain its overall social liberal orientation, in relation to privatisation, wage increases and relations with financial capital.

The confirmation of the social-liberal orientation of the leaders of social democracy could deepen the internal crisis of certain social-democrats, indeed cause the emergence of left currents of left and even of small left splits as in the PS in France. This evolution is often presented a return to a traditional social democracy. Some of these currents take a step to the left but they have as reference the policy of Die Linke and in particular its policy of alliances with social democracy to govern.

The crisis also will strike the global justice movement: some currents will be radicalised while orienting towards a break with capitalism, others to centre on "realistic" proposals. This is the case of the president of ATTAC-Germany who recommends new regulations of capitalism through the governance of a "G23", i.e. a "G20" extended to the new powers of Asia and Latin America.

In the same direction, that of adaptation, it is necessary to underline the extent of the process of integration of the trade-union leaderships in the economy and the institutions, in particular in Europe. The strategy of the ETUC and the trade-union leaderships is confined, faced with the crisis, with proposals which are presented more in the form of good intentions than as concrete measures: less credit for speculation, better control of the banks, control of tax havens, reform of the rating agencies, changes in accounting standards, regulation of speculation funds. As the leaders of the European Union have just rejected any plan for economic recovery and any mechanism constraining the financial markets, the trade-union leaderships remain stuck within the neoliberal framework.

Some programmatic axes in relation to the crisis
The situation requires a "programmatic redeployment". With the crisis neoliberal policies have undergone a stinging failure. Two questions are again central, the distribution of wealth and the question of ownership. In the coming social struggles, there is a formidable point of support: thousands of billions of dollars granted to the banks... in a few hours or a few days... whereas the coffers are always empty for wage earners, the unemployed, and the people. It is necessary to reverse the tendency taken for 25 years in the distribution of wealth, to devote this wealth to employment, wages, social security, and public services and not to financial speculation. The management of the crisis, the bankruptcies of banks and companies place on the agenda the problems of organization of the economy: by whom? And at the service of who? Will we leave the fate of millions of people in the hands of the profiteers, speculators, and the creators of mass unemployment? We need public and social intervention, public ownership or the nationalization of the banks and companies under the control of the workers.

Many questions, topics and demands can pass from propaganda to agitation, from general explanations to specific proposals, to objectives of mobilization or struggle.

a) The starting point on the social emergency: defence of employment against dismissals, creation of public employment, wage increases, a halt to privatizations. It is not the workers who should pay for the crisis, it is the capitalists. "Save the people, not the banks!"... This is the approach which must be ours: to defend the working and living conditions of millions of workers who are hit by the crisis and to state this policy in concrete demands which will mobilize in unity the whole of the labour movement and the social movements.

b) On the financial and banking crisis, there are a series of documents which can be points of support: the Caracas declaration, interventions and documents from left economists in Argentina, the Beijing appeal. These documents stress demands against financial deregulation, for taxes on financial transactions and tax havens, non-payment of the debt, control of capital, the lifting of bank and commercial secrecy, the nationalization of the banks without compensation and their creation as state and para-state bodies, like the Bank of the South supported by

Cuba and the progressive regimes. We must support this programme of demands and partial rupture with imperialism and globalized financial capitalism, in particular by the expropriation of the imperialist trusts which have appropriated the natural resources and the key sectors of the economy in many countries of Eastern Europe, Africa, Asia and Latin America. This program must be counterposed to nationalization or state control of a "temporary" or "partial" kind. It must be accompanied by a questioning of the private ownership of banking, by full nationalization of the whole banking, financial and credit structure. This nationalization, so as not to revert to the "old" nationalizations, must be accompanied by the control of the workers, employees and people.

c) Facing the bankruptcy of the banking structure or the collapse of certain sectors like large companies, if it is necessary, to save employment, to make incursions into the private ownership of these large companies, we should not hesitate to go in this direction by defending their nationalization under workers' control.

In the discussion between reformists or regulationists and anti-capitalists or revolutionists there is the question of challenging property. We do not defend only a new distribution of wealth but also a change in the relations of ownership. We want to replace the private ownership of capital and the big companies by the public and social appropriation of the economy through control or management by the workers. That must impel us to restore life not only to a series of transitional measures but also to the actuality of socialism, with the taking in charge of the economy by the workers. In this socialist combat, there is an ecosocialist dimension, in connection with another economic model, based on the struggle against global warming, another organization of transport policy, energy policy, the struggle against pollution and the degradation of neighbourhoods and the countryside. It is necessary to start from the demand for durable development in the ecological area to restore some meaning to the idea of economic planning. Here too the crisis will lead to clarifications.

The implementation of this programme requires governments at the service of the workers, relying on the mobilization and self-activity of the popular classes. This battle - and it is a central battle today - implies the rejection of any participation or any support for social liberal governments managing the business of the state and the capitalist economy. More than ever, this crisis must lead us to combine the social emergency plan, measures of radical transformation of the economy and socialist solutions around the management of the economy by the workers and the people, it is the content which we give to the socialism of the 21st century

November 2008

The Economic Crisis and its Effects
Andy Kilmister

Introduction

There are three important starting points for understanding the current economic crisis[1]. Firstly, what is happening at the moment represents the break-up of the interlocking set of arrangements by which the world economy has been governed since the mid-1980s. These arrangements represented a temporary `solution' for capital to the crises which emerged a decade earlier. Secondly, the crises of the 1970s and the attempts to resolve them of the 1980s arose from a central contradiction within capitalism between the creation of profits in the sphere of production and the realisation of those profits in the sphere of circulation and exchange. Thirdly, the historically weak situation of British capital, at least that section of British capital territorially located in Britain, has left Britain especially vulnerable to the crisis.

The crisis itself has a number of dimensions but three in particular are crucial. The first is the build-up of debt, both corporate and household debt, but especially household debt. Linked with this is the likelihood of a return to international monetary instability and of the refusal of the rest of the world to fund US (and UK) trade deficits. The third factor is the effect of the ecological crisis on the world economy, which brings with it the prospect of an end to two decades of low commodity prices. However, these should be seen as medium-term developments, determining the underlying tensions within which more immediate changes take place.

A Marxist analysis of the crisis needs to be based on an analysis which can both grasp these underlying structural factors, see how these play themselves out in surface phenomena and also understand the competing strategies of capital as it attempts to manage the crisis.

The Recent Financial Turmoil

The key development of the second half of 2008 has been a dramatic worsening of the first of the dimensions mentioned above; the financial crisis based on the accumulation of debt. The main cause of this has been growing recognition that the quantity of bad debt in the system was much larger than was previously thought. This in turn led to confusion amongst the US ruling class about the way to respond to the rising number of loan defaults. Unwillingly forced to nationalise the mortgage companies Fannie Mae and Freddie Mac (largely as a result of pressure from Chinese and Japanese investors in these companies) they then switched abruptly to allowing a leading investment bank, Lehman Brothers, to fold.

This threw the banking system into a deeper crisis in three ways. First, the rising tide of bad debt threatened the solvency of the banks. Second, the apparent change in Federal Reserve policy from the earlier rescue of Bear Sterns created a panic in the inter-bank lending market. Uncertain of which banks would survive banks ceased to lend to anyone at all in this market causing the system as a whole to seize up. Thirdly, stock market investors also panicked sending bank shares into freefall. Since bank regulation is based on the idea that loans can only be a certain multiple of bank capital and since the decline in shares reduced capital significantly, this looked likely to lead to a massive decline in bank lending, which would have further threatened the stability of the system. While these problems were first apparent in the US and UK, where housing booms and bank deregulation had been especially strong, it quickly became clear that banks from many countries, particularly Continental Europe, had also made loans in these markets so that the banking crisis affected the major industrialised countries as a whole.

The result of this has been an abrupt change in policy towards bailing-out the banks. The form of this has varied across countries. The US response, led by Treasury Secretary Henry Paulson, who is rooted in Wall Street, has been particularly shameless (the original proposal by Paulson was simply that the US government, funded by taxpayers, would buy up the worthless debt from the banks – a straightforward subsidy with no control over future bank behaviour whatsoever). The UK government plan, which has effectively been adopted by the EU, provides some potential leverage for political debate in that it involves buying shares in the banks. This allows for discussion about the nature of state control over the banking system and about who should pay for the crisis. But it is clear that the initial aim of the government was to have the minimum amount of state involvement in the financial sector and to provide funds which would then be used to restore the banks to profitability in the hope of a quick sale of the governments' stake. The model was the Scandinavian restructuring of the banks following the financial crisis there in the early 1990s.

Who Pays for the Crisis?

The starting point for Marxists in understanding these developments must be in terms of the devalorisation of capital. The immediate effect of the recognition of the bad debt in the housing market is that a large amount of capital which was valued at a certain amount, on the basis that the housing loans would be repaid in full, is no longer worth what was originally envisaged. This capital falls into two categories. Firstly, there is the capital directly tied up in providing housing linked to sub-prime mortgages, both the loan capital used to provide the mortgages and capital employed in construction and housing development. Secondly, there is the capital in other industries which has been invested in the expectation of demand originating from a booming housing market; in particular that which depends on high levels of demand resulting from homeowners borrowing against the equity in their houses – something now unlikely to happen in the foreseeable future.

Any devalorisation of capital of this kind raises the question of who will pay for the loss – capital or labour. The financial sector has been quite brazen about trying to shift the cost of the crisis onto labour – even to the extent of formulating plans to use taxpayers' money to maintain bonus payments. The mechanisms for ensuring this shift include the following:

· Direct subsidies for the banks funded by the taxpayer.
· Rebuilding of the profit base by refusing to pass on interest rate cuts to borrowers. This may well be made easier by mergers like the Lloyds-HBOS merger, which will reduce competition and increase the dependence of households on a small number of large institutions.
· An attack on the job security, wages and conditions of bank staff in order to cut costs. Again, state-sponsored mergers may help this process by providing the means to close branches.
· Reduction of the interest rate paid out to savers and depositors.

To the extent that the state has attempted to act as something other than an agent of capital and to enforce terms on the banks, the banks have responded by threatening to bring the system down if they don't get their way. This has led to some conflict between the government and the banks, particularly with regard to the enforcement of cuts in interest rates. However, the cuts which have been achieved here have come at the expense of even larger cuts in rates paid to savers which have serious implications for both current and future pensioners. In addition, the bail-out as a whole has resulted in a considerable ideological cost both in terms of the reputation of the financial sector within society as a whole (which is probably now at an all time low) and in terms of the increased legitimacy of regulation and even state ownership.

Stabilising the Financial Sector
While it is difficult to predict events with any certainty, it appears most likely at present that the injections of funds made so far have restored a measure of stability to the banking system. While the housing boom in the

US and a number of European countries was a significant speculative bubble, it did not represent sufficient lending in itself to bring down the financial systems of the industrialised world (*The Economist* of September 27 2008 reports a June Federal Deposit Insurance Corporation estimate of about $500 billion worth of `seriously delinquent' residential mortgages in the US out of a total of $10.6 trillion). It should also be remembered that even if mortgages are not repaid in full the houses on which they were secured are not entirely worthless.

In assessing the cost of this stabilisation we should be cautious about the headline figures such as the $700 billion attached to the US bail-out. The bail outs comprise three different kinds of spending. First, there is direct financial assistance to the banks. This is a real cost. Second, there are loan guarantees. These will only become a real cost if the loans that are made from now on result in defaults. Basically they are confidence building measures and it is not expected that they will require much if any actual spending. Thirdly, there is direct government lending to get the money markets flowing again. Again this will only be a real cost if the interest rates at which the lending takes place are unrealistically low or if the loans made result in default.

The real cost of the UK bank bail-out at present appears to be around £37 billion; i.e. the actual financial assistance being given to the banks. Even this will not necessarily be a long-term cost if the stake taken in the banks can be resold at a higher price at a later date. Nonetheless, it is a significant amount of money and will lead to a record government budget deficit this year. The sums involved in other European countries appear rather similar – for example the *Financial Times* of 5 November reports that Italy is planning to allocate £24 billion to recapitalise its banks.

Here it is also important to recognise that the immediate impact of this government spending is only a small part of the projected increases in budget deficits in the medium term. More important is the loss of tax revenue and the extra expenditure resulting from the slowdown in growth arising from the crisis. Analysing Alistair Darling's pre-budget statement in the *Financial Times*, Martin Wolf points out that tax receipts are now expected to fall by 3 percentage points of GDP in 2009-10 and observes that `these changes are overwhelmingly due to revisions in the fiscal capacity and level of GDP; a permanent reduction in taxes on financial sector profits and housing transactions; and, more strikingly, a lasting loss of GDP. In 2010, the economy is now expected to be some 5.5 percent smaller than forecast in the budget' [2]. This raises serious questions about the ability of governments such as the British government to fund their increased deficits by issuing bonds without either a sharp fall in bond prices which will raise interest rates and worsen the crisis or an increase in public borrowing from abroad which will further weaken the value of the pound.

What is more even important though than the immediate possibility of financial meltdown and the impact of the rescue of the banks on government spending is the longer-term impact of the financial crisis both on the financial sector and on the economic situation more generally.

The banking crisis has also raised the issue of the kind of financial system which will emerge if and when the initial stabilisation has been achieved. It is very difficult for New Labour to avoid this debate now because by taking stakes in the banks they have inescapably raised the issue of how these stakes will be used to enforce control over the financiers. However, while this would seem to be a golden opportunity for social democracy to reassert ideas about regulation of the system the ideological hegemony of neo-liberalism over the last two decades has left it unable to articulate any very convincing vision of an alternative. The main ideas about regulating banks currently being discussed include strengthening the capital requirements for making loans (basically a stronger version of what already exists), regulating bank bonuses and banning certain kinds of market transaction (such as `short-selling' where traders sell shares they do not actually own in the expectation that they can buy them up more cheaply before completing the transaction). None of these will lead to any significant differences between the financial system which emerges from the current turmoil and what we have seen in recent years.

However, if social democracy is unable to put forward a convincing alternative to neo-liberal financial deregulation that provides an opportunity for socialists to enter the debate. A space is opening up both for defence of public ownership and for arguments based on need rather than profit in a way which has not been the case for many years.

Recession and the Financial Crisis

The most important current development in the wake of the banking crisis is the transmission of that crisis to the rest of the economy and its interaction with the more general economic crisis now emerging. The most obvious issue here is the onset of recession. The central reason for the recession is the dependence of consumer demand in particular but also business investment on high levels of debt over the last two decades. Now that lending is contracting this debt-fuelled expansion is no longer possible and a sharp economic slowdown looks inevitable. The fall in house prices is also worsening the slowdown in consumer spending as households can no longer borrow against rising equity values.

There are two fundamental reasons for the reliance on debt. Consumption has come to depend on debt because of the contradiction between driving wages down to generate profits in production and needing to ensure demand in order to sell the goods produced and realise these profits. The most obvious manifestation of this is growing income inequality and it is no accident that the build-up of debt has been worst in countries with the greatest disparity in incomes, notably the UK and USA.

Linked to this is the way in which production in general, but especially investment, has come to rely on debt as a result of the weakness of profitability in the productive sector. As Robert Wade puts it `the rate of profit of non-financial corporations fell steeply between 1950-73 and 2000-06 – in the US, by roughly a quarter. In response firms `invested' increasingly in financial speculation'[3]. Consequently, without debt being available to fund expansion recession appears inevitable.

The response of governments to the recession has been firstly to increase their own borrowing and secondly to encourage central banks to cut interest rates. But both of these create their own problems. Government borrowing is limited by the cost of the bank bail-outs. High levels of borrowing can also push up interest rates or reduce currency values as discussed above. Both of these effects lower household real incomes and decrease spending frustrating the original purpose of the borrowing. The strategy adopted by the British government in response to this is to make tax cuts explicitly temporary. But this risks making them ineffective since households will simply save any extra income in anticipation of future tax rises.

Cutting interest rates is also difficult. Central banks only directly control short-term interest rates and private banks have simply refused to cut long-term rates in response to central bank policies. Cuts in interest rates also have the effect of lowering both the actual returns of current pensioners living off savings and the prospective returns of future pensioners both of which may lower consumption.
More fundamentally, the room for government policy to boost the economy is limited so long as spending depends on debt because of low wages and inequality and so long as new debt is not forthcoming. Consequently, the slowdown is likely to be protracted and severe.

The Internationalisation of the Crisis
The growth of debt over the last two decades in countries like the USA and UK has been dependent on international flows of capital which in turn have

resulted from a significant degree of exchange rate stability compared to the turbulence of the early 1980s. Conversely, a move towards a different pattern of accumulation will inevitably put great strain on global monetary arrangements.

So far the crisis has mainly manifested itself in domestic monetary developments in the largest economies, although countries like Iceland, Ukraine, Hungary and the Baltic States have been driven to seek IMF or EU help. But this is now changing and the crisis is being internationalised in three ways.

The first of these is the effect of current developments on so-called `emerging market economies'. Nobel Prize winning economist Paul Krugman gives the example of Russia where `while the Russian government was accumulating an impressive $560bn hoard of foreign exchange, Russian corporations and banks were running up an almost equally impressive $460bn foreign debt...This truly is the mother of all currency crises and it represents a fresh disaster for the world's financial system'[4]. The unwinding of the `carry trade' (where financiers borrow in markets with low interest rates such as Japan and lend abroad) is beginning to have a devastating effect on such currencies.

Secondly, countries like the UK and USA which have been at the centre of the crisis see their currencies in danger of sliding, both because their governments need to borrow abroad and because of a general lack of confidence. At the time of writing the dollar remains relatively strong simply because of the weakness of other currencies, but sterling has fallen dramatically against both the dollar and the euro.

The third factor is increasing pressure on countries to devalue their currencies in order to boost exports at a time of falling demand. Even the Chinese government is now considering this to American consternation[5]. All of these developments are likely to herald a period of much greater turbulence for exchange rates and capital flows. Yet underlying the immediate changes in currency values is a deeper disagreement about future strategies amongst the international capitalist class.

The central long-run task for capital is to develop a strategy of accumulation which does not depend on the build-up of unsustainable debt (Martin Wolf's article in the *Financial Times* of November 5 entitled `Why agreeing a new Bretton Woods is vital and so hard' is in many ways a manifesto for this process). This process involves a wide range of different potential conflicts but one issue in particular is seen as increasingly central. This is the rebalancing of world economic growth away from the USA (and UK) towards the surplus economies of Asia and elsewhere, especially China.

The more far-seeing representatives of capital, such as Wolf, are very clear that if the current pattern of global imbalances persists, so will recurrent financial crises of the kind we have seen recently. Large flows of funds into the US and UK will result in risky lending whatever the regulatory structures created. The only way this can be avoided is through a shift towards domestic consumption in countries like China and a move away from consumption towards investment and, especially, exports in the US.

This kind of strategy is extremely difficult to implement in practice because the unplanned, spontaneous nature of capitalism makes this kind of rebalancing very destabilising and risky. This was shown in the mid-1980s when the decision to co-ordinate a rise in the value of the yen and shift the Japanese economy towards domestic demand and away from exports triggered a speculative frenzy of lending resulting in a slump lasting almost two decades.

Yet, an even more serious problem today is that there is no clear agreement on the way forward between the representatives of different national capitals. That has been shown within Europe with regard to the arguments between the German and British governments over the degree to which government spending and fiscal deficits are an appropriate response to the crisis. More serious, however, are the underlying tensions between the US and Asian governments[6]. These tensions reflect not just economic concerns, but also shifts in the balance of power within international capitalism.

Commodities and the Ecological Crisis

The third aspect of the crisis of capitalism raised at the outset of this article is the question of commodity prices and the constraints on production arising from ecological factors. There is a strong temptation at present to downplay this issue as oil prices in particular fall. There are four reasons why this would be a serious mistake.

Firstly, oil prices remain at high levels compared to five or ten years ago, as do food prices in much of the world. Even in countries like Britain rising energy costs are seriously affecting working class living standards while for the poor in developing economies food costs are still devastating.

Secondly, to the extent that energy and food prices have declined it has only been because of the severity of the recession. Any sustained upturn in growth that does take place, in particular one based on a shift towards domestic consumption in countries like China, is likely to lead to renewed price rises. Here it is important not to assume that all the commodity price inflation of 2006 and 2007 was due to speculation. This did play a role, especially as speculators moved away from the dollar during this period, but it was by no means the only factor. The price rises of those years also indicated a genuine constraint on global capitalist growth arising from ecological limits.

Thirdly, given the irrationalities of capitalist decision-making any sharp decline in commodity and fuel prices which does take place over the next few years is likely to stop the development of new sources of supply and worsen the price rises that will occur if growth restarts.

Fourthly, the current recession is not slowing down the process of international environmental degradation, especially climate change. The impact of this on food supplies in particular represents a long-run trend which will assert itself increasingly sharply in future years whatever the level of global output.

All this means that, while at present governments and central banks are not worrying about inflation when trying desperately to restart production, any sustained recovery from the crisis is likely to reawaken inflationary fears. This will constitute a severe constraint on the economic options available to them in the longer term.

An End to Neo-Liberalism?

An important question here is that of the extent to which the current crisis represents an end to the political hegemony of neo-liberalism. Linked to this is the issue of the revival of Keynesianism. Here it is important to recognise that state expenditure is by no means incompatible with neo-liberalism provided such expenditure is in the interests of capital[7]. The initial aim of New Labour in rescuing the banks was very much within this framework, as discussed above.

However, this does not mean that the resolution of the crisis will remain within the bounds of neo-liberalism. A neo-liberal outcome in which the banks are restructured and re-privatised while accumulation is restarted on a free-market basis remains one possible outcome but by no means the only one. Already, in the UK the government has been driven to be more interventionist with regard to management of the banks than it had originally intended and to adopt fiscal policy measures which were also not planned even a few months ago. So, far such measures – pressuring interest rate reductions and raising income tax to 45 percent for higher earners – do not represent a significant break with past policies. But they do indicate a space for debate around political alternatives which is opening up. The way in which this space will be occupied will depend partly on how the crisis develops but also on the ability of socialists to articulate alternative responses to what is happening to that proposed by capital.

More generally, the way in which the crisis has thrown into question the way in which the world economy has functioned since the mid-1980s indicates that even if neo-liberalism is able temporarily to resolve the situation on its terms the way in which it will do this will differ significantly from what has been seen in recent years. It will also involve turbulent and difficult adjustments which in turn will open up further opportunities for socialists to present alternatives.

What should socialists demand?

In raising demands in response to the crisis it is important that socialists emphasise the nature of the crisis as a general crisis of capitalism, which has its roots in the contradictions of productive capital as much as in the financial sector and which is caused by global factors, not the economic policies followed by a particular national capital. In this context the following demands seem especially important:

- Nationalisation of the banks coupled with popular control over the allocation of credit and use of savings

- A massive programme of public works to combat the recession with particular emphasis on ecological production and a shift in the economy towards `green' technologies. Investment in alternative forms of transport and energy.

- Taxation of the income and wealth of the rich and limits on higher earnings to remove the reliance on debt to maintain consumption.

- Opening of the books of both the financial institutions and industrial companies to public scrutiny in order to prevent any use of the crisis as an excuse to force through cost-cutting and redundancies.

- Indexation of wages, pensions and benefits to protect workers against rises in food and energy prices.

- An extensive programme of publicly-owned and financed house building to avoid another housing bubble. A moratorium on any re-possessions for mortgage arrears.

- A government guarantee for pensions. Future pensions to be paid for from taxation of the rich and not to be reliant on returns from shares and bonds. Current pensioners to be compensated for loss of income resulting from interest rate reductions.

- Control over international financial speculation both through controls on capital movements and through taxation.

Conclusion

The current crisis represents the most significant set of economic events internationally since the decade spanning the mid-1970s and the mid-1980s. The economic order created following that turbulent decade is now breaking down. What replaces it will depend not just on `objective' circumstances but on the ability of the left to put forward its own vision of an economy based on need rather than profit as a replacement for the finance-driven accumulation of the last twenty years.

NOTES

[1] For a more detailed account of the following argument see A Kilmister `What's happening to the economy?' (*Socialist Outlook* no.14, February 2008), A Kilmister `The world economy and the credit crisis' (*Socialist Resistance* no.51, Summer 2008)

[2] M Wolf `How Britain flirts with disaster' (*Financial Times* Nov 28 2008, p.11)

[3] R Wade `Financial regime change? (*New Left Review* Second Series no.53 September/October 2008 p.11). There is a lively debate amongst Marxist economists about the extent to which the crisis can be seen as the result of falling profitability, which in large measure centres on different ways of measuring the profit rate. However, even those who see profits as being to some extent maintained (and who point to the fact that the share of profits in national income has risen) accept that the link between profits and productive investment has weakened significantly in recent years – presumably because of a change in expectations of future profits.

[4] P Krugman `We all go together when we go' (*The Guardian Weekend* Dec 6 2008 p.31)

[5] G Dyer `Paulson in last stand against weaker renminbi' (*Financial Times* Dec 4 2008 p.11)

[6] D Pilling `Prudent Asia is unlikely to bail out the west' (*Financial Times* Dec 11 2008) p.13)

[7] For a development of this argument see A Kilmister `Understanding neo-liberalism' (*Socialist Outlook* no.3 Spring 2004)

Green Keynesianism and its Limits

Sean Thompson

In July, the *new economics foundation* published the *Green New Deal*, whose authors include Larry Elliot of the Guardian, Anne Pettifor, of Advocacy International and Caroline Lucas of the Green Party. In the pamphlet, they recognise what most other 'experts' have still signally failed to; that the current crisis is not just financial, it is the first of three overlapping and global crises that we face. This "triple crunch", as they call it, is a combination of the banking crisis we are still experiencing, the ongoing and ever growing threat of climate change and the explosion of energy prices caused by the imminent approach of peak oil. *"These three overlapping events"* they say *"threaten to develop into a perfect storm, the like of which we have not seen since the Great Depression."*

They propose that we should deal with these interlocked crises with twin strategies; first, *"a structural transformation of the regulation of national and international financial systems, and major changes to taxation systems"* and second, *"a sustained programme to invest in and deploy energy conservation and renewable energies, coupled with effective demand management."*

These strategies are fleshed out by a number of specific policy proposals, which include:

- A big reduction in the Bank of England interest rate.

- Tight controls on lending and on the generation of credit.

- The forced de-merger of large banking and finance groups.

- The divorce of retail banking from both corporate finance and securities dealing.

- The reintroduction of government controls on capital flows.

- Strict regulation of derivatives and similar spivvy wheezes.

- The long term downsizing of the financial sector in relation the rest of the economy.
- Minimising corporate tax evasion by clamping down on tax havens and

ensuring transparent and honest corporate financial reporting.
- The establishment of an Oil Legacy Fund, financed by a windfall tax on the profits of the oil and gas companies.

- An energy conservation programme (including a massive domestic insulation and micro CHP installation scheme) and the development of renewable energy generation capacity.

- An environmental reconstruction programme, along with the recruitment and training of the hundreds of thousands of workers required.

- Significant increases in fossil fuel prices on order to force energy efficiency and to make alternative energy sources more attractive.

- The negotiation of international agreements that allow national autonomy over domestic monetary and fiscal policy, set an international target for atmospheric greenhouse gas concentrations, establish Kyoto 2, financing poor countries' investments in climate change adaptation and renewable energy generation and assisting the free transfer of new energy technologies to developing countries.

The authors of the *Green New Deal* are right to say that the current crisis undermines the credibility of the whole neoliberal project and to point out the need for good old-fashioned direct government spending and job creation, putting new demand into the economy through investing in infrastructure and public services. In their recognition of the scale and urgency of the environmental and resource aspects of the crisis, they are a good deal more far sighted than is the myopic norm among economists, and their advocacy of a full blooded Keynesian approach in response to it has produced a more radical package of proposals than anything currently on the desk of any finance minister or central banker.

However, the proposals have a narrow – if entirely understandable – focus on the immediate desire for economic stability and the urgent need for big reductions in carbon emissions. This is the result of two fatal flaws in the *Green New Deal's* analysis.

First, the pamphlet's authors fail to recognise the cyclical instability that is an inherent characteristic of the capitalism, or the speculative impulse that lies at its heart The fact is that it is the structural instability and impossible unpredictability of the financial system that is the prime mover of the credit crunch rather than the sleight of hand of a relatively tiny number of spivs and hucksters. As the Canadian economist Jim Stanford has said "*Capital-*

ism is nothing if not creative and the financial industry has lured some of humanity's smartest minds to focus on the utterly unproductive task of developing new pieces of financial paper, and new ways of buying and selling them. Despite the finger pointing at mortgage brokers and credit rate, therefore, the current meltdown is rooted squarely in the innovative but blinding greed that is the raison d'être of private finance."

Second, the *Green New Deal* fails to deal with the issue of inequality that it identifies. Gas and electricity prices have risen by 30% in Britain over the last year, and over the past two years average disposable household income (after housing and all other bills are paid) has dropped from £541 to £382 per month. Unemployment is rapidly rising and repossessions are currently running at more than a hundred a day. A central plank of the *Green New Deal* strategy is that fossil fuel costs should be increased in order to make investment in energy efficiency and renewables more profitable and of course that would bear most heavily on the elderly, the unemployed and the low paid. The pamphlet's authors only response to this is to propose that the UK *"could set up an Oil Legacy Fund, paid for primarily by a windfall tax on oil and gas company profits"*, and that *"Part of these increased revenues would need to be used to raise benefits for the poorest people in our society, who would otherwise be too adversely affected by such price rises during the transition to a low-carbon future."* mention of a meaningful redistribution of wealth, merely a nod towards the amelioration of the plight of the very poorest.

It is, of course, true that the current global financial crisis has been triggered by the collapse of the credit fuelled property bubble in the United States. It is also undeniable that the bubble was the inevitable outcome of the financial deregulation of the late seventies and eighties that led to an enormous expansion of financial markets, an explosion of credit and the development of ever more exotic and arcane speculative vehicles. For twenty five years or more there has been an ever flowing torrent of cash pouring into the financial markets. In the United States, total financial assets averaged around 440% of GDP from the early '50s to the late '70s. Then they started to climb steadily; to over 600% in 1990 and over 1000% by 2007. With a few unpleasant interruptions (the stock market crash of the late '80s, the Asian and Mexican financial crises of the mid '90s, the dotcom bubble of the early 2000s) it seemed as if Wall Street and the City had entered an eternal bull market. Thus, the globalised economy become a giant Ponzi scheme.

In reality, this ready access to credit - for speculative financial ventures (on the part of the rich) and for housing and unsustainably cheap consumer goods (for the rest of us) - helped disguise the ongoing relative decline of western (particularly US and UK) manufacturing industries and the hollowing out of their real economies. What this has led to is both an increase in personal indebtedness and a dramatic inflation in the value of assets (stocks and shares, houses etc.). Commodity inflation was suppressed by falling labour costs, which were kept down by the introduction of 'flexible labour markets', heavily reinforced labour discipline through the imposition of draconian labour laws and the export of manufacturing to China and the Far East. As the *New Green Deal* puts it, this asset inflation *'explains why the rich have got richer within the liberalised financial system and the poor have become poorer and more indebted.'*

All this make it irresistibly tempting to call for the re-regulation of finance – and indeed, that is desperately needed. But this crisis hasn't happened just because Thatcher and Reagan's deregulation of finance introduced instability into the capitalist system, and that after each crisis since the late '70s the system, when it bounced back, was even more unequal, unbalanced and distorted than before. The underlying cause of the crisis is the inherent boom/bust instability that lies at the heart of the capitalist system, particularly the financial markets.

Why Capitalism Has To Keep Expanding & Is Inherently Unstable

In pre capitalist economies, where money played an enabling role, the circuit of commodities and money existed in a form in which particular commodities (or use-values) constituted the end of the economic cycle. A commodity embodying a particular use-value is sold for money which is used to purchase a different commodity, or *C-M-C*. So each circuit is closed by the consumption of a use-value.

However, in the case of a capitalist economy, the circuit of commodities and money begins and ends with money. Money is used to purchase commodities which are sold on for money, or *M-C-M*. Of course, since money is simply the abstract expression of a quantitative relationship, such an exchange would be meaningless if the same amount of money was exchanged at the end of the process as at the beginning. So the actual formula in reality is *M-C-M**, where *M** is in fact *M+m* or profit, or capital, or, as we dried out bitter old Marxists say, surplus value. Of course, the big difference between this and simple commodity production is that there is no end to the process, since the object of the process is not final use but the accumulation of capital. So the *M-C-M** produced in one year leads to the *M* being reinvested, leading to *M-C-M*** the next year, *M-C-M**** the next, and so on ad infinitum. Just like a shark needs to continually keep on swimming in order to survive, so capitalism needs to continually go on expanding.

The mainspring of this drive to accumulate is competition. This competition forces every player in the market to grow through continual reinvestment in order to survive. In the case of banks, the commodity to be bought and sold is credit (or conversely, debt). Competition puts banks and brokerages continually under pressure to try to expand their markets by issuing loans to riskier and riskier customers and speculate on riskier and riskier financial paper.

So the financial system is both structurally unstable and impossibly unpredictable – although this crisis, triggered by the bursting of the US and UK housing bubbles, should have been predictable enough. This inherent instability, compounded by the deregulation of the markets demanded by financiers and the consequent global mobility of capital, has led us to shift, seamlessly and almost overnight, from a situation where credit was sloshing around our knees to one where credit has virtually dried up.

Credit creation is an essential social and economic function, but it has been largely handed over to private banks – with, it appears, bugger all regulatory or social oversight – whose raison d'être is to maximise their own profit. When their cost-benefit or risk analyses diverge from those of society as a whole (and they do frequently), the economy finds itself with too much credit, too little, or in a really desperate crisis (like now) none at all – despite, in the case of the UK, the exhortations of a government which has effectively nationalised a significant slice of the banking system and recapitalised it with £37b of state funding. Of course, we need credit as an essential lubricant to ensure the liquidity of institutions and ordinary people in the real economy, but that credit supply needs to be stable and at the right level. We have the living proof before us that 'the market' cannot ensure that; only governments can – if they have the will.

Beyond Stabilisation To Transformation

For that reason, we need to go beyond the proposals in the *Green New Deal*, which look more modest by the day. The pamphlet's key proposals for financial renewal include a big reduction in the Bank of England interest rate, tight controls on lending and on the generation of credit, the forced de-merger of large banking and finance groups, the divorce of retail banking from both corporate finance securities dealing, the reintroduction of government controls on capital flows, strict regulation of derivatives and similar spivvy wheezes and the long term downsizing of the financial sector in relation the rest of the economy.

Now all these proposals are fine as far as they go, but the pamphlet is very shy about dealing with the central issue; the inevitable necessity to exert direct state control over the domestic financial system in order to implement any of the proposals in a meaningful way. To quote Jim Stanford again; "*At the end of the day, the risks associated with private finance will always be socialised (as they have been in the current crisis) simply because the costs of the major financial failures are too severe, and too widely distributed, to tolerate. So why don't we socialise the whole process, or at least part of it?*"

This certainly means making our central bank (the Bank of England) the main tool in the government's strategy of financial intervention by reversing its so-called independence and by changing its current narrow and negative neo-liberal remit of limiting price inflation to a much more positive one of actively promoting economic health and full employment.

Nationalisation of the banks, through receiving equity in return for recapitalisation, is a perfectly practical option. The Government has already nationalised Northern Rock and Bradford and Bingley and is in the process of effectively nationalising RBS and Lloyds/HBOS, while Barclays has only avoided the same fate by throwing itself upon the mercy of investors in Qatar and Abu Dhabi to the tune of $7.3bn at eye watering rates of interest.

However, neither the dramatic lowering of the Bank of England base rate, with more to come, nor the state taking over or becoming the largest shareholder in three of the five clearing banks and two of the largest players in the mortgage market has had any significant effect on the behaviour of the financial sector in general or the supply of credit in particular. There is absolutely no point in the state taking all or part of the equity – and toxic debt – of the banks simply to ride this crisis out and then to return to business as usual. We have to find more equitable and publicly accountable ways to create a stable supply of credit without recourse to the anarchic and irrational monster that private finance has become. Rational lending in the real economy – to consumers, home buyers and productive undertakings – is a necessary public service we all depend on, but we can't trust the market to provide it reliably. So we need to develop alternative vehicles, including banks brought into public ownership, credit unions, building societies and other mutuals and not for profit institutions.

In September, one commentator said that the Government's apparent policy of allowing, or even encouraging, the development of ever larger financial institutions through amalgamations or take-overs in order to deal with the weakness of institutions like HBOS and B&B was in danger of creating a situation where instead of there being institutions the government couldn't afford to fail, there would soon be institutions the Government couldn't afford to save. The authors of the *Green New Deal* are quite right to suggest that we must reverse this policy, but I fail to see how the forced de-merger of behemoths like Lloyds TSB, Barclays, RBS etc. could be effected without complete state control – if not ownership - of their assets.

A New Industrial Revolution

The authors of the *Green New Deal* have taken their inspiration, as well as the title of their pamphlet, from the programme developed by Franklin D Roosevelt in response to the post 1929 Depression. Like him, and like Keynes, they propose an ambitious programme of public works and infrastructure development. Only it isn't ambitious enough.

All the indicators for global recession are at red. Commodity prices are undergoing a dramatic fall; copper, iron and oil have all at least halved in price over the last few months. These falls reflect a sudden reduction in demand as a result of the collapse of the construction industry and of car and retail sales. The Baltic Dry Index (a daily assessment of the price of moving major raw materials by sea) has fallen from 11793 points in May 2008 to 815 (a drop of 93%) in November. The lack of credit has led to a disappearance of letters of credit, and combined with the debt load of ship construction and the collapsing price of raw commodities, created a perfect storm for the world's marine commerce.

At the beginning of October, the Guardian reported that the UK manufacturing sector is shrinking at the fastest rate since records began 17 years ago. It reported that levels of output, new orders and employment in the manufacturing sector had recorded unprecedented declines in the previous month. The British Chamber of Commerce has reported that all the main indices in its most recent quarterly survey – sales, orders, profitability and confidence – were down for manufacturing and services firms of all sizes, findings that are described as 'exceptionally bad'. It is now predicting that unemployment will exceed two and a half million by the end of 2009. There can be no doubt that this situation can only get a great deal worse.

While the proposals to spend £50-70b a year on a massive programme of energy conservation measures coupled with a similarly vast programme for the development of renewable energy sources are admirable, they are so tightly focussed on the trees that they don't notice that the wood is in danger of rotting away. Manufacturing in the UK now only amounts for around 25% of the economy.

Our manufacturing base has been withering since Thatcher decided that a

Post Industrial Britain didn't need to concern itself with making things; there was far more money (for some) in manipulating financial paper. In particular, our engineering and construction industries have been hollowed out and our previous army of skilled engineers and builders dispersed, with no one replacing them. So now, if we need more trains (and we do) we must buy them from Germany or France, because we have no locomotive building industry any more. If we want large wind turbines we have to wait in the queue for them at Danish, US, Spanish or German manufacturers, because we currently have no large turbine manufacturing capacity, despite having the best conditions for wind power on earth!

The *Green New Deal* pamphlet predicts that the development of the admirable low-carbon energy system and environmental reconstruction programme it proposes will *"see hundreds of thousands of.... jobs created in the UK. It will be part of a wider shift from an economy focussed on financial services and shopping to one that is a an engine of environmental transformation."* That is certainly a desirable goal, but it will not happen without the most massive and rapid programme of investment in the retooling of industry and reskilling of labour that we have seen since the Second World War.

If our aim is to build a whole new low-carbon energy system, along with other aims not mentioned by the pamphlet, such as a totally renewed public transport system, a sustainable water supply system and a massive programme of social housing to meet the needs of the four million families on waiting lists for a home, we are going to need nothing less than a new industrial revolution. We need to develop/redevelop the capacity to implement a huge production programme encompassing mini and micro CHP equipment, wave and offshore wind turbine plant, a whole new grid infrastructure, energy efficient buses and rail/light rail vehicles, low impact buildings and building materials etc., etc. (which, incidentally, would almost certainly place us on a collision course with the EU Commission). As the pamphlet's authors put it, there is a *'need for mobilisation as though for war.'*

Although hundreds of thousands of jobs would be created by such a programme, the major changes in industrial strategy that are implied by the pamphlet – for example, contraction of the motor vehicle, armaments and aero-space industries and the run-down of much of the existing electricity generation capacity - would lead to a need to transfer and retrain workers moving from declining to rapidly expanding sectors. To gain the support of the workers effected, such changes would have to be accompanied by an absolute guarantee of jobs and retraining with no loss of pay or security and a guarantee of rehousing rights where necessary.

Funding And The Market

But of course, such a huge programme must be financed, and it is here that the pamphlet is either at its most optimistic or at its weakest, depending on the hue of your tinted glasses – and mine, I'm afraid, are not very pink at the moment. Having listed the three key planks of FDR's New Deal, authors of the pamphlet tell us that; *"The Green New Deal will, however, differ from its 1930s predecessor in that there will be a much bigger role for investments from private savings, pensions, banks and insurance."* Every fund raising measure, in fact, apart from flag days and bring and buy sales. Strangely, even though the pamphlet points out that the programme will cost the equivalent of 3.5% of GDP – much the same as was committed to FDR's New Deal – it doesn't explain why, though FDR funded his programme largely with public spending, we should not do the same.

The pamphlet suggests that the government funding required could come in part from the increase in its income from rapidly rising carbon taxes and carbon trading. The pamphlet doesn't mention either the potential for the redistribution of existing government spending (reducing the defence budget by two thirds would free up £22b for example) or increased direct taxation, both personal and corporate, so the prosperous, not to say the filthy rich, could pay their fair share (potentially over £40b). However, it does mention government bonds.

Now, there is nothing safer than a government bond. However, monetarist policy was to reduce government spending and debt and thus to reduce the supply of government bonds, encouraging institutions to go for riskier assets. Increasing the supply of government bonds not only produces a valuable stockpile of public debt, it can also serve as a stabiliser to the financial system. So the idea of using government bonds as a funding vehicle for the project, along with local authority bonds and various novelty variations aimed at suitable sections of the public, particularly in the form of 'green gilts' is a sound one.

And the pamphlet is quite right to look to the pension funds as a long term source of funding. However, as the pamphlet itself says *"Pension funds are not charities. They are governed by the obligations of fiduciary duty to pursue the best interests of their members* [in other words, to maximise profits] *rather than the ethical whims of their trustees."* In reality, their policies have tended to be steered more by what is good for the fund managers' bonuses than anything else. The pamphlets authors suggest that two factors might lead pension funds to change their investment strategies; a growing realisation of the threat of climate change and the tightening of regulations on pension fund disclosure and valuation.

The first of these factors can, I think, fairly confidently discounted. It requires a long term view that is, for most fund managers, an unaffordable luxury, rather like expecting a football manager to plough most of his transfer funds into a training school for young players. however, the second factor is potentially significant. In practice it is about using the power of the state to determine the investment strategies of the fund managers. But why not simply cut through the Gordian Knot and require pension managers to put a minimum percentage of their funds into government bonds?

The pamphlet points out that the Norwegian state has used its oil and gas income to establish a huge investment fund that underpins its state pension scheme. It suggests that we could follow Norway's lead (three decades late) and set up an Oil Legacy Fund, paid for primarily by a windfall tax on oil and gas company profits. Part of these increased revenues, it is suggested, would be needed *'to raise benefits for the poorest people in our society'* who would otherwise suffer from the inevitable rises in the prices of fossil fuels that peak oil and carbon taxes would generate. We already have five million households in Britain classified as suffering fuel poverty (that is, more than 10% of household income going on fuel). The recent huge increases in gas and electricity will be, literally, the death of hundreds, possibly thousands, more pensioners this winter. The pamphlet suggests that: *"grants would be required to cover 100% of the cost of changes needed to the dwellings of the most disadvantaged, to increase energy efficiency and fit renewables."* Is that it? What about challenging poverty? What about equality?

Taming The Market?

If we seriously want to gain popular support for the New Green Deal or similar strategies, we should be arguing that the policies we propose will constitute a war on poverty and unemployment right now, rather than a programme of grants and benefits to ameliorate the worst of effects of peak oil on the poorest. We must be clear, both to ourselves and to the mass of ordinary people, who stand to gain from such a strategy and whose active support is necessary for its successful implementation, that it is going to be necessary to challenge both the domination of the market and its powerful defenders, whether they are financiers, EU Commissioners or the boards of multinational corporations. And here we come to the key limitation of Keynesianism. whether green or any other colour; essentially it has always been about trying to stabilise a fundamentally unstable system rather than transform it. It seeks to civilise the market rather than challenge its domination and tame it.

Not only can we not trust the market to find the funding for the sort of measures advocated in the *New Green Deal*, we can't trust the market -or its functionaries – to implement them. The pamphlet's failure to recognise this is a major weakness, as is its exclusive focus on energy conservation and renewable energy as the vehicles of economic restructuring.

In reality, there is little point in a new low-carbon energy system without a completely renewed public transport system, since transport accounts for 24% of our carbon footprint. And it is impossible to develop a sensible energy conservation programme for our homes, workplaces and public buildings, particularly the pamphlet's *'every building a power station'* policy, without dealing with the inextricably linked needs for a renewed and sustainable sustainable water supply system and a massive programme of social housing.

There is a consensus that we cannot trust the market to deliver or maintain a national railway service and that therefore the railways should be brought back into public ownership. I think that it is self evidently true that we cannot trust the power companies to develop a sustainable and equitable energy service, not the water companies to deliver water and remove waste in a socially and environmentally just way. Therefore, one of the preconditions of the sort of vast infrastructural reconstruction advocated in the pamphlet is the taking into public ownership not only the railways, but all public transport services and the power and water utilities.

While the idea of an Oil Legacy Fund is an excellent one, using it to continue to subsidise poverty rather than challenge it is hardly likely to excite the popular imagination. Far better that we use it, together with a hypothecated National Insurance Fund, to underpin a decent pensions scheme that does not leave the old, the disabled and the vulnerable in poverty. Fuel costs could be dealt with by a variation on Mayer Hillman's carbon rationing proposals; the allocation to all households a free energy allowance (weighted so that single person households were not disadvantaged) with all energy consumed above the free allowance charged at a progressively higher rate. Clearly, such a proposal would not be practicable in the context of privatised oil, gas and electricity suppliers.

Conclusion

The pamphlet is right to say that the current crisis, in which the US banks alone have lost something like $1.6 trillion so far and in which financial institutions across the world are likely to end up with liabilities to the tune of at least $500 trillion (more than the global GDP), undermines the credibility of the economic orthodoxy that has dominated almost all governments and their policies for over thirty years. In the words of one of the Green New Deal Group, Ann Pettifor *'Flawed monetary policies are turning a crisis into a catastrophe.'*

It is right to point out the need for direct government spending to put new demand into the economy through investment in infrastructure and public services. The pamphlet correctly argues that we should be shifting the focus of the economy away from the financial sector and back to the real economy, where real people produce real goods and services that actually contribute to our collective well being. It highlights the next crisis that is likely to sweep over us quite soon, that of peak oil, rightly emphases the scale and urgency of the threat of global warming, and points out that coping with those threats has to be an integral part of our infrastructural renewal.

However, the pamphlet does not sufficiently recognise that this crisis, like all those that have come before, is rooted in a deeper and more fundamental problem than the greed and recklessness unleashed by neoliberalism. The fundamental problem is that of a financial system orientated towards maximising private profit rather than assisting real progress for ordinary people. As a result, many of its proposals rely to a dangerous degree on the goodwill, common sense or long term thoughtfulness of the very groups who have got us into this mess and who will pull the world down round their ears rather than concede power. What is needed is a programme of infrastructural renewal even more ambitious than that envisioned by the pamphlet's authors. Such a programme will require determined government and popular action to end the domination of the market and to use society's resources, including the banks, building societies and other financial institutions and most importantly, the pension funds, for the common good.

This isn't the final crisis of capitalism. Capitalism will always find a way to recover – but at huge cost to us all. As John Bellamy Foster wrote recently; *"It is important to remember that a breakdown of capitalism as a whole will not occur by mere economics alone. Given time to work things out on its own terms the system will no doubt recover — though a full recovery could be many years away, if possible at all.*

The real historical issue before us is to what extent the world's population is willing to wait for this crisis to be resolved on capitalist terms, so that the whole irrational process of exploitation and boom and bust can gain steam again — or whether they shall decide to insert themselves into the *process to say `Enough!'"*

We must be able to show working people, through the daily experience of their own lives, that we need to transform the system; that it can't be satisfactorily or permanently reformed. But we won't do that by chanting "one solution, revolution". So the correct course for socialists is not to simply dismiss the *Green New Deal* pamphlet as reformist (which of course it is) but to point out how and why the programme it proposes is inadequate and needs to be extended, and the radical implications of such a more developed programme – in other words, developing transitional demands and politics.

November 2008

Sub-Prime Driven Recession: Coming Soon To A Neighbourhood Near You - The New Global Financial & Economic Crisis

Raphie de Santos

Introduction

Already millions of people are feeling the chill wind of a global financial and economic crisis that is beginning to sweep the world. In the United States (US) where the present crisis has its roots, there are scenes that are the 21st century equivalent of the great 1930's slump. Homes are being abandoned and stripped of all valuable fittings and are being occupied by the homeless. The police are being employed by the mortgage companies and banks to evict them. Empty homes are boarded up everywhere across the country. Home ownership has fallen to the lowest level since 1945 and house prices have collapsed by 11% in the last 12 months. In the US they are calling it a sub-prime crisis as if the people affected are some inferior sub-species of the human race. We could see the same pattern repeated in the UK and Scotland as the housing bubble here starts to deflate.

At the same time there are almost daily reports of panic and meltdown in the financial markets affecting every corner of global finance. The UK government had to step in with the largest nationalisation in history using $220bn* of tax payers' money to effectively prop up the global financial system. In the US the Federal Reserve, Bank (The Fed) essentially the US government, has orchestrated the rescue of one of the US's largest Wall Street investment banks in the fear that its imminent collapse would create a financial panic. Such was this bank's interconnection with the whole financial and economic system.

The language and participants of global finance are shrouded in mystery with such terms as LIBOR, hedge funds, derivatives and collateralised debt obligations designed to confuse and keep ordinary people in the dark.

In the real economy we are starting to see major problems as people experience levels of inflation not seen for decades. The government tells us it's about 2% but it feels much higher as food, housing, petrol and utility bills rocket. At the same time these mature economies of the West face new competition from a growing large capitalist economy – China.

What lies behind this crisis and why is there talk of a 1930's style slump? That is what I set out to do in this chapter.

This is not the first time that the capitalist economic system has been on the verge of a big meltdown. Capitalism has been prone to periodic economic crises ever since it first emerged. This must suggest that there is something inherently unstable about the way capitalism functions, going from boom to bust and back to boom to be followed by bust.

Indeed as capitalism expands, the gap between supply and demand becomes ever greater because, sensing the good times, capitalists rush to expand their productive output in order to make greater profits. As a result there is then a crisis of overproduction and oversupply. As soon as this point is reached, capitalists, fearing a fall in profits, scale back on production, thus sacking workers, depressing demand and deflating the economy. The crisis then becomes of a crisis of lack of demand. But as the bottom of the cycle is reached, some capitalists take advantage of the situation, buy up their competitors which in turn creates the conditions for growth again.

These economic crises are inherent and endemic to capitalism because each boom provides the basis of the next slump and each slump provides the basis for the next boom. This becomes a perpetual cycle that will endure so long as there is capitalism.

What's more, each boom and slump tends to be bigger than the last one because each cycle brings about the ever-greater concentration of capital into a smaller and smaller number of bigger and bigger capitalists. As a consequence if one of these ever bigger capitalists goes under, then it threatens to bring the whole system down with it.

The structure of the pamphlet is that in Section One, we start by trying to get behind the smoke and mirrors of modern global finance and explain in lay terms how the different markets operate and how they are linked to the real economy and real people. We find that the interconnectivity of global finance can transmit a problem such as the sub-prime crisis round the globe to its every corner so that millions of people are affected in some way by it. This is a marked difference from the 1930s slump where a crisis in the banking system was limited to the United States. Modern finance has the ability to magnify and transmit a financial crisis in one major economy to all the world's economies.

You can read the whole of this section in one go, dip into when you want a fuller understanding of some other sections, or skip it all together and come back and read it once you have read the rest of the chapter.

We then take a look at the global economy since the end of the Second

World War and see that it has been stagnant since the late 1960s and that the tools that have been used to avoid slumps such as those that happened in 1974/75 and 1979/1980 have come to the end of their shelf life.

Next we turn our attention to the current UK housing crisis and show it is very complex. Various problems have come together at the same time which could lead to a bigger slump than in the 1930s.

We examine the possible effects of the crisis on ordinary people around the world with a particular focus on it's affects in Scotland.

Finally, we look at a long term socialist alternative to capitalism's crises and a different economic system which could put and end to booms and slumps and provide everyone in the planet with a good standard of living – housing, food, health and culture – and a dignified and fulfilling existence. However, we also show the immediate policies socialists would put forward to defend the living standards of people in Scotland today.

* In this chapter we measure all financial quantities in US dollars and one billion will represent 1,000,000,000 US dollars and one trillion will represent 1,000,000,000,000 US dollars and they will be abbreviated as $1bn and $1tn respectively.

1. The Global Financial System

The global finance system has developed into a beast that can spread a crisis around the world almost instantaneously leaving no corner or person untouched. It is shrouded in mystery and is given almost god like status as it is worshiped in awe by the media. Terms such as "the Footsie reached new highs", "LIBOR has an inverted yield curve", "the Fed has cut rates", "CDOs are blowing up in all sorts of unexpected places" and "hedge funds are synthetically short", leave the ordinary person puzzled. They represent a barrier set up by financiers to create a reverence around the system and an almost obedient servitude to it. Here we will try to demystify it, showing its inner workings and how something, such as poor people in the United States unable to meet their loan repayments, can create a global meltdown of the whole financial system.

The roots of the modern financial system lie in developments in the early 1980's when investors of capital could not find avenues where they could obtain reasonable returns after a decline, from the early 1970's onwards, in the profit levels of traditional companies. Changes to the financial system were created largely by the neo-liberal governments of the US and the

UK to find fresh outlets for under achieving investments. These changes were:

- The deregulation of financial markets.
- The ending of international investment restrictions abroad.
- The introduction of cheap new powerful technology.
- The ability to use financial models previously too cumbersome and expensive to run on less powerful expensive computers.
- Instantaneous communication between financial markets around the world.

The new global financial system became more interconnected and based on products based on a whole raft of financial theories. These could not have been previously implemented without today's cheap desktop computing power. We will take a look at the different markets, the participants and how assets are transacted on these markets.

We show by example how the global system is now so interconnected that this could mean that any major financial crisis could dwarf that seen in the US banks during the 1920's/30's. That set off a global slump (depression) that ended in world war, the death of hundreds of millions and the destruction of whole societies.

The key financial markets can be divided into the following distinct categories:

- money markets
- bond markets
- currency markets
- equity share markets
- derivative markets

The participants in these markets can be broken down into the following categories:

- investors
- speculators
- hedgers
- arbitrageurs
- executioners
- risk takers
- lenders and borrowers

We will first examine the key financial markets. Then we will see who the participants are and how they operate.

2. The Financial Markets
Money Markets
This is where the financial institutions and corporations raise and lend cash to run their businesses in the short-term, i.e. for periods of less than 1 year. The box below explains how it operates and relates to a central bank (essentially the government's bank).

Bond Markets
Bonds are nothing but loans for a period longer than one year. They are a way of raising money by corporations and governments by lending a named amount which is normally in multiples of 100 of the currency of the loan. The issuer or borrower will guarantee to pay the lender a fixed sum of interest expressed as percentage of the named amount. There is a risk that the lender will default on the loan. As consequence this will reward the lender with a higher rate of interest than can be obtained from a lower risk investment, say in a bank's deposit account. Corporations are particularly likely to do this. Governments rarely go bankrupt although the Russian government did default on its loan repayments in 1998. UK government bonds are called gilts (gilt edged stock) and US government bonds are called treasuries. It is a way of governments raising money to spend on large public projects or trying to reduce any deficit in their finances.

Currency Markets
This is a market for the exchange of one currency for another and this involves private transactions between very large banks. For example a sterling exchange rate of $2 means that you would exchange two US dollars for one pound sterling. The markets main centers are Tokyo, London and New York with London being the largest. The currency market is the biggest financial market by value in the world, trading on average over $3tn a day. All the market participants are active in this market, as well as corporations meeting their foreign currency requirements.

Equity Share Markets
More commonly called the stock market after joint stock companies which buy and sell shares there. Companies issue ordinary equity capital called ordinary shares to raise money for investment. These are traded on regulated markets and unregulated markets across the world. The price of these shares is driven by supply and demand, information on the economy and news affecting particular industrial sectors and companies. Indices are cal-

culated to give investors a general feel for the direction of the overall market and its particular sectors. These are based on the market value of each company (the price of the company's shares times the number of ordinary shares issued by a company). The market values of a group of companies are added together to calculate an index. Examples are the FT-SE 100 (Footsie) which is an index of the largest 100 UK companies. The Dow Jones 30 is an index of 30 leading US companies and the Nikkei an index of 225 leading Japanese companies.

Derivative Markets

Derivatives are paper contracts, which allow you to buy or sell an asset at some point in the future. There are two basic types. The first gives you the obligation to buy or sell. These are easy to value and are based on the fact that you do not have to buy the asset until some point in the future and the money you need to do that is deposited in a bank account until such time. The second type of derivative gives you the right and not the obligation to buy an asset in the future. These derivatives are called options, they are difficult to price and there are a variety of approaches and assumptions to do this.

All derivatives are highly leveraged with only the requirement to make a small deposit (margin) at the outset of the trade and then make or receive daily payments based on the value of the derivative to you.

Derivatives trade in two ways. The first is the listed market in the huge daily values quoted on a basic range of underlying assets – currencies, bonds, interest rates, stock market indices, commodities and even animals. These are the most simple and easy to trade and have the highest value of trades per day. Though without the proper controls they can be very dangerous. It was listed derivatives, which were at the root of the recent Barings Bank collapse and the Soc Gen trading losses.

The second way they can be transacted is over-the-counter (OTC) – a private agreement between two parties. This tends to happen for the more complex, bespoke and large value derivatives such as the CDOs(collateralised debt obligations) which we will describe later on.

All the participants use the derivatives markets for a wide range of purposes. In a controlled fashion they are excellent at reducing risk and transaction costs. But the complexity and lack of understanding of some products, such as with CDOs, can mean they are a time bomb waiting to explode.

3. The Participants
Investors

These are the largest group of participants, by value of investments. They buy and hold financial assets for 1 to 35 year periods (medium to long term). These investors are largely ordinary people who have their money invested through:- pension fund contributions, life insurance policies, endowment policies and collective investment schemes. These allow individuals to invest any excess money they have in financial assets. Examples of these would be ISAs and special funds e.g. UK equities. These investments are bought and sold and managed by large institutions e.g.:

- a pension fund company (e.g. Lothian Pension Fund)
- an insurance company (e.g. Norwich Union)
- a fund management company (e.g. Baillie Gifford).

Through ownership of these institutions, about 75% of financial assets belong to ordinary people. For example the breakdown of the average pension fund in the UK is as follows:

- 28.7% UK equities
- 26.4% Non-UK equities
- 23.9% bonds
- 9.6% index-linked investments (inflation protected government bonds)
- 11.4% property and money market instruments (cash)

The majority of shareholders in private corporations are similar people to those they employ and exploit. This is the irony of global finance in modern capitalism. Not only do we make the corporate profits, but we own much of them and raise the capital for them to exploit us more!

Speculators

There have been speculators since the first financial markets. They take positions (buy or sell financial assets) in anticipation that the financial assets will appreciate or depreciate because of the influence of some outside factor. A recent example was Black Wednesday when many speculators thought the UK government would be forced to withdraw from the European Exchange Rate Mechanism and cut interest rates dramatically. Some sold sterling and bought other currencies. They expected sterling to weaken against these other currencies as interest rates in the UK fell below European interest rates. This meant that investors would rather deposit money in Europe than the UK because they could obtain a higher rate of interest. A more subtle form of speculation was the buying of property related shares – property companies, building companies and building material companies – anticipating that the likely cuts in UK interest rates would create a revival in the UK housing market. This would lead to more business for all these sectors and higher profits. These types of 'trades' were executed by traders in investment banks. Some later left the investment banks and set up their own leveraged companies. Together with speculative fund managers, they set up hedge funds. They combined speculation with other investment strategies, which we describe below.

Speculation can lead to financial bubbles when more investors pile into a particular product (strategy).

Hedgers
Hedgers are investors who want to protect the current value of assets from falling in the future. Take for example a UK pension fund that owns UK equities. If it is worried about the prospects for the UK economy, and hence the value of its UK equities, it can sell a derivative or something else on its portfolio and eliminate all potential losses or some of the losses. Corporations also hedge for example if they have to pay for something in a foreign currency at some date in the future. They are worried that their own currency will depreciate against the currency they have to make the payment in. So they buy an 'insurance' or hedge, through a forward foreign exchange contract to cover any shortfall in what they have to pay. Hedging has grown dramatically since the early eighties with the introduction of derivative markets. The strategy has spilled over into speculative investing where hedging can reduce the risk of a "trade" but also the potential profit.

Derivatives can be used to increase speculation too as they are highly leveraged. In some cases, they are easy and cheap to buy and sell. A recent example of speculation going awry is the Soc Gen Futures trader who lost nearly $8bn in speculative trades using derivatives based on equity share indices. There will be more on those indices later in this section. Many hedge funds use them as a leveraged speculative tool or for reducing the risk of a speculative trade.

Arbitrageurs
These are a group of investors who try to take advantage of differences in prices of similar assets or groups of assets. They will buy (go long on) the cheaper asset and sell (go short on) the more expensive one expecting over a period of time that the prices of the two assets will converge. They will make a near riskless or low risk profit depending on how alike the two assets are and other technical factors. The simplest case is an arbitrage between the shares of the companies in an index such as the FT-SE 100 and a derivative based on the FT-SE 100 index. These arbitrage trades can be

quite complex and there is no guarantee that they will result in a profit. Especially if the relationship between the buy and sell sides of the arbitrage becomes more tenuous.

One such arbitrage transaction, which went wrong and nearly caused a meltdown in financial markets was one involving Long Term Capital Management (LTCM). They lost $4 bn in 1998. LCTM had bought less easily tradable cheaper Russian government bonds and had sold the more expensive bonds of the developed countries expecting the prices to converge over time. But in August 1998 the Russian government defaulted on its debt payments. There was a flight from low quality cheap government bonds that LCTM had bought to the more expensive developed governments bonds, which LCTM had sold. This resulted in massive losses. Because LCTM had bought and sold the bonds from investment banks, there was the possibility that their failure to make payments to these banks could lead to a domino effect through the financial markets. So the US Federal Reserve Bank stepped in with a $3.5bn rescue package.

Arbitrage trades mostly originated within investment banks. They have been taken into the hedge funds by traders who have helped set up these funds.

Executioners

These are financial intermediaries who simply carry out financial transactions on behalf of financial institutions or individuals. They take no risk and take a fee for facilitating the transaction. Mortgage brokers are the first example. They arrange a mortgage between an individual and a bank and take a fee for doing so. A second example is the case of a pension fund that wishes to buy UK equity shares and goes to an investment bank to buy them. The investment bank acts as agent in the UK equity share market and takes a commission for executing the transaction. These executioners are essentially living off the crumbs that fall off the slices of a big cake, our cake, when it is cut into lots of small pieces.

Risk Takers

These are institutions which commit their own capital in a financial transaction. Take the two examples above. In the first, a bank will raise funds and pay for the house and take this house against this loan as security. If a person defaults on the loan repayments then the bank will repossess the home and sell it to raise the money to pay off the initial sum it borrowed. There is the risk that if house prices have fallen since the date the loan was taken out then they will have shortfall on the original loan and make a loss. This will become an increasing problem in the UK as house prices fall from their all time highs.

In the second case the investment bank may go to another investment bank and buy equity shares that the second bank is offering to sell at a guaranteed price on the electronic equity share market. The second bank will have the equity shares on its books and it bears the risk that these equity shares may fall in value.

Lenders and Borrowers

Lenders fall into two basic categories. The first loans money to individuals. They are called retail lenders and there are retail arms of banks such as the Halifax Bank of Scotland and the Royal Bank of Scotland.

The second are the large banks which lend to other banks and financial institutions. These banks have large amounts of capital. They are highly rated by the credit rating agencies being given a triple A rating. This means they have a low probability of defaulting on loans or going bust. An example of such a bank is HSBC. But many of the banks have been downgraded over the last few months leading to higher rates of interest for loans.

4. The Global Capitalist Economy since World War Two

You cannot understand the current economic crises without understanding how capitalism has evolved from its last major crises – the 1920/30s depression and the 1974/75 and 1979/80 recessions.

In the 1950's and early '60's, capitalism was able to expand rapidly from this lower base level. Initially it had a more a compliant workforce. The introduction of new technology was linked to space exploration and the armament industries. There was also a growing arms economy, which excess capital could invest in, as a result of the 1950'sand '60's Cold War.

Company profits expanded and the rate of profit increased steadily over the period from 1945 to 1965. There was growing investment and accumulation of capital (profits). This all came to an end in the late 1960's as profit rates stagnated, then started to fall and the accumulated capital could not find new markets to invest in. The profits of companies are based on the extra value that labour contributes to the production process. But labour was being replaced by machines, labour saving devices and other new technology. These, in themselves, create no new value. They merely pass on the value (manual and intellectual) of the labour incorporated in their production. The amount of profits that corporations made therefore fell. This together with an over capacity of production led, in 1974/5, to the first generalized synchronized recession since the end of the Second World War.

There was a massive crisis of over-production as stock piles of unsold goods and services built up in warehouses all round the capitalist world. This was compounded by a fall in the rate of profit for corporations and on top of that a hike in the oil price. After a partial and hesitant recovery the world capitalist economy entered a second recession in 1979/80.

Capitalism tried to deal with this crisis using several approaches. One was to create new avenues for excess capital. They did this in two ways. One was to privatise large chunks of state industries - that is open it up to private capital. The second was to liberalise the financial markets to encourage cross-border investment and the invention of new financial products that excess capital could speculate in.

Another solution was to create a larger level of consumer demand amongst working people so as not to repeat the previous crisis of overproduction of 1974/75 and 1978/80. They did this by expanding the credit markets for mortgages, loans and credit cards. It is this boom in credit, a credit bubble, which has come to end with the sub-prime crisis in the US and the start of the bursting of the housing bubble in the UK. This has ended one of late capitalism's tools to dampen and reduce the frequency of recessions.

New Markets?
An unexpected event happened in the 1990s which offered capitalism some reason for hope. It was the restoration of capitalism in the former Soviet Union, Eastern Europe and China. This opened up potentially new markets for capitalism to sell its goods. It was hoped that this could help solve the crisis of over production. The first two regions have proved to be less fruitful than at first expected. Although trade with the regions has doubled with the capitalist West, it was originally at very low levels. Their economies, infrastructures and capitalist systems have not developed and are still largely controlled by the local "mafia". As a consequence they have not produced a vibrant economy and financial system. Western companies are not willing to commit large investments to these new 'capitalist regimes'. However, China has followed a different path.

China: the New Competition
China has proved to be a double edged sword. While it has opened up new markets and is a source of cheap labour it also becoming the West's main competitor. It has much lower wage costs and a much lower level of automation in its production processes, which means it can achieve much higher profit levels than Western corporations. It is also a source of competition for natural resources and food as it develops a growing workforce spending more money and rapidly expanding industries able to suck up

global commodities. This has led to food and commodity price inflation. This has come at a time when the West wants to cut interest rates to try and stimulate its own economies.

However, the US has cut its interest rates dramatically. It prefers higher inflation to a deep recession. The UK and Europe have cut rates very slowly or not at all. They are more concerned about inflation. More of this will be imported if their currencies weaken.

As we will show later the effect of cutting interest rates is limited because of the 'Credit Crunch' and the US may in the end have inflation and a recession a phenomenon known as stagflation.

At the same time in the West the rate of profit has stagnated and shows no sign of improving. Capitalism has really come to an impasse with low profit rates, a credit crunch, a global as yet not fully understood financial crisis, growing inflation, food shortages for the poor, commodity shortages and competition from China.

The Effect of the Crisis on the Emerging Economies

How will the emerging economy of China, along with India and Brazil, be affected? Their economies are largely based on export sales to the richer countries of the West. The effect of the global economic and financial crisis will be to slow down these emerging economies considerably. The reduction in demand for goods from these emerging economies from the US, Europe (including the UK) and Japan (which has already slipped in to a recession), together often called the Triad block, will put the brakes on their economic growth. The global corporations of the Triad bloc will also reduce their production in these emerging economies. This will also cause a reduction in the amount of goods produced there as demand for their goods decreases.

Inflation

A second major problem for these emerging economies is the growth of domestic inflation fuelled by an increase in the wealthy minority amongst their populations. Although this minority is small in proportion to these countries' total population it is, given the huge populations of these countries, significant compared to the Triad's population. This growing now wealthier population is putting pressure on the goods they are demanding – property, food, consumer goods. This is resulting in inflationary pressures both in their domestic economies and in the international economy as a whole. This demand is the largest contributor the rise in global food prices representing about 70% of the price increases we have seen in the last year.

The other contributor is the conversion of wheat products into bio fuels.

Ironically, the Chinese and Indian governments have raised interest rates to try and dampen this demand and hence reduce their domestic inflation. This is a bit like what Tweedledee and Tweedledum (Brown and Darling) did just before the sub-prime crisis broke in August of 2007. The effect will be to further slow the emerging economies more just as they were starting to slow as a result of the growing recession in the Triad economies.

A third major factor in slowing these emerging economies is that the property and stock market bubble in these economies has started to deflate – the Chinese stock market has declined 45% since August 2007. Therefore, the wealthy minority will start to feel less well off as the value of their assets in property and shares falls. This will lead to a reduction in their consumption.

A fourth factor is the weakening currencies of the Triad block – particularly the $ - will reduce the income in their domestic currencies from the sale of goods from the emerging economies to the Triad block.

Finally, the banks and financial institutions of these emerging countries have exposure to the sub-prime market via instruments such as the CDOs. A combination of all these factors could well push these emerging markets into recession.

The Effect of the Crisis on Third World Debt

The mountain of Third World debt on the poorest countries and people on the world was created in the 1970s. The $182bn that was owed in 2006 by the public authorities of these poor countries to the international banks of the Triad countries is a multiple of the original debt. This is largely as a result of a big increase in interest rates by the Federal Reserve in 1982. This multiplied the size of the original debts because of the consequent increase in the debt repayments.

The Triad's international banks have already written off $300bn as a result of the sub-prime crisis. Many experts, including the International Monetary Fund (IMF), believe this figure will grow closer to $1 tn. In addition the UK government has spent $220bn nationalising Northern Rock basically to save the global financial system. Why then can these banks and their governments not write off a smaller debt which was imposed upon the poor of world via despotic dictatorships and has multiplied because of the fiscal policy of the US central bank?

Effect on Climate Change and Natural Resources

Capitalism will now resist any effective measures to reduce the effects of climate change. Such measures cut into the profitability of corporations and, as they face declining profits because of recession, they will oppose any further green measures which further eat into these already falling profit levels.

At this same stage of a global recession /downturn you would normally expect that commodity prices would decline as the commodity markets anticipate a slowing demand as global industry slows down. This is not the case as commodity prices, particularly oil, continue to rise. This is a result of several factors: the growth of the Chinese economy and its demand for commodities. The fall in the US dollar, which most commodities are priced in, means producers need more dollars to match the local currency value of the commodity. Added to these factors, there is the fear that key commodities are close to reaching their peak production again particularly oil. Since the turn of the new millennium commodities have become a major investment asset attracting both long term investors but also speculators. These higher commodity prices have started to feed through into producer prices (the price of factories producing goods) – the UK has reported the biggest increase in these in seventeen years.

Extreme weather that is a one of the byproducts of climate is reducing and wiping out harvests in the poor south. This is leading to food shortages, more starvation and rising food prices for the poorest people on our planet. However, price rises in foodstuffs and fuel are having a far more devastating effect in the Third World countries. There is no actual shortage of food in the world, but the poor millions in the shanty towns and countryside can not afford to buy basic necessities. This is why we are seeing pictures of people in Haiti eating mud pies to fill their stomachs. Capitalist barbarism has already arrived in much of the Third World.

5. UK Housing Market: A Bubble about to Burst
A Brief History of Economic Bubbles

The latest news of the first monthly decline in the average selling price of a UK house indicates that the bursting of one of the great economic bubbles of modern times is well underway. We will show that the UK housing bubble is much larger than in the US because the low interest rate policies of the early part of the new century have been compounded in the UK by two other factors. The graph shows that the average UK house price has increased 4.5 times since the start of 1987 this is compared to about a peak of 3.5 times in the US. We are therefore likely to see a much larger fall in house prices in the UK than in the US where house prices have already fallen 11% from their peak. In the UK we expect to see a fall in house prices of between 20% and 40% from the peak, meaning that the average peak house price of £184,000 would fall to approximately between £147,000 and £110,000.

This will have serious consequences for the economy and individuals. We will discuss this later in this section. We will also, show that, despite what Brown is saying, the main reason for the housing bubble in the UK was the Bank of England's policy of dramatically cutting interest rates to avert a recession and to revive the stock market at turn of the last century.

"...that he could not calculate the madness of people" – Isaac Newton when asked to comment on the South Sea Shipping Bubble.

Economic bubbles are not new of course and below we describe some of the most notable ones.

Average UK House Prices (£) Q1 1952 to Q1 2 2008

Bubbles are characterised by a frenzied greed where all rational decision-making and valuation is thrown out of the window. Investors bury their heads in the sand refusing to acknowledge the real value of the assets they are buying and the fact that buyers will eventually run out. External factors beyond their control will also affect the value of the asset itself or the economic position of the investors.

Today's situation in the US and UK housing markets most resembles what happened in the famous Wall Street Crash of 1929. This started around a recovery in the US economy in the early 1920s as individuals started to buy shares in US companies. They borrowed heavily from banks to do this and they were highly leveraged – the shares in companies were paid for by borrowed money from the bank. The banks took the bought shares as security against these loans. A speculative frenzy drove the price of US shares to way above what their real economic prospects indicated. A correction on Wall Street started panic selling as investors tried to sell their shares to repay their loans. This drove the stock market down by 89% over a period of 3 years and it took until 1954 for the market to recover to its pre-crash level. Banks across the US went bust as they could not recover the loans and the price of the shares they held as security had fallen in value radically. This slowed the whole economy to a halt as both individuals and banks went bankrupt and the economy slipped into the Great Depression of 1929-39 which spread throughout the world.

The 1929 Crash was a reaction to the performance of the US economy. It transferred itself into the stock market, then into the banks, from there to individuals and finally back into the economy.

The Great UK Housing Bubble

The great 1980s UK housing bubble, which is now deflating rapidly, started with problems in the economy in 1970/80s and was inflated by:

- Government policy around selling council houses.
- A disastrous entry into the European Exchange Rate Mechanism.
- Central bankers cutting interest rates to avoid a deep recession at the turn of the millennium.

The last major economic recessions in 1974/75 and 1979/80 saw a massive overproduction of goods and services with factories and warehouses stock-piled with unsold goods. Capitalist governments sought to stop a repeat of such a crisis of overproduction. One way was to find alternative avenues for investments; the other was to increase consumer demand for goods. The US and the UK in particular did this by privatising state industries. Excess capital flowed in and created a climate and appetite for credit amongst their working and middle classes.

One way this was carried out in the UK was to sell off council housing. This allowed spare capital to be invested in a growing private housing market and created a shortage of social housing meaning that ordinary people were forced to look at buying private housing rather than renting a council home. The second way was to create a feeling of wealth through home ownership. This encouraged people to borrow money through credit – loans and credit cards. Thus, at the beginning of the 1980s, these factors started the great UK housing bubble.

Another factor, was also absent in the US, was the UK's entry in the European Exchange Rate Mechanism (ERM). Before the creation of the Euro, the ERM ensured that the different members' currencies exchanged against each other within defined limits. However, because of the weakness of the UK economy and hence sterling, the UK was forced to keep interest rates high to attract investors into sterling assets to keep it within the restricted bands of the ERM. This was not sustainable and on Black Wednesday in September of 1992, the Tory Chancellor put interest rates up from 12% to 15% and then announced Britain was withdrawing from the ERM and slashed them to 12% again. This allowed the UK to cut interest rates dramatically and bring the country out of recession but at the same time create a boom in the housing industry and a growth in credit.

The final stimulus to the UK housing market came at the turn of the millennium when the US had slipped into recession and the Dot.com shares bubble burst. The US central bank, the Federal Reserve, cut interest rates aggressively and Chancellor Brown followed suit. This fuelled a massive boom in credit and house prices. All types of liberal lending practices developed - buy to let, no deposit mortgages, loans of a multiple greater than three times one's income, re-mortgages, loans secured on equity in homes, and low fixed rate mortgages. These are the UK sub-prime loans. This is why the UK housing bubble has just come to an end.

The Fed and Bank of England Inflates the Housing Bubble

The US central bank, the Federal Reserve, cut interest rates aggressively, during 2000/2001 to dampen the domestic recession and lift the stock markets after the dot.com shares bubble burst. They cut interest rates to as low as 1.0% - in the UK they were cut to a low of 3.5%. This created the conditions for a credit boom and in particular a house lending boom which because of the low level of interest rates was aimed at low income families or even families on social security. They could be charged a much higher rate than the market interest rate to compensate for the increased risk of these borrowers defaulting on their loans.

Mortgage brokers sought out these loans and then laid them off onto investment and commercial banks who repacked them as complex securities called collateralised debt obligations (CDOs). These were then sold on to hedge funds, pension funds, insurance companies and banks all over the world reaching every corner of the global financial system. The model that is used to value these products was flawed and based on a very low default rate by the sub-prime borrowers in the US and a very low estimation of the close relationship between these borrowers.

When the Federal Reserve started to put up interest rates to cool the credit boom and curb creeping inflation, the default rate amongst the sub-prime borrowers picked up dramatically. The closeness of the relationship between these borrowers turned out to be much greater than at first estimated. This caused the value of these CDOs to fall rapidly leading to losses throughout the global financial system. Losses so far are estimated at $300bn to $500bn with the International Monetary Fund believing that the final losses could be nearer $1 tn.

The Chickens Come Home To Roost

In August 2007, these losses caused the money market to dry up as nobody would make loans to each other as lenders did not know what risk the borrowers were carrying. This is an unsecured lending market (i.e. not guaranteed by the government). The interest rates quoted are based on the borrowers and lenders having the highest credit rating called triple A. There are now only two major banks which still are rated at triple A and one of those is on a negative watch – that is it could be downgraded. This means those lending money put a premium on the rates they will lend at to other financial institutions depending on their view of how risky was the borrowers business. No matter how low central banks cut interest rates – where they would lend to the triple AAA rated banks – it made no difference to the rate where these banks would lend on in an unsecured manner to other financial institutions. This is the so called 'Credit Crunch' and it is filtering through to every level of society right across the world.

The 'Credit Crunch' is causing the deflation in the UK mortgage market. As all the exotic cheap deals end, lenders put up the rate that people borrow at to buy a house. They will only lend to the most secure borrowers because they can now only access a much smaller pool of money.

Therefore, the demand for property will fall sharply with fewer buyers seeking to purchase houses. It's a simple economic law of over supply and under demand which leads to a decrease in the price of an asset. This decline will go on for some time as it will take one to three further years to unravel the global sub-prime lending products and losses.

Recession on its Way
The consequences for the UK economy are severe. There will be a big drop off in consumer demand as credit dries up rapidly – we are already seeing this from consumer confidence surveys. The UK economy is almost certain to go into a recession some time at the end of 2008 or the beginning of 2009. Spain and Ireland are the other economies, apart from the US and UK, which are already experiencing house price declines. They both have large speculative housing markets. There are also property hot spots in the emerging economies of China, India, Brasil and Hong Kong which will follow the same fate as the US and UK housing markets. It is too difficult to estimate if we are going to enter a full blown global slump of 1930s or 1974/75 proportions but the odds of it happening are shortening all the time.

Conclusion: Capitalism as a casino economy
One of the key points to emerge from this discussion is that there is an inherent madness in the way the capitalist economy works. Both financiers and producers speculate widely and endlessly in their drive to increase profits. This is where the phrase 'If you don't speculate, you can't accumulate' comes from. There is no sense in which the capitalist economy is planned. Nor is there any real coordination between the different competing units of

capital. Capitalists play in a casino and the problem is the chips they play with are our lives.

6. How The Crisis Will Affect Scotland

We can see several developments in the Scottish economy as result of the global and economic financial crisis. We have already noted that the tightening of credit will mean that lenders will be more aggressive in chasing up bad personal and mortgage debts. In 2008 and 2009 there will be more personal bankruptcies and repossessions than in 2007.

The mortgage market will shrink and become more competitive with no growth in new customers. This will hit the two large Scottish banks Halifax Bank of Scotland (HBOS) and Royal Bank of Scotland (RBS). HBOS will be hit the hardest. It has the largest share of the UK mortgage market and is the most exposed to money market loans. But the RBS has greater exposure to sub-prime products and has further exposure through selling other derivatives to hedge funds, fund managers and investment banks. Its recent intention to raise $26bn in a rights issue is to cover loses on sub-prime products and protect it against any future loses in its' other derivative products. We expect to see attempted redundancies at both banks.

As the chart below shows Scotland is now very dependent on the business and financial sector with 18% of Scotland's workforce, or 450,000 people employed in this sector. The tightening of credit and falling asset prices will see a fall off in business right across the sector with thousands of jobs at risk from redundancy. Falling profits in this sector will see business and financial companies try and keep wages rises down and attempt to increase productivity.

The next biggest private sector is tourism (hotels and restaurants) and this will suffer a double whammy. First, Scots, as they tighten their belts, will cut back on luxuries such as going out for meals and short breaks, Secondly, the international recession will mean less foreign visitors and therefore less spent in hotels and restaurants. Manufacturing is smaller than it was ten years ago but still employs nearly 225,000 and this will be hit by the global downturn in demand.

Scotland's biggest employer is the public sector. It will be hit by a big reduction in tax revenues especially from 2009/2010. We can expect to see threatened cuts and redundancies in this sector as the government tries to make good its shortfall in revenues.

These will be added to the cutbacks in front line services, already being imposed across Scotland, as a result of the SNP Scottish Executive's freeze on council tax revenues, and the real cut in New Labour's Westminster block grant.

7. A Socialist Alternative to Neo-liberalism

As we have shown in this pamphlet the real economy is now intrinsically linked to the global financial system. The historic role of the financial markets has been to raise capital for corporations and public funds for governments.

But financial markets have always attracted speculators, who have created financial bubbles where the assets in the markets are priced way above where they should be realistically valued at. These bubbles invariably burst and as well as causing bankruptcy and the ruin of the individual speculators have a damaging consequence for the wider economy and as a consequence the innocent majority of the population.

We saw that it was such a speculative bubble which was one of the main causes of the 1929-39 depression.

Neo-liberalism, which was the main capitalist solution to its slumps of 1974/75 and 1979/80, has since the early 1980's opened up and deregulated financial markets. This was to ease the raising of and movement of capital around the world and to create an alternative home for underperforming investment capital. This was to avoid a repeat of the crisis of the over-production of goods and services seen in the depressions of 1974/75 and 1979/80.

This has created a wave of speculators – by US investment banks and latterly the new hedge funds – who have exploited these deregulated and globally connected markets.

New Labour

New Labour has been amongst the biggest supporters of this neo-liberal project. Gordon Brown has made two major contributions to this. The first was to remove control over interest rates from an elected government. This was the major instrument for regulating the economy. Now, control is in the hands of an unelected committee of the representatives of global finance. This committee decided to cut interest rates aggressively at the turn of the millennium and then to put them up in the spring/summer of 2007. This has exasperated the problems in the UK credit and housing markets.

The second was to create an ineffective body to regulate the financial markets in the UK, the Financial Services Authority (FSA). The FSA has proved to be a toothless organisation lacking in the expertise, skills, experience and powers to police the financial markets. One has only to witness their low level of prosecutions of financial crimes in the City. The most damning indictment of their ineptitude was their failure to spot the crisis in Northern Rock which most of the financial markets had detected at the start of 2007. They have admitted their failure in this case and Brown has announced there will be an investigation into it. It is an investigation to be carried out by the FSA themselves!

New Labour's privatisations and the use of Private Financial Initiatives (PFIs) are other examples of their love affair with neo- Liberalism. PFIs basically allow private companies to build projects and then lease them back to the government for a period of years. We pay exorbitant rates of interest and at the end of the lease it is the private companies that own the schools and hospitals to do as they want with them.

The SNP
The new SNP administration in Scotland is repeating the same mistakes. Their main objective is growth for the Scottish economy; for growth read more and easy profits for private global and local companies. It's an unattainable target given the current and likely future state of the global economy and the crisis in the financial markets. We can see this by the SNP's attempts to curry favour with individual business people such as Brian Souter and Donald Trump.

Their replacement for PFI's is essentially the same beast in the form of a Scottish Futures Trust. They have frozen council tax but this is leading to cuts in services and jobs across the country and they have no plans for a radical progressive local income tax that would carry out some wealth redistribution from the rich to the less well off.

Their plans for independence are within the European Community, with Scotland remaining part of the Sterling Zone. This would mean that control of interest rates would remain with the Bank of England. Even if Scotland were to later join the Eurocurrency Zone, this would mean handing decisions over to a European Central Bank which is also more concerned with fighting inflation than relieving the effects of a recession. Either option would also mean a limit to the size of the budget deficit a Scottish government could run to fund public spending projects such as schools, hospitals and housing. This would mean a dependence on PFI type schemes for any public services.

The Alternative - An Economy under Common Ownership and Democratic Control

There is an alternative to the speculation of the money markets and the booms and slumps of a capitalist economy. It is an economy owned by the people, run by the people, for the benefit of the people.

Instead of hundreds of types of different goods being produced without any idea if anybody wants them or if they will serve any useful purpose, the consumers and producers and the locally communities will democratically decide what is needed by society. We live in a world of limited and declining resources and it is only rational to plan what should be produced and what needs should be met by these goods.

It would mean that the major components of the economy would be taken into common ownership. Industries and services would be run by the people who work in them with democratically elected management boards. It would require a new style of revolutionary democracy based on mass participation, with people discussing and voting on proposals. All shades of opinion would be able to be represented and allowed to put their plans and proposals to a network of local, regional and national assemblies.

Planning and its implementation would take place at the level of society most appropriate to the plans themselves.

This type of participative, decision making, pluralist socialist democracy is a million miles away from the Soviet bureaucratic command style economic planning that took place in the former so called "socialist" countries.

A vibrant planned economy decided on by a mass participatory socialist democracy is the only rational alternative to capitalism's four horseman of death - slumps, war, climate disaster and poverty - for the billions in the poor South.

It is an alternative that the Scottish Socialist Party is campaigning and fighting for.

8. Immediate Socialist Solutions to the Crisis

Socialists also have answers to the immediate crisis. We would:

* Provide sustainable and affordable social housing for rent. The £110 billion that the UK government spent on saving Northern Rock would alone pay for 2 million of such houses!

- Take under common ownership all banks involved in house lending and turn their mortgages into cheap social loans.
- Take under common ownership the house building companies and task them with building social housing.
- Set in law the right to open the accounts of any financial firm or pension fund to inspect its investments and strategies.
- Set up an empowered independent body of people with market experience to regulate the financial markets. They would be elected and accountable to an assembly of individual investors and enforce stiff penalties and sanctions.
- Pass legislation to stop repossessions happening and turn the property involved in the loan into socially rented housing.
- Raise the threshold for personal bankruptcies from £1,500 to £10,000.
- Freeze all food prices and bring the production, distribution and sale of food under social ownership - food meets a basic human need.
- Demand the triad banks and their government write off the developing world's debt.
- End the massive expenditure on arms and nuclear weapons and use this to pay for social amenities and services.
- Raise taxation on the rich and on companies to provide the funds for expanding social provision of housing and social services.
- Cut the excise duty on petrol prices and increase the tax on the oil companies profits.
- Introduce a free public transport system to reduce are dependency on the car and reduce pollution and oil consumption.
- Bring the Oil industry under common ownership.
- Introduce a food for oil and technology and skill programme with countries in the poor south.
- Bring the power and gas companies under common ownership and reduce prices – heating and cooking are a basic human need.

The UK's deflating housing bubble is just but one manifestation of an interconnected global financial and economical crisis.

Socialists will have plenty of opportunities in the coming months and years to show there is a rational and humane alternative to the disease that is capitalism as the global crisis challenges its very foundations and its accepted ways of running our lives.

Bibliography
The Economics of Global Turbulence, Robert Brenner, 2006.
Your Money or Your Life -The Tyranny of Global Finance, Eric Toussaint, 2005.
Late Capitalism, Ernest Mandel, 1972.
The Second Slump, Ernest Mandel, 1980.
Long Waves of Capitalist Development, Ernest Mandel, 1995.
Options, Futures and Other Derivatives, John Hull, 2006.
From Black-Scholes to Black Holes, Risk, 1992.
Money Market Madness, Scottish Socialist Voice 321, 2008.
Between Northern Rock and a Financial Crisis, Scottish Socialist Voice 322, 2008.

Case Study: Leverage
Leverage is when you buy something with borrowed money because you cannot afford the full price. For example, you want to buy that new car that costs £30,000. You don't have the full £30,000 but can only put a deposit of £3,000 down on it. You borrow the rest from a finance company hoping to repay this loan from your monthly salary. If you lose your job and can no longer pay the loan the car is taken from you by the finance company.

Case Study: Interest Rates
The Bank of England (BOE) cut interest rates on 10 April 2008 to 5.0%. Why can't ordinary people borrow at this rate and why have mortgage rates not moved down? The BOE controls the base rate and they moved this down by 0.25% to 5.0%. This is the rate they will lend to national banks. These banks then lend and borrow in the interbank lending market. To make any money they have to lend at a higher rate than they are able to borrow at. They also, have to consider if the bank or institution they are lending to will default on the loan. The most highly rated banks – called triple A – will be quoted a LIBOR (London Interbank Offer Rate) number which they can borrow money at. This figure only fell by 0.05% in the wake of the BOE's rate cut. This reflects the uncertainty over the financial future of all institutions – that is the likelihood that they will default on any loan which is unsecured. There are only two large triple A banks left in the market and one of them looks like it might be downgraded to double A. This means its chances of defaulting on a loan have increased. The mortgage lender that most people use will not have such a high credit rating as tripe A. They will have to pay a higher rate than LIBOR and they will to want to make a profit on the mortgage. Banks such as HBOS are paying a large premium over LIBOR. This reflects the lenders' views that HBOS's financial position will deteriorate because of its exposure to the UK mortgage market and its high dependence on the money markets to fund its loans for borrowers.

Recessions & Depressions

Recession – This occurs when a period of economic growth comes to an end due to falling profit rates, leading to overproduction and stockpiling of goods. It can also be triggered by a financial crisis following a speculative bubble.

The last two major recessions in the UK occurred between 1974-5 and 1979-80. Japan has suffered a prolonged recession since 1990, which spread into much of the rest of the Far East (except China).

Depression – This is a major downturn in economic activity, leading to long-term unemployment and great hardship.

The Long Depression (1873-96) mainly affected the agricultural regions of Europe. New farmlands, particularly in the Americas and Australia, were able to produce food and raw materials more cheaply. Large scale emigration eventually helped to relieve hardship.

The Great Depression (1929-39) affected the whole world. It was triggered by the speculative bubble in US shares. Closures of factories and mines led to large-scale unemployment. Low agricultural prices forced many small farmers out of business. It took the destruction caused by the Second World War before a full recovery was made. The organizations of the working class had been greatly weakened.

Some Financial Bubbles

1. The Tulip Bubble (1636-7) in the Netherlands saw the Dutch population taking part in a speculative frenzy based on borrowed money. This resulted, when it burst, in many individual bankruptcies and the Dutch economy slipping into what we would now call an economic depression.

2. The South Sea Bubble (1720) in the UK saw wild speculation in a company to which the government had given exclusive trading rights in the Pacific. When it was found that there were few market prospects the bubble burst.

3. The Railway Mania (1847) in the UK led many people to invest in railway projects which had little basis in reality. The 1847 Crash also coincided with the Great Famine in Ireland. Poverty stricken peasants died in their hundreds of thousands because they could not afford the plentiful wheat crop but had to live on blight-destroyed potatoes.

4. The Wall Street Crash (1929) in the USA was preceded by a frenzy of share buying in industries which believed the 1920's American consumer boom would never end.

5. The Dot,com crash (2000) saw the biggest ever drop in share prices ($2tn) when it became clear that the many dot.com companies which had been set up were grossly overvalued.

What is a Mortgage?

Mortgage lending is a form of leveraged borrowing. Home buyers borrow from a bank or building society multiples of their income to buy an asset, their house, paying some initial (or in some cases no) deposit. The bank or building society takes the house as security against the home buyer not being able to meet their loan. As long as house prices stay the same or increase and the homeowner remains able to meet their mortgage (loan) repayments which relate to the inflated price the house was bought. The problems now are that house prices are starting to fall and some homeowners are beginning to have problems meeting these repayments.

In the past, mortgage borrowers had to put down a substantial deposit. This ensured that the building society or bank making the loan retained substantial funds to pay off any unforeseen demands. Building societies and banks were not highly leveraged, i.e. there were limits on the amount of money they could provide. Recently, mortgage borrowers have not had to make any prior deposit. This means that building societies and banks are more highly leveraged and can loan much greater sums of money. It also means they are in a much worse position if borrowers are unable to pay up. This is the kind of situation that caused the Wall Street Crash in 1929.

Case Study: HBOS (Halifax Bank of Scotland)

HBOS has over 20 million customers and 63,000 employees. It has the largest share of the UK mortgage market at about 20%. However, after Northern Rock, it was the biggest user of the money markets to fund its mortgage book - about 30% of its mortgages are funded this way, 50% more than its rivals. It therefore has to pay more for its funds and this is reflected in HBOS putting up its mortgages for its less credit worthy customers. Faced with a shrinking and more competitive mortgage market and higher borrowing costs than its rivals explains why its share price has fallen by 54% since the credit crunch broke in August 2007. We can expect attempted:redundancies and "productivity increases" and cuts in real wages for its workforce in the months ahead.

8. Postscript – September 2008

The effective nationalisation by the US government of Freddie Mac and Fannie Mae highlights the very origin of the current global financial and economic crisis. These two agencies control the almost half of the US mortgage market. They were originally set up by the US government to stimulate the housing market and hence the market for credit. They were the pioneers of repackaging house loans into mortgage backed securities (MBS). These MBS were forerunners of the CDOs which are at the centre of the so called sub-prime credit crunch. Both entities faced the prospect of not being able to renew over £200 billion of borrowings on the money markets in September 2008. Because house prices are still falling in the US their mortgage book looks very unattractive to both investors and lenders of cash to them.

It this drying up of credit to consumers and the fall in their house prices that is reducing demand for goods and the driving force in slowing world economies. House prices and have fallen by over 20% from their peak in the US and by nearly 13% in the UK. As we have shown, that along with Spain, these are housing markets with the largest house price bubbles. These declines will continue as the supply of money available to lend to potential house owners shrinks and banks remain reluctant to lend when the asset (the house) they are using as security is declining in price. Demand for mortgages is falling to as recession bites and people are losing their jobs or not feeling their job is secure. Brown's removal of stamp duty on house purchases will do nothing to change the supply of funds for house purchases or the falling demand for houses.

This means that a prolonged recession or slump (more than two successive months of negative GDP growth) is on the card for the world's major mature economies. In the second quarter of 2008 all the major mature economies slipped into negative GDP growth or flat growth apart from the US. The US has escaped a decline in GDP because it cut interest rates very aggressively, pumped money into the money markets, gave tax cuts and the declining value of the US dollar meant that its import export revenues came in higher. All these factor have disappeared and the US is almost certain to have negative GDP growth in third and fourth quarters of 2008. The other major economies have reacted less swiftly to the crisis and have focused on fighting inflation by keeping interest rates high and have not cut taxes. They have paid the price with negative or flat growth and any measures they take now will have a much smaller positive effect on their economies.

The financial system is paralysed and despite central banks – the US and European in particular - pumping money into the system, lending has not increased. Instead banks have hoarded money to replenish their capital against further potential losses from complex derivatives. Several medium sized banks – Lehmans and Merrill Lynch – are in trouble because their smaller capital base and exposure to complex derivatives make them potential bankrupts. Investors are unwilling to pump fresh capital into them because of this risk. A second complex instrument hangs over the whole banking industry: credit default swaps (CDSs). These have been heavily sold by banks to insure against companies going bankrupt. The prices of these instruments has been rising hitting the balance sheets of the banks. The real crunch comes when companies start to go bankrupt and the banks have to pay out on the insurance. These products were sold in large volumes from 2001 onwards when the global economy had just comes out of recession – it is estimated that there is over $30 trillion of this insurance outstanding. As we enter a recession the rate of bankruptcies will increase and the recovery of assets from bankrupt companies will likely to be lower than estimated in pricing these CDSs. Banks will take big hit globally – up to £5 trillion worldwide. This is likely to take some banks down with a domino effect through the banking system. This is why the financial markets are so worried about Lehmans because it has exposure with CDSs and other mortgage related securities to other banks and financial institutions.

The major emerging economies – China, India and Brasil - have been hit by the global downturn in the mature economies. China's GDP and manufacturing growth rates have slowed down as the demand for their exports has slowed. While not in recession these big slow downs have resulted in pain for Chinese workers as factories have closed and workers have been laid of. Domestic demand has been dampened in these economies as their governments have chosen to raise interest rates to quell inflation. China's massive infrastructure spending programme is keeping its economy growing and also keeping up demand for natural resources globally.

Inflation – both food and natural resource – hangs over the capitalist system. Food inflation will continue as climate change affects crops and the demand from China for western style foods will only diminish slightly as the rate of Chinese economic growth only slows. Natural resource inflation is likely to slow after the speculative bubble of the last two years had burst and global demand from the mature economies slows as they slide into recession. However, we expect it to continue rising at the rate of growth that we saw from 2000 to the middle of 2006 when natural resources as whole saw their prices rise by 250%. This is largely as a result of the massive infrastructure programmes going on in China and the other emerging economies. This will give capitalism little room for manoeuvre.

Lehman Brothers effective bankruptcy in filing for chapter 11 protection marks the second leg of the greatest financial and economic crisis that capitalism has faced since the great depression of the 1930s. Lehman Brothers is the largest financial bankruptcy in US history. On the same day one of the big three investment banks, Merrill Lynch, was taken over by Bank of America. The Thundering Herd as Merrills was once known, does not have as much mortgage backed exposure as Lehmans and the Bank of America' capital base could easily absorb any further potential losses that Merrills may incur. On the same day the major bond insurer AIG failed in its bid for buyout of its trouble hit business and is now looking for a short-term loan of $40 billion from the US government!. Such were the unknown extent of Lehmans future potential losses on mortgaged backed securities and other derivative instruments that no bank or institution was willing to step in and buy it for virtually nothing. The US government has taken the gamble that the global financial system can absorb the losses that investors all around the world will be hit with as a result of Lehmans defaulting on its obligations.

The implications for the financial system and hence the global economy are far reaching. The money markets have frozen up again with short dated interest rates rising as nobody knows who has exposure to Lehmans and more importantly credit default swaps (CDS). CDS are the second leg of this great financial crisis. CDSs are insurance sold by banks to protect against companies going bankrupt. This price has risen from about 1.5% to 2% overnight wiping about $150bn off banks' balance sheets.

We will come to be as familiar with CDSs as we are with sub-prime collateralised debt obligations (CDOs). As we have pointed out some $30 trillion has been sold over the last seven years by banks to investors. There is a double whammy as bankruptcies rise the value of these contracts increases to the investors and the banks have to pay out any of the debt not recovered when a company or companies on which the CDSs have been sold goes bankrupt. The banks that have sold these products have seriously underestimated the bankruptcy rate – not foreseeing a recession at or one of this severity and overestimated the rate of recovery of a bankrupt company's assets. We could well see losses to the global banking industry of $5 trillion. As nobody knows who has sold these CDSs – they are unlisted, unregulated instruments – or on what companies, banks will be reluctant to lend to each other no matter if interest rates are cut or money is pumped into the money markets by central banks. This will dry up lending and push up the cost of credit. This will lead to further declines in house prices and the removal of credit as a tool to try and reflate the global economy.

The global recession will therefore be deeper and more prolonged with natural resource prices falling as the financial markets anticipate much reduced demand for them. Several medium and small banks are almost certain to go down as a result of CDS losses with the possibility that one of the major banks will follow leading to a domino meltdown of the global financial system.

Capitalism's solutions to the crisis are unlikely to work. Tax rebates will be used to clear credit or be hoarded for that rainy day. Budget deficit spending will be inflationary and carried out on a modest scale. Much of the demand for materials from such projects will not benefit local economies but the natural resource companies and add further inflationary pressure. Energy savings' packages proposed by governments will be passed back to the poor with higher energy prices.

The workers and poor of the world are starting to fight back and say it is not our crisis and we won't pay for it. Workers from Boeing in the US to council workers and civil servants in the UK are striking for higher pay to maintain their living standards. The very poorest of our fellow civilians, who make up the overwhelming majority of the world's 6.6 billion population, are marching and demanding basic foods in wake of shortages.

Capitalism has runs its course and its latest crisis has shown the emptiness of neo-liberalism. It has opened up a debate about housing, the financial system and the right to affordable food and energy. Socialists have an opening to put the case for a rationale society based on meeting the needs of the entire world's population and that can use our finite resources in sustainable way. It is one we should all go out and seize.

Acknowledgements

"To Marilyn for her wonderful love & encouragement throughout 2008"

My thanks also to the many comrades who encouraged me to write this pamphlet. In particular for their many suggestions and contributions: Gregor Gall, Frank Martin, Marilyn Sangster, Kevin Leetion and Allan Armstrong. Eddie Truman did page layout, Gillian Tyrer proofread.

Last but not least to the memory of Ernest Mandel who inspired me to try to understand modern finance and ecomonics and to try and change the system that brings such misery to the majority of the world's population.

A F T E R W O R D
Looking Back and Looking Forward

There is no doubt about it capitalism is teetering on the edge of its second great depression. While a recession is defined as two successive quarters of negative growth in an economy – set by economists as all the goods and services that are produced domestically or the gross domestic product (GDP) - there is no formal definition for a depression. Here we will define a depression as a prolonged recession lasting more than two years of successive quarters of negative growth and resulting in a 10% shrinkage in GDP. How did capitalism get to the edge of the precipice? In this afterword we try answer that question.

First, we will shows that at the root of this crisis for the world's economy and global finance lay a series of economic and financial policies that were used to deal with capitalism's last great economic slump: the 1974/1975 recession. We will identify what lay behind this crisis and what policies were put forward by capitalism to solve it. We will show that these policies were later extended, modified and added to by mainly the governments' of Clinton, Bush, Blair and Brown to pull capitalism out of a speculative bubble. We will show that the world's central banks implemented monetary policies without understanding the complexity of the financial system and products that they had helped create and the impact of their policy changes on them

Next we will try to explain the dynamics of the current crisis. How it has interacted with the real economy and the global financial system and has created a beast that is eating up the capital of global finance. These losses are so great that the whole global financial system is frozen and is on the verge of bankruptcy.

Following this, we will look at the strategies that governments have come up with to fight the crisis. Many governments and commentators are reviving the memory of Keynesian economics with their crisis fighting policies. We will show how these policies did not work, contrary to popular myth, in the first place, what actually solved the first great depression and how Keynesian solutions are even more unlikely to succeed this time round given the dynamics of this financial crisis. We will then examine the Marxist theories of economic crisis and see if they can explain the current crisis or if some new theory or modification of an existing theory is required to do so.

Next we will chart how capitalism is likely to evolve from this crisis and what solutions it will try to inflict on the working class and poor of the world to save itself. We will ask if there may be a further rise in fascism as means to this end.

Finally we look at how the effects of the crisis will make the workers and poor of the world fight back against capitalism' offensive and how socialists could organise to help transform this great crisis of capitalism into an opportunity to create a new society based on cooperation, that is democratically run and sets out to meet the needs of people and not the needs of capital.

At The Root of This Crisis
At the root of this crisis lies:

- A bubble in housing prices.
- A liberal lending regime to everyone from the poorest in the rich worth to whole countries.
- The deregulation of the financial system.
- The breaking down of the demarcation lines in finance and banking.
- The creation of new complex financial instruments that can multiply the exposure to the assets they are based on.
- Independent carefree interest rate policies.

These factors evolved from solutions to the 1974/75 economic slump. This slump marked the first synchronised economic recession since the end of the second world war. The recession came about as profit rates started to decline as more and more human labour (mental and manual) was replaced by automation. In addition there was an over accumulation of capitalist profits that could not be profitability invested. This led to a massive over production of goods and services which could not be sold.

Capitalism tried to solve the problem of declining profits by weakening the organisations of the working class, increasing productivity and moving its production base to South East Asia where the rate of exploitation was greater. The problem of the over accumulation of capital was to create new avenues for it. Some of this was done through the privatisation of state industries and housing. The deregulation of financial markets and institution, allowed some of this excess capital to be invested in financial speculation. Finally, to solve the crisis of producing too many goods capitalism created an easy market for credit on the back of private home ownership and the deregulation of financial markets and institutions.

The governments of Clinton, Bush, Blair and Brown further extended these neo-liberal policies. Their central bankers made a major error at the turn of the millennium when they cut their central bank lending rates dramatically – US rates fell to 1% and UK rates fell to 3.5%,. They did this as the so called dot come bubble burst and the US economy went into recession. This created a major housing bubble and because of the liberal deregulated financial markets and institutions, a wave of credit related products were created on the back of these very low interest rates which helped feed back into the housing bubble.

The Dynamics of the Crisis

Having created a giant housing and credit bubble and a raft of products and strategies that sought to take advantage of the very low interest rate environment central bankers on both sides of the Atlantic then unknowingly burst it rapidly. Worried about growing inflation , the by product of so much credit and increased demand from China, and the housing bubble, central bankers started to raise interest rates in 2006/2007. They had no idea of the vast network of products that were linked to the US house market or the depth of poor peoples' borrowings – the so called sub-prime market. Up to 20% of US lending is sub-prime and an incredible 60% of US mortgages are in some form of derivative security. These were repackaged around the world and sold to all sorts of banks, financial institutions and pension's funds. The US central bankers did not realise how sensitive the sub-prime lenders were to rises in interest rates. These lenders soon started to default on payments and this helped, as well as the increase in interest rates, to bringing about a fall in house prices. Products based on these sub-prime mortgages fell in value and financial institutions who bought them started to have financial problems and suffered huge losses – Bear Sterns being a good example. Those other institutions that had borrowed short-term in the money markets and lent this money long term – Northern Rock and HBOS are good examples of this – run into trouble as the cost of short-term borrowing rose. Nobody would lend to them either as they feared they may go bankrupt as a result of this failed business model.

The dynamic of a falling housing market has continued and now has gone beyond sub-prime loans to prime and even super-prime loans as these borrowers face the same problems as the very poorest borrowers did. The US housing market was worth over $12 trillion at its peak and 60% of this as we mentioned has been repacked as some form of derivative and sold round the world. Other types of loans such as credit cards and car loans have been repackaged this way and in other countries as well as the US most notably the UK. These are the toxic assets that have been talked about and they are becoming even more toxic.

The banks were first afraid to lend to other banks and financial institutions because these borrowers may be potential defaulters and go bankrupt. Now the lending banks are suffering such losses on these repackaged loans and something called credit default swaps (CDS) that they need their money to cover day to day losses and quarterly write downs of mortgage and loan based products.

This has caused a complete freezing of the credit markets to everyone form the individual right through to small businesses to large corporations and governments and countries. This drying up of credit is and has pushed the world into an economic recession as consumer demand dries up and capitalism is unable to function because it cannot service its day to day running without credit. Of course the recession feeds into lower house prices and this feeds into more bank losses and more tightening of credit and a deeper recession and so on.

In a recession companies go bankrupt and here is a further problem for the banks. They have sold insurance against companies going bankrupt called CDSs. The value of this insurance has risen in value and hit the daily cash reserves of the banks and now as companies start to go bankrupt then the banks have to make a full payout to those who have bough the insurance on the bankrupt company. Recent examples have been Lehmans and an Icelandic bank. Up to $60 trillion of CDS insurance has been sold and the losses to the global banking system could be in the region of $10 trillion if we have a long severe recession as seems likely. This of course further freezes up credit which deepens and prolongs the recession which leads to more bankruptcies which feeds into more bank losses and so on! It is literally a spiralling dynamic that will be very difficult to stop.

The interacting dynamic of recession, falling house prices and corporate bankruptcies is taking us to the edge of a great depression. It is a dynamic that governments don't fully understand and will be sucked into with disastrous consequences.

Solutions to The Crisis
Governments and central banks, particularly outside the US, have been kept on the hop in trying to deal with the crisis. They have moved from one fire to another mainly throwing money at the banking and financial system as they tried to stop financial institutions going bankrupt or the haemorrhaging of their capital and cash.

Governments have literally thrown trillions of tax payers dollars putting these fires out – it was revealed that the US Federal Reserve (FED) have spent over $US2 trillion over the last few months under existing legislation onto top of the $US700 billion recently announced rescue plan.

Because of the dynamic of the financial system losses the FED have abandoned buying the toxic mortgage backed securities as they had spent so much on keeping financial companies from going under. They understand that they will need more money in the near future as the recession deepens and the financial system losses spiral further out of control. There in lies the seeds of another problem. Just as governments want to spend money on capital projects and giving tax cuts to try and boost demand they will have very little money left to do this as they spend so much money on the bailouts.

These bailout which lead to a huge borrowing requirements which will be difficult to meet because nobody wants to hold the assets of a weak economy as that country's currency will also be weak. Recently the German government failed to sell all its issue of government bonds and Germany is perceived to have the best quality of state debt. Too much debt financing by governments issuing bonds will also lead to high long-term interest rates which will push up short term interest rates as well. There is the possibility that governments could go bankrupt themselves and have to be bailed out by the International Monetary Fund – global capitalism's central bank. Of course lending of the scale needed to bring the world out of recession also fuels inflation.

The other Keynesian policies of cutting interest rates and giving tax rebates can limit the depth, length and onset of a recession but not avoid one. This is what happened this time round in the US and their policies delayed the recession starting by three months. The rest of the world was slow to follow such policies and using tax rebates and cutting interest rates will now lead to individuals hoarding money for those unexpected bills or as insurance against losing their income in the future or the future tax increases to pay for it all in the first place!.

All these policies do not deal with the two fundamental requirements for a recovery in the global economy: capitalists to invest in fresh new projects and individuals to increase their spending, leading to a need to increase the production of goods and services.

In the 1930s it was massive arms expenditure, which in itself is inflationary, and a second world war which destroyed huge amounts of capital, that created the conditions for the recovery of capitalism after 1945.

Marxists Theories of the Crisis
These broadly fall in to two camps. One camp thinks that too much profit is being produced and being accumulated and this tries to find fresh avenues of investment. But too many goods and services are produced and these end up being unsold and this leads to a crisis of an over-production of goods.

The other camp believes that as workers are more and more exploited by increases in productivity that their real wages decrease and as a consequence their demand for goods and services falls. Capitalism has to do this because their rate of profit is decling as more and more of the human labour in the production process – physical and mental – is being replaced by automation. This tends to happen as capitalism's boom cycle approaches its peak.

Accompanied by every boom particularly as the peak is being approached is speculation in credit and credit based investments. This has happened with every cycle. In this crisis governments and central banks laid the basis for a massive bubble in credit and speculation which was able to be leveraged several times by the use of complex financial instruments called derivatives. As the name suggests they are not actual physical assets but are derived from the performance of a physical assets or in some cases economic measures which only have a mathematical reality – such as inflation or interest rates. Capitalism needed new avenues to put it's over accumulating capital and financial speculation was one of them. It also kept demand up as a real wages fell by giving everyone from the poorest in society to the affluent middle classes unlimited access to credit.

Ultimately, it was the drying up of credit which led to a huge decrease in demand that is fuelling this slump and recession. As Marx emphasised on several occasions in Capital 'the ultimate reason for all real crises always remain the poverty and restricted consumption of the masses, as opposed to the drive of capitalist production to develop the productive forces as though the absolute consuming power of society constituted their limit'.

But it is the complete paralysis of the financial system with its exposure to recession multiplied several times by the use of derivatives that could take the world into its second great depression. This financial crisis is unprecedented either in scope, depth and complexity in capitalism's history.

A New State Capitalism
There is a debate emerging between the left and right wings of capitalism. The right want to let private companies go the wall and have some bank bailouts but under bankers control to keep the financial system afloat. This right wing view is represented by the Republican administration in the US and the German Christian democratic government in Germany and Cameron's Tories. The left view is a move to state control of the financial system, tighter financial regulations and the taking over of troubled major private enterprises such as General Motors in the US. This wing of capitalism is represented by the Democratic Party in the US and Brown government in the UK. Salmond's SNP is somewhere between theses two camps.

China is likely to emerge as a stronger capitalist power as although its economy is slowing rapidly and it may go into a light recession it has less exposure to credit or to house bubble related assets. It is keen to attract international investors and private equity firms and corporate financiers may pile their money into China. They see it as the best bet of a recovery amongst the capitalist economies after they have suffered heavy losses, and the banks that lent them the money, on their projects in the mature economies of the north.

We are unlikely to see an emergence of fascism as a capitalist tool as happened in the 1930s when it was used to break a highly organised and politically conscious working class. This has already happened with the big defeats of the working class in the northern hemisphere in the early 1980s. Capitalism too has moved its production base to Asia and other emerging countries where it has much higher rates of exploitation and a more compliant work force.

There will many struggles world wide against capitalism onslaught to restore profitability and save itself. Many of the struggles against factory closures, redundancies and increased productivity will be led by the emerging working class in Asia. In the rich north there will be resistance as well and the opportunity will arise to build a new combative working class rank and file current as the ineffectiveness of the unions and their leaders becomes evident to the broad mass of the population.

Socialists have the opportunity to help build such an alternative current in and outside the workers movement as well as engage in the defence of public services which will come under attack as governments' finances become stretched with the bank and industry bailouts.

We can help generalise these struggles and question the legitimacy of capitalism, its solutions of common ownership under capitalist control. We can counter pose our vision of a society under common ownership and under common control for the common good. A rationally planned society which is democratically decided upon and meets the needs of people and not the needs of profit and can end world hunger and stop the destruction of our fragile planet.

These are exiting times indeed.

November 2008

A C r a s h   C o u r s e   I n   C a p i t a l i s m
Claudio Katz

The seism on Wall Street has surprised the world Establishment. At the summits of power, panic and alarmist declarations dominate. Everyone is absorbing an event which could be the beginning of a change of epoch. The comparison with the fall of the Berlin Wall gives some indication of this historical dimension.

The present crisis started to incubate in June 2007, with the collapse of the insurance funds managed by Bear Stearns, and demonstrated its force with the nationalization of the British bank Northern Rock. From this gestation we moved on to events the profundity of which is obvious to everyone.

Dimension And Costs

The rapid conversion of problems of liquidity into insolvent deficits illustrated from the beginning the enormous dimension of a crisis which could not be contained by partial patching up. The reduction of interest rates proved to be useless, just like the attempt to form rescue funds managed by the banks. Nor was making large sums of money available or the assistance of the external sovereign funds sufficient.

The government of the United States undertook several contradictory initiatives to attenuate the explosion. By allowing Lehman Brothers to go bankrupt it opened up the possibility of a brutal cleansing of the banks which were failing and tried to place certain limits on rescue operations. It thus granted the Federal Reserve full powers to judge who should be saved and who could drown. But since that sowed terror among financiers, it quickly backtracked.

The opposite alternative, aiming at nationalizing all the losses, was consolidated by the nationalization of AIG. The official support granted to the largest world insurer (and to its gigantic portfolio of pension funds) thus supplemented the previous rescue of Fannie Mae and Freddie Mac, which finance half of housing in the United States. The fact that these semi-public institutions were contaminated indicates to what point the initial problems of bad quality debts (subprimes) had already been surpassed.

The new series of nationalisations came to the aid of the latest victims of the hurricane: hedge funds, venture capital funds (which operate with highly speculative financial products) and money market funds (which accumulate investments that are less audacious and not without government guarantee). But in fact it was the commercial banks that constituted the critical point.

The bankruptcy of Washington Mutual inaugurated the collapse which threatens to extend to 117 minor entities surveyed by the FDIC (the official guaranteeing body). Certain estimates forecast that the last rites will be said over half of the 8,500 US banks. In any case, the crisis has already reached the investment banks (which raise money directly in the financial circuits) and is affecting the entire system, with interbank operations becoming paralysed and insinuations of deposits being in danger.

We are also seeing a vertiginous wave of acquisitions within this framework. Merrill Lynch was captured by Bank of America, Bear Stearns was taken over by Morgan Stanley, Wachovia passed into the hands of Citigroup (or Wells Fargo) and Goldman Sachs put its package of shares up for sale. This virulent change of owners extended on an international scale, with the acquisition of Britain's HBOS by Lloyds and the absorption of subsidiaries of Bradford and Bingley by the Spanish bank Santander.

Some buyers (Barclays) are pocketing the small change of their old competitors (Lehman) or foraging among their leftovers. The result of all that will be a new level of banking concentration. Those who will survive their gambles (possibly the trio JP Morgan Chase, Bank of America and Citigroup) will take the leadership of the whole of the American financial system. This centralization is being preceded by a furious devaluation of the capital concerned, handled up until now in the financial sphere.

Another option underway is that of the nationalization of toxic mortgages, an option that Congress is examining in a climate of blackmail by the Stock Exchange. The financiers (presented as "the market") demanded government aid to stop the economy going under ("restoring confidence"). They asked the government to purchase the depreciated securities in order to revalorize them before reselling them.

This rescue resembles that obtained by Mexican financiers in 1995. There too the state bought the devalued securities, thus cleansing companies' balance sheets, and marketed bonds at a pure loss for the state budget. The speculators had created a climate of panic so that this new swindle would come as a blessed relief.

But this time the shameless aid brought by the state to those responsible for the collapse produced indignation against the bankers, which called into question their sacrosanct rules of the free market. This rejection of Wall

Street - which had not been seen since Roosevelt's time - obliged the legislators to incorporate some restrictions on the blank cheque initially asked for by the Federal Reserve. The amendments thus include tax reductions of various kinds, to create the illusion of a more equitable distribution of the load.

The widespread malaise expresses, moreover, a massive intuition that there has been a useless waste of resources. If the future confirms that two thirds of mortgage credits are completely irrecoverable, a mountain of money will have been frittered away. It is obvious that no financial engineering can resist the continuing collapse of property prices, nor the unending deterioration of the income of house-buyers.

For this reason Congress is also sponsoring a certain form of renegotiation of mortgages between those in debt and the banks, with the mediation of the state. But only a context of economic recovery - which appears distant - could provide support for such an initiative.

For the moment, what predominates is a crisis without a foreseeable solution, which has put into question all the neo-liberal principles. In a climate of state intervention and subsidies, the regulator is welcome and the market is challenged. But as the rescue is not free, it will be necessary to resort to an operation whose cost is unknown. The emission of securities on securities was so sophisticated that nobody is in a position to calculate the amount concerned. In July 2007 the Federal Reserve estimated the losses at around 50 billion dollars. At the beginning of the year 2008 the figure leapt to 512 billion dollars and current evaluations turn around 1,000 to 2,000 billion dollars. How will such a bill be paid?

The great banking crises of recent decades had colossal costs for the underdeveloped countries. They represented 55.1 per cent of the Gross Domestic Product (GDP) of Argentina (1980-1987), 55 per cent of that of Indonesia (1997-2004) and 34 per cent of that of Thailand (1997-2004). But this percentage hardly reached 3.2 per cent of GDP at the time of the last great financial rescue operation in the United States (1981-1991). This is the first time in decade that the leading world power will have to face a full-scale financial loss.

Global Recessionary Impact

The outbreak of the crisis transformed the economic slowdown into a clear recession. Braking is already perceptible in the fall in investment, the stagnation of consumption and the fragility of US exports. The discussion between the optimists and the pessimists with regard to the future level of economic activity has already been settled by a common diagnosis of a drop in GDP.

There are already no more margins making it possible to act by reductions in the interest rate, while the financial operation aiming to take over losses and purge portfolios precipitates the contraction of credit and a deflationary escalation. Since the 1960s all recessions precipitated by collapses of the property market have been long-lasting.

Consumption on credit, which held up the US economy, has been hit head-on and we are headed for a profound social crisis. The desperate debtors who abandon their homes to avoid liquidation are the first victims of this nightmare. The disorder in the housing market threatens a population already irritated by the rise in the price of petrol, and which fears unemployment in a country that does not have significant social protection. This climate increases indignation against the executives of Wall Street, whose revenues have, over the three last decades, gone from 40 to 344 times the wage of the average worker.

The international role of the US economy is determining the accelerated transmission of its recession. Wall Street alone handles a volume of funds higher than that of all the European Stock Exchanges. The United States concentrates 20 per cent of world GDP, but its imports determine world trade and its transnational corporations set the tone for the production of the whole of the planet. Moreover, the leap that globalization represents has increased the international synchronization of business cycles.

The initial hope of a cyclical decoupling led by Europe was abandoned following The nationalisations which followed the US wave (Fortis in the Benelux countries, Bradford and Bingley in England, Glitnik in Iceland...). The old continent is confronted with the same problems of irrecoverable debts as the United States, while carrying out, moreover, a tough monetary policy which is trying to homogenize different national situations around the euro.

The crisis has not only undermined this attempt but divided the governments, between the partisans of a general recovery fund and the promoters of rescues taken in charge by each national budget. This rupture obviously indicates that the health of the banks is very differentiated across the region. Moreover, any European attempt aimed at supporting the project of neo-liberal unification through high interest rates is seriously threatened by the slowing down of economic activity which it would impose.

For its part, Japan did not resist the recession either, having furthermore to face up to its own depression. The Japanese economy has less autonomy than that of Europe to exert pressure outside its own narrow field of influence. It had hardly started to recover when it was hit head-on by the US collapse.

The compensatory role that some were hoping would be played by China and India has been diluted, because there is no locomotive capable of pulling a train which has completely derailed. There has been much discussion as to whether China would be able to resist the world slowdown because of the expansion of its internal market. Certain economists have put forward this possibility, whereas others ruled it out, pointing out the dependence of the US market on growth in Asia. But in any event the possibility of China acting as a counterweight was only conceivable in the case of a moderate slowdown in the centres of the world economy and not in the case of the brutal recession which has taken place. This is why the decoupling that was announced is tending to be transformed into a recoupling of Asia to the general crisis.

Comparisons

Many analysts are seeking in preceding crises a guide to imagining the possible developments of the current shock. The initial analogies with the stock exchange crash of 1987 or the bursting of the technological bubble in 2001 have already been completely left behind. In both cases it was shares that were involved and not housing, and none of these crises led to banking collapses. They precipitated only recessions of limited intensity and duration, which the reactivation of consumption absorbed within a relatively short time.

The fact of ruling out the resemblance to these declines in economic activity, whose impact was weak, has led to generalized comparisons with the depression of the1930s. Many economists underline the points of coincidence with this traditional antecedent of generalized collapse. But they are comparing the possible depth of the fall and not the modalities of the crisis. Will the intensity of the drop in production and of social regression attain this scale? For the moment this is an unknown factor. But the dynamics of the process that is underway show many differences with the road which led to 1929.

The measures which were applied eighty years ago after the crash were this time implemented in an anticipated way. The injection of liquidities that has been carried out over the last few months would have horrified Hoover and provoked applause from Keynes. Similarly, at present they are limiting the fall of the banks and not envisaging increases in interest rates. It will have to be seen whether these measures attenuate economic collapse or if, on the contrary, they worsen it. But they are being employed in an international context that is very different from the past.

During the 1930s the present-day intertwining of capitals did not exist. Nor was there any coordination between the Federal Reserve and the central banks of Europe and Asia. Instead of there being international currency of reference, a conflict then reigned over who would inherit the primacy of the pound sterling and it was in function of this aspiration that the great powers devalued their currencies. The protectionist context of commercial sectors engaged in a struggle with each other is also very far removed from the present-day interconnection that is imposed by the transnational corporations.

The Great Depression led towards a military confrontation and to war between the principal powers, something which no one any longer envisages at the beginning of the 21st century. A military confrontation between the United States, Europe and Japan is unimaginable.

Another fashionable comparison presents the stagnation of the Japanese economy as a mirror of what is waiting for the United States. This Asian economy experienced a very similar property bubble: prices tripled (1986-1991) before collapsing by two thirds. But Japan hesitated to implement the measurements that have been quickly orchestrated by the United States, thus confirming the distance which separates a subordinate power from a dominant power. Moreover, the Japanese economy has never acted as the locomotive of the world economy and, depending on US military protection, it re-modelled its economy by commercial and monetary measures (revaluation of the Yen and opening up of its economy). Measures that nobody dares to suggest in the United States.

Perhaps the most adequate comparison with the current economic collapse would be with what happened in 1975-1976. This crisis put an end to a stage (the boom of the post-war period) in the same radical fashion that the collapse of 2008 could put an end to neo-liberalism (founded by Thatcher and Reagan). In taking into consideration this historical reference it is necessary to take into account the measures which lead to significant modifications. Three decades ago these sharp turns were the inconvertibility of the dollar (1971) and the increase in interest rates (1978). The current crisis will certainly include transformations on this scale and we will know fairly quickly whether these measures, which have already been adopted, will attenuate or on the contrary exacerbate the intensity of the upheaval.

The Barometers

Rather than trying to guess the future extent of the crisis, it is more productive to characterize its tendencies. Their contours are concentrated in the weaknesses and the resources accumulated by the leading world power. The indicators of American fragility are visible, in particular in the political field. Bush is a corpse of the neo-conservative project, undermined by the adventure in the Middle East. This military adversity limits the capacity of American imperialism to transfer the crisis to its competitors.

But the sudden loss of presidential authority to act in the face of a banking collapse is more significant. It is not the proximity of the elections which have eroded his power, but really the division in the United States elite faced with the seism on Wall Street. There has not been such a volatile scenario since the time of Nixon.

The economic weaknesses of the United States are also well-known. A trade deficit of 6 per cent of GDP does not make it possible to turn towards an export-based model, after so many years of buying euphoria. The country has the biggest debts in the world, half of its Treasury bills are in the hands of foreigners and it is approaching a record tax deficit.

But the other face of this reality is the ability shown by the Federal Reserve to protect the dollar and the Treasury bills from general collapse. Up to now it has proved capable of conducting a controlled fall in the American currency, preserving a rate that is attractive for the inward flow of capital and at the same time stimulating exports. Since the two levels are contradictory, for them to maintain the equilibrium requires a great predisposition of the creditors to maintain the monetary primacy of the United States. This subordination has continued up to now, in spite of the economic and financial collapse.

During the fall of Wall Street the predisposition of capital for quality favoured the currency which was in great danger. The capitalists of the whole world paradoxically took shelter by acquiring the dollar and its Treasury bills, i.e. the currency and the bills which were formally the most threatened. No other economy could provoke such a reaction, which obviously flows from the central role of the United States in the reproduction of world capitalism.

This reaction of complicity is based on the protection which the Pentagon guarantees to all the ruling classes. This is a decisive guarantee which modifies all the conventional models of evaluation of the economic process. It is important to point out this characteristic, in order to avoid analyzing the

US economy with parameters identical to the analysis of any other nation's economy.

The dollar serving as a refuge also illustrates the increasing internationalization of exchanges around a currency which monopolizes 70 per cent of world trade and 65 per cent of world reserves. By supporting the dollar the majority of the world's creditors are defending their own skin.

After the tsunami that we have seen over the last few weeks it is difficult to imagine a simple continuity of this monetary hegemony. If it manages to maintain itself as the world reserve currency, the dollar will have to adapt to the new relationships of forces which emerge from the crisis. The acceptance of a greater presence of foreign banks in the United States (by reducing old restrictions on it) could be part of this adjustment. The transfer of the shares of Morgan Stanley to China Investment and to Mitsubishi, the sale of Goldman Sachs to Sumitomo Mitsui and the transfer of the external operations of Lehman to Nomura anticipate this tendency.

However the possibility of a rupture of the monetary system, which would oblige the dollar to share its domination with other currencies, cannot be excluded. In this case we would see the appearance of geographical monetary zones, similar to the competitive model of the inter-war period. Until now the indices of such a possibility do not exist, because contrary to the past no country is aiming to establish its power by crushing the dominant imperialism. But the candidates for the division of power in the world will not accompany the dollar to the point of suicide, if the US currency collapses. The various scenarios that are possible thus depend mainly on one factor: the extent of the crisis.

The Orthodox And The Heterodox

Interpretations of the crisis are more important than descriptions of it or forecasts. The orthodox economists have remained devoid of arguments, confronted with a collapse which refutes all their principles. They maintain a low profile while waiting for the storm to pass, and even find certain justifications for their approval of the nationalisation of the banks. But as the hypocrisy of neo-liberalism has been revealed to the light of day and its spokesperson are discredited, we can expect the ideological retreat of the right-wing ideas that have been the most influential over the last several decades.

We can still hear voices which explain what has happened by "insufficient control over credit" and the granting of "bad loans" to "doubtful customers". But the generalized impact of the housing bubble indicates that it was not a question of occasional errors. The bad quality loans became massive because of the competition that the banks were engaged in, taking advantage of permissive legislation.

The financial collapse also calls into question orthodox confidence in the sophisticated ("securitised") debt packages. As these constructions included debts of very varied consistency, they imagined that diversification reduced the risk. The crisis pulverized this belief, producing the typical scenario of everyone seeking to save their own skin.

The eclipse of the talibans of the market brought into the foreground their heterodox rivals. Krugman, Stiglitz and Soros have been endlessly repeating their theory that the crisis was caused by insufficient control, attributing the disease to deregulation and postulating its treatment by the application of a dose of supervision. They question the weakness of the control exerted by federal agencies, criticize the elimination of the compartmentalisation of banks that was imposed after the 1930s and propose governmental measures aimed at evaluating the estimates of risk and controlling international movements of finance.

But deregulation was not a whim. It was generalized in order to restore profits and it will be again if this variable is seriously affected. Under capitalism controls are articulated by profitability. They are reinforced or decrease according to profits.

Regulationist fantasies are inspired by the way bankers are being presented as the only people responsible for the crisis. We must suppose that they act independently of their colleagues of industry and agriculture, being particularly and perversely inclined to speculation.

But to bet on a fast profit in the financial sphere is an intrinsic characteristic of capitalism. It is the product of the competing constraint which governs a system characterized by blind rivalries and periodic bubbles. The effects of these movements remain occult in periods of prosperity and become sharply obvious only in times of crisis.

The novelty of the present period lies only in the scale and the sophistication of speculative activity. Unwonted forms of packaging and marketing debt were introduced, as were operations with derived financial products whose prices are established depending on another financial product.

We have witnessed the expansion of securitization (getting rid of portfolios by the emission of securities that are acquired by other investors), credit

derivative swaps (CDSs) (separation of the creditor's risk in order to negotiate it separately) and Collateralised debt obligations (CDOs) (fragmentation of debts into segments with differing degrees of risk).

This type of operation was extended at a frenetic rhythm, especially after
2001, between the investment banks, in which the relationship between the
credits that were being offered and the patrimony (capital) reached an
alarming level. The traditional relationship of 1 to 8 between the banks'
own capital and the loans provided was amplified by 25 or 30 times.

The dynamics proper to capitalism stimulated these actions and what happened to Wall Street offers us a crash course in this system, in its web of
complicities (Paulson running the Federal Reserve under the auspices of
Goldman Sachs) and its contradictions (Bush nationalizing the banks).

A Particular Crisis Of Over-Accumulation

In the face of the heterodox simplifications it is necessary to turn again to
Marxist interpretations which explain the crisis by the intrinsic contradictions of capitalism. These imbalances erupt periodically and cannot not be
eliminated as long as a system governed by the supremacy of profit subsists.
But what are the singularities of the present crisis?

The present shock has several specific causes. First of all, it expresses the
tensions created by the capital that has been over-accumulated in the banks
at the end of a long process of fictitious expansion of funds, free from any
real counterpart in the productive sphere. This atrophy developed during
the years of the expansion of credit and the generalization of derived products and is the result of the strengthening of the power of the financiers.
But the promotion of this banking elite to the summit of capitalism took
place in support of a regressive project shared by all the oppressors. It made
it possible to impose the social discipline that the ruling classes demanded,
by shareholder management of companies, pressure aimed at maximum
profitability and the empire of the Stock Exchange. The explicit purpose of
these transformations was to increase profits to the detriment of popular
revenues. The supremacy of finance was an instrument for the flexibilisation of work and served as a guarantee of the increase in exploitation.

This financial hegemony put in place a veritable time bomb, which exploded
in Wall Street. The expansion of "personal finance" transformed the worker
into a customer anguished by debts. American workers were imprisoned
in a network of compromises with the banks in order to be able to pay their
costs of housing, education, health and retirement.

This house of cards started to collapse when insolvency invaded it. The impossibility of reimbursing subprime credits - granted to those whose incomes were not regular or sufficient enough to acquire a home - was the spark for the present collapse.

This crisis of over-accumulation was delayed by refinancing by means of a mountain of securities on securities, offering high yields. The skein of emissions was so complex that it effaced the trace of the debts themselves in a generalized environment of ignorance of the nature of the credits. The bankers themselves no longer know what contracts they own, because by abandoning the traditional estimates of risk they have lost contact with their clients.

Faced with fictitious valorization on such a scale the present collapse was inexorable. What nobody had imagined, in spite of the many warnings which had announced it, was the impressive scale of this crash.

All the collapses which had since the 1980s shaken Latin-American, European, Japanese and Asian finance announced the cyclone which was about to reach Wall Street. The most explicit signal was given by the bankruptcy in 1998 of the big Long Term Credit Management (LTCM) hedge fund, which operated with the same derived products as those which have rotted the US financial system. Since the hunger for profit does not cease because of warnings, the crisis of over-accumulation finally reached the centre of the system.

National And World Overproduction

To avoid financial phantasmagoria it is important to analyze the productive contradictions which underlie the banking crisis. These imbalances correspond to a cycle of production and are the result of the periodic inequality between the increasing expansion of production and the restrictions on purchasing power which characterize capitalism. Competition aimed at increasing the rate of exploitation widened the breach of surpluses.

Overproduction openly manifested itself in the property sector (housing) which had experienced strong growth over the previous decade. The big rise in property prices and the multiplication of high-risk credits generated the present surplus of housing in relation to solvable demand. Financial speculation certainly reinforced this tendency, but the most significant bubbles have all related to the commodities that were most in demand at the time. The valorization of these investments awakens the hope of increasing profits, which collapses when the tendency is inversed. The recession demonstrates the same mechanism for other goods whose prices have taken off.

The present overproduction nevertheless has a large international dimension, which derives from competition to lower wages. This schema stimulated the opening of frontiers to the advantage of the corporations, which competed to multiply production while seeking to lower their costs, leading to a plethora of commodities. These surpluses were nourished in particular by the Asian manufacturing pole, which flooded the world with its exports, favouring the general depreciation. Since the crisis of South Korea and Thailand (1997) this deflationary tendency has affected many industrial goods.

Overproduction is also the result of the internationalization of production that is stimulated by the transnational corporations. The application of micro-electronics in industry and the fall in the prices of transport and communications contributed to multiplying surpluses. In the anarchistic competition aimed at reducing costs, no company asked itself the question: who will be able to acquire the new goods?

The fight for production at low cost ended up by encumbering the shops. This is the result of the restriction of purchasing power which is still the case in the periphery and of the instability of consumption inflated by debt that the flexibilisation of work imposed in the central countries. The United States is the epicentre of this mercantile artifice based on the extension of working time and on putting all family members to work.

As long as the capitalist class maintained its optimism - produced since the 1980s by the recovery in the rate of profit - these tensions remained in the background. But surplus goods overflowed, indicating the absolute limits of United States consumption, provided by Asia and financed by the whole world.

Under-Production Of Raw Materials

The increase in the prices of raw materials was the third pillar of the present crisis. The rise in the price of oil (which in a few years went from 10 to 120 dollars a barrel) affected the central economies, and the rise in the price of raw materials (+114% since 2002) troubled the world economy. This rise reversed the downward tendency that had been in progress since 1997, but it went beyond cyclical variations, both by its duration and its scale.

The rise in the prices of raw materials reflects the weakness of investment in the sector of production of natural resources. But it was reinforced by speculation by financiers who, faced with potential losses in other sectors, sought refuge in oil and raw materials. The bankers introduced into the raw materials market all the derivative engineering of Wall Street, so much so that the purchase of fuel or corn has been transformed into a sophisticated mathematical operation.

But the rise in the prices of raw materials also influenced the structural process of destruction of the environment after several decades of capitalist competition for control of essential supplies.

This combination of conjunctural, structural and historical tendencies exerted an inflationary pressure on raw materials, which many specialists think will be more lasting with regard to fuels (few discoveries, rise in the costs of extraction, conflicts in the production zones) than with regard to food.

This rising cycle confirms that the relative prices of raw materials are not subject to systematic and permanent deterioration. They experience periodic oscillations and when they increase the modalities are abrupt because they are less sensitive to the increase in productivity, in comparison to the products of industry. The imminent world recession will impose a ceiling on the inflation of raw materials. But we will have to see if this fall in prices will reach the level of the preceding cycle. For the moment we are dealing with indices of a fall in these prices, but not with their collapse.

Consequently, the current crisis is the confluence of three processes: underproduction of raw materials, financial over-accumulation and industrial overproduction. In that it presents similarities with what occurred in 1975-1976 and will have a very unequal regional impact.

Periphery And Semi-Periphery

The peripheral countries were the main victims of the neo-liberal stage and they are candidates to suffer from the worst effects of the present crisis. They suffered from the degrading effects of the world polarization which marked the 1980s and 1990s. Certain areas, such as Africa, were crushed by the foreign debt, trade liberalization and capital flight. They face the tragedy of emigration, refugees and massacres because of local wars.

The recent beginning of famine constitutes another example of this impact. Following financial speculation, trade deregulation and forced specialization in crops for export, the rise in the price of food threatens the survival of 1,300 million people.

If during the period of consumption-led prosperity in the United States the impoverished economies of the planet suffered from a massive drain on their resources, the imminent recession foreshadows major sufferings. The

Third World countries which are driving out their desperate inhabitants will face new financial restrictions and serious trade difficulties.

The panorama is more contradictory in the semi-periphery. An intermediate layer of non-central countries - with autonomous ruling classes and which play their own game on the world market – have limited world polarization over the last few years. This group of economies concerns in particular China, India, Russia, South Africa and Brazil. The capitalists of these nations benefitted from the rise in the prices of raw materials and developed their own industrial activity, in partnership with the transnational corporations. They even forged "emergent multinationals" which operate on a world scale.

The change of the financial cycle also reduced the weight of the debt in various medium-sized countries. Growth associated with continuing social inequality produced sufficient profits to remove the foreign debt. This is the reason for the emergence of Asian and Arab sovereign funds.

The crisis that is underway can prolong this promotion of semi-peripheral countries, as already occurred in 1975-1982 during the period of petrodollars, of a rise in the prices of raw materials and the United States' defeat in Vietnam. This process could even be consolidated if forms of growth, similar to those observed during the world instability which followed the crisis of the 1930s, made their appearance. At that time the stagnation of the central economies opened up a space for the industrialization of certain underdeveloped countries.

But the current recession can also precipitate opposite dynamics, brutally putting an end to the forward march of the semi-peripheral economies. We would then witness a repetition of the scenario of 1982-1990, when the neoliberal offensive precipitated a fall in the price of raw materials and asphyxiation by debt, which spread distress across the planet.

It is premature to anticipate which of the two tendencies will prevail, or whether it is a combination of both which will emerge. Capital flight - which affects Russia and Brazil – is so far coexisting with the affirmation of the sovereign funds which are taking part in the rescue of American banks and which will be able to be paid for their assistance.

Contrary to all the financial collapses of the last two decades, Latin America is the recipient and not the originator of the present crisis. But the unequal dependence of its various countries towards the United States produces differentiated effects from the recession that is underway. Whereas Mexico and Central America are very much linked to this epicentre, the Southern

Cone maintains a greater degree of autonomy. The financial transmission of the crash is also unequal according to the importance of the external refinancing of each country. The peripheral and semi-peripheral economies of the region have followed divergent paths.

But in the immediate future the difficulties for US imperialism to intervene in its back yard will be accentuated. This limitation reinforces the room for manoeuvre for the implementation of economic policies in rupture with these countries' creditors and for carrying out the nationalization of natural resources. Such orientations could reduce social inequalities and benefit the popular majority, if they are implemented in opposition to the local ruling classes.

Socialism As The Objective
The crisis in progress will be solved on the political level. To examine the significance of this event in exclusively economic terms does not make it possible to grasp what is at stake between the contending forces. Without understanding the capitalist nature of the financial tsunami we cannot seek effective remedies for its consequences. The struggle against the social regime which is at the origin of current misfortunes is the only way to prevent sufferings from coming down on the popular majority.

In the struggle to clarify the capitalist character of the crisis we should not enter into competition with the press with regard to the forecast of even bigger collapses. The fear that the media propagates tends to provoke paralysis rather than indignation. Instead of predicting dark scenes it is advisable to work with proposals which open up popular alternatives.

This attitude is at the antipodes of conformism or the resigned belief in the eternal duration of capitalism. It is false to suppose that this system will always be able to find a way out, whatever the tragedy that it imposes on the majority of society. To imagine that capitalism is immutable is as fatalistic as to disregard action and strategy for its eradication.

Certain thinkers on the left formally accept these premises, but make the point that now is not the time to work in an anti-capitalist direction. They justify this attitude by "the absence of favourable conditions" or "the weight of accumulated defeats".

Such an attitude blocks any appreciation of the political and ideological transformations that are taking place. Socialism is not an anthem for special days, nor is it a nostalgic dream. It is a project to be established at critical moments and energetically diffused when capitalism exhibits its most nefarious visage.

The new conjuncture can be felt in the brutal change in the language of the press. From despair or confusion the mass media are no longer singing the praises of capitalism. With panic and stupor they write ironically about the "socialism for the rich" which accompanies the rescue of the bankers. They do not know that real socialism is the antithesis of this rescue that it aims at helping those who are abandoned and penalizing the rich. At the beginning of a great political turning point this simple message can once again become as popular as ever.

October, 2008

Capitalism's Worst Crisis Since The 1930s

By Joel Geier

The United States and the world are now in the opening stages of the worst economic crisis since the depression of the 1930s. This crisis represents the greatest failure of the free market since the Second World War. For some time now, economists have argued that the market is self-regulating and self-correcting; this fantasy has been destroyed. The crisis has led to a run on the international banking system, a stock market crash, and has opened the door to what will be the longest and deepest recession of the post–Second World War period. This is not a typical cyclical crisis, which capitalism generally has every decade or so, but a systemic crisis, a crisis of the financial system, which provides money for the circulation of commodities, of trade, and of investment. There is no alternative, we were told, to the free market. What we are now told is that there is no alternative to government intervention and regulation.

As Karl Marx pointed out many years ago, capitalist crises do not come about because of a shortage of goods or crop failures, but because of overproduction. This overproduction is not overproduction of things that are needed by people, but overproduction in terms of what can be sold profitably on the market. If products cannot be sold profitably, whether they are physical commodities or debt securities, profits cannot be realized, and the system goes into crisis, as lending and investment seize up. Workers are laid off, plants are closed, and the banks go bust, in a downward spiral. Capitalism's only way out of the crisis is by lowering labor costs (wage-cutting) and the massive devaluation of capital, as businesses are destroyed and surviving capitalists swallow up the weaker businesses on the cheap. There has already been an enormous destruction of capital. In the last number of months, more than $7 trillion has been wiped off the U.S. stock market. Indeed, $1.1 trillion was wiped out in a single day on October 15.

As of mid-October, $27 trillion had been erased from stock markets worldwide. Housing values in this country have already declined by $5 trillion; pension funds by $2.5 trillion; and bank write-offs are now at $600 to $700 billion and expected to be $1.4 trillion. Large, conservative, seemingly stable companies have disappeared. Lehman Brothers, which had been capitalized at $30 to $40 billion, has gone bankrupt, and AIG, which until a few months ago was capitalized at between $150 and $200 billion, required a $123 billion lifeline from the government to survive. This has led to a massive credit crunch. Banks and other financial institutions now no longer trust each other not to totter and collapse underneath the weight of toxic debt, and refuse to lend to each other, producing a credit meltdown affecting the entire global financial system.

All of this is opening up a longer, deeper recession. In the U.S., profits, the motor force of the capitalist system, are now in free fall. They peaked in the third quarter of 2006, and already are down 29 percent, not counting the banks' write-offs. The failing housing market, which was the catalyst for this current financial crisis, continues to decline. Housing prices are now down 23 percent nationally—and are down even further in California, Nevada, and Florida. One sixth of all homes are now under water—the mortgage is now greater than the value of the home. There are millions of unsold homes, and four million homes are expected to be in foreclosure; and this before the recession and layoffs have really begun to hit hard. Unemployment is already 6.1 percent, and economists are predicting that next year it may rise to 8 or 9 percent. In the last recession in 2001, unemployment peaked at 6.3 percent. In the last year, unemployment has gone from 7.3 million to 9.5 million people. The U.S. Department of Labor has reported that the rate of unemployment is 11 percent, if you count the 5 million "discouraged" workers who have recently stopped looking for work, and a portion of the 6.1 million involuntary part-time workers. Moreover, real wages have declined even before this recession has gotten under way. In the last year, weekly wages rose 2.8 percent, but after adjusting for inflation, they fell 2.5 percent.

And the credit contraction has only just begun. Even if the latest moves of the European and American governments—who have decided at the eleventh hour to partially nationalize the banking system by injecting trillions of dollars into the banks—are successful, nonetheless the credit contraction, the rationing of credit, will continue.

The government has stepped in to provide capital for the banks in order for them to continue to function. In the U.S., a plan to invest $250 billion in nine of the country's largest banks superseded the previous plan to spend $700 billion of taxpayers' money to buy the banks' toxic debt. Nonetheless, all the banks are still holding huge amounts of mortgages and other loans at highly inflated asset prices. Even with the bailouts, they will have to sell off those assets in order to be able to raise capital. The banks are also being de-leveraged, that is, they are being forced to pay off some of their debt and to cut back on the risky loans they've made over the past several years. Rather than loaning ten times more than their capital, they were loaning thirty and forty times their capital; and in Europe the banks were leveraged at an even greater rate.

There will have to be a protracted period of restructuring and recapitalization of the banking system. During this period there will be less money for loans for business investments and consumer purchases, which is only going to exacerbate the recession, leading to more corporate bankruptcies. This in turn will lead to more layoffs, higher unemployment, and a continued downward spiral.

The restructuring of the banking system is not the only thing that will occur during this crisis. There are going be all sorts of industries—not just corporations, but industries—that will be on the verge of bankruptcy, such as auto, home construction, and the airlines. All those industries will have to be restructured through mergers and acquisitions, through leveraged buyouts, and through the sale of companies and assets at fire-sale prices. Capitalism's only way out of this downward spiral, as in all capitalist crises, will be the massive devaluation of capital and a lowering of wage costs to the point where profits and investments are restored.

An International Crisis
Meanwhile, the international character of the recession will deepen it. Already, all of the advanced industrial countries—Germany, Italy, Britain, France, Japan are in deeper recession than the United States. The banking situation in Europe may be even worse in than in the U.S., because the housing bubbles in a number of countries were bigger, and because, as we have already mentioned, there was even more leverage in the European banking system than in the United States. The collapse of the commodities boom—prices of oil, copper, grains, and other commodities have declined dramatically since the summer of 2008—has thrown a number of emerging markets into chaos. In Russia, the stock market has crashed, and as of mid-October was down 60 percent from its peak. In a number of countries there have been currency collapses. The value of Brazil's currency declined by 40 percent in the last two months, and Korea's currency declined by 50 percent. Whole countries (of which Iceland is only the first) face the possibility of bankruptcy. The Baltic dry index—the cost of shipping commodities—dropped 80 percent from where it was just a few months ago. It is an indication of the collapse of world trade.

This will be the first time since 1973 that the entire world has gone into recession at once. This will make the recession deeper, since it will be impossible for countries to export their way out of the crisis to countries that are still expanding.

The Origins Of The Crisis
The current crisis is a product of the contradictions of the twenty-five-year-long neoliberal boom, which started in 1982. The postwar boom ended in

1973, and from 1973 to 1982 there were three recessions in the United States. The restructuring that went on in the United States, and to a lesser extent internationally, with the introduction of neoliberal, free-market measures, led to a twenty-five-year-long boom. It is the contradictions of those neoliberal measures that have produced this crisis.

The first contradiction to note was the creation of a giant debt bubble. The increase in debt during the Clinton and Bush years was staggering. Over the two decades preceding 2007, credit market debt roughly quadrupled from nearly $11 trillion to $48 trillion, far exceeding growth rates. To put it in perspective: according to the *Wall Street Journal*, since 1983 debt expanded by 8.9 percent per year, while GDP expanded by only 5.9 percent. The nation's debt grew to enormous, unsustainable proportions starting with the Asian financial crisis of 1997–98. There are a number of elements that contributed to creating this debt bubble. The first is the use of monetary policy as a way to handle economic problems. When the Asian crisis arose, the United States pumped tremendous amounts of liquidity, of money, into the banking system, and cut interest rates dramatically, even though the nation was still in boom. This led to the creation of the dot-com bubble—the wild inflation of technology stocks—that burst in 2000.

The second contradiction was that the United States became a buyer of last resort, establishing a trading system with Asia in which the Asian countries exported to the United States, which kept up spending through debt. The American balance of payments went from approximately $200 billion a year to $700 to $800 billion per year. All of this was borrowed. The U.S. government had a budget surplus under Clinton. But under Bush, with the tax cuts and war spending, the budgetary surplus disappeared, and the U.S. went from having a $250 billion government surplus in 2000–2001 to a $300 billion deficit in 2002. This stimulated the economy, but it meant that the United States became dependent on foreign capital, since the savings rate in this country had collapsed and was negative in the last years of this boom. Foreign capital, in particular from China, Japan, and the Middle East oil exporting countries, financed the American debt. When the dot-com bubble collapsed and recession came in 2001, Federal Reserve Chairman Alan Greenspan lowered interest rates to between 1 and 2 percent for three years. This led to massive asset inflation, particularly in housing prices.

An important factor contributing to the explosion of debt was the phenomenal increase in income inequality. The neoliberal boom was the result of a shift in the balance of class forces, in which the rate of exploitation was increased, real wages were depressed, and almost all wealth created went to capital. Some figures will indicate how dramatic the shift was. In 1973, GDP per person, in constant non-inflationary dollars, was $20,000 a year. By 2006, it was $38,000 a year—a more than 90 percent rise. Wages, however, in that same thirty-three-year period, declined. Real wages in 1973 were $330 per week; and in 2007, wages were $279—a decline of 15 percent.

This shift of wealth from the working class to the capitalist class produced a tremendous amount of capital for potential investment. But in this last business cycle, that capital could not find all that many profitable outlets domestically. There was no expanded reproduction, no accumulation of capital in the U.S. during the 2000s. In this last business cycle, there were fewer factories at the beginning of the recession a year ago than there were in 1999. Instead of investing in new technologies, new plants and equipment, capitalists invested money overseas, domestically, investments went to the most profitable industries—housing, construction, and finance. "In 1983, banks, brokerage houses and other financial businesses contributed 15.8 percent to domestic corporate profits," writes James Grant in the October 18 *Wall Street Journal*. "It's double that today."

These investments stimulated the housing and debt bubble. Between 2000 and 2005, housing prices increased by more than 50 percent, and there was a frenzy of housing construction. Banks and other financial institutions went on a mortgage-lending spree, creating a massive market in subprime mortgages—adjustable rate mortgages sold to borrowers with weak credit. There was also a big increase in housing speculation, with small investors buying second and third homes with the expectation that housing prices would keep rising and that these houses could be resold at a profit. Merrill Lynch estimated that in the first half of 2005, half of economic growth was related to the boom in the housing sector.

Meanwhile, workers tried to maintain their standard of living despite the decline in real wages. In the 1980s and 1990s, they worked longer hours, took on more than one job, and increased the number of family members working. This could prop up household income to some extent. Yet even household income declined from 1998 through the boom of the 2000s. The only way to maintain living standards in the midst of declining wages was by borrowing against the rising value of their homes through home equity loans and mortgage refinancing. In the period of the last boom, homeowners took $5 trillion out of their home equity ($9 trillion since 1997), fueling an increasingly unsustainable debt structure that finally popped with the decline of inflated asset prices in housing.

The third contributing factor to this debt bubble was the deregulation of the banking system, which led to the creation of a shadow banking system. This shadow banking system grew to be bigger than the regulated, insured commercial banks, which through this shadow system, were able to keep all sorts of loans and investments off their books, Enron-style.

In this shadow system, banks did not have to put up adequate capital reserves. As a result, they were able, through this unregulated system, to borrow thirty, forty, or fifty times above the value of their capital in order to invest in the stock market and in various new exotic debt products, such as collateralized debt obligations (CDOs), credit-default swaps (CDSs—essentially a form of insurance against debt default), and various other financial swindles, many of which were based on the packaging and repackaging of housing mortgages. These were bundled and sliced up into investment vehicles that contained a good deal of potentially toxic debt—$900 billion worth of subprime loans, for example.

The unregulated banking system provided a lot of the credit for this asset inflation and in the creation of these new credit instruments, mortgage-backed securities like credit derivatives, CDOs and CDSs, led to a speculative mania that drove prices higher and higher. At the same time, these unregulated instruments were so complicated that no one really knew what they were really worth. This setup provided enormous profits to the banks at first. The feeding frenzy drove up asset prices, creating an environment in which everyone was eager to participate, setting the stage for the inevitable crash. The house of cards started to collapse when the housing market went south.

The End Of The Debt-Fueled Trading System

The trading system that emerged out of the Asian crisis of 1998 was always unsustainable. What is remarkable is how long it continued. The current crisis now makes it impossible for it to continue. The United States developed an enormous trade deficit, which was financed through foreign borrowing of dollars, the international reserve currency. If the dollar weren't the international reserve currency, it is unimaginable that this trade deficit could have gone on for so many years. Now that the world has entered recession, the U.S. is going to be running higher budgetary deficits. Those deficits will be increased also by the expansion of U.S. military spending, which has increased from $300 billion a year in 2000 to more than $800 billion a year now, if you include the supplemental costs for the wars in Iraq and Afghanistan. On top of this spending, the U.S. has introduced a hugely expensive bailout plan. That means it will in all likelihood be running deficits of three-quarters of a trillion dollars, and possibly more, in the coming years.

Where will the money for that come? At the moment there is no savings in this country, though that may change dramatically. But it is highly unlikely that China, Japan, and other countries are prepared to continue to finance an American trade deficit to the tune of $700 or $800 billion a year when the balance sheet of American finances, the huge national debt, has gone from $5 trillion when Bush came into office to $11 trillion today. It is unlikely that the Chinese and others are going to continue to finance this debt—although at this point in time U.S. treasuries are still a safe haven. This is particularly true because China's trade surplus is going to contract considerably as a result of the world recession.

The Chinese population only consumes 35 percent of what it produces. The rest goes for reinvestment and export. China's economy has the highest rate of exploitation in the industrial world. But its export markets are going to constrict—they've already started to decline. As a result, China's desire to lend greater amounts to the United States is problematic, particularly if interest rates in the United States are low. The United States therefore can no longer continue to run an enormous trade deficit while it is building an enormous budgetary deficit, and sustain both of them on the basis of foreign borrowing. There will have to be a restructuring and reordering of the system. At the same time, the U.S. may become more dependent on direct foreign investment from countries like Japan and China that, as we've mentioned, have developed large cash reserves. That is what we mean when we say that this is not just a typical cyclical crisis of capitalism. All of the contradictions of the neoliberal boom have burst asunder and now have to be addressed.

Government Intervention

There has been some talk on the right that government intervention is "socialist." Even Treasury Secretary Henry Paulson, after he agreed, in response to Britain's bailout plan, to shift the government's commitment from buying bad debt from the banks to injecting capital into them, said that "[G]overnment owning a stake in any private U.S. company is objectionable to most Americans — me included." Living in the rarified world of bankers and speculators, he apparently has not seen the polls showing that a majority of Americans want single-payer health care and better social services.

For those free market hacks who fear that the bailout plan represents some kind of creeping socialism, the words of a *Financial Times* editorial are instructive:

- Does this rescue mean the end of private financial capitalism? Of course not. Although the size of the crisis requires an exceptional response, this is but the latest in a long line of banking crises and state rescues. Nationally owned banks seem likely to be a reality in many countries for a decade. In the next great financial crisis—rest assured, there will be others—bank rescues with equity purchases may be a first step rather than a last resort. But stakes in banks will, eventually, be sold back to private investors. Governments—rightly—will regulate to avoid further crises. They will fail, and then be forced to act to pick up the pieces. There is no alternative.

- Modern capitalism needs well-functioning banks. Businesses and individuals need liquidity and an effective means of turning their savings into productive investments. But banks perform this function by making bets on the future. This is the purpose for which they exist—but it makes them inherently unstable. They tend to overextend themselves in the good times and are over-cautious in the bad, exacerbating booms and busts....

- These leaders are not putting capitalism to the sword in favor of the gentler rule of the state. They are using the state to defeat the marketplace's most dangerous historic enemy: widespread depression. And they are right to do so.

The editorial goes so far as to admit that the boom-bust cycle is endemic to capitalism, and that credit, while it fuels and extends the boom, also makes the crisis worse. The old neoliberal mantra TINA—There Is No Alternative to free market capitalism—is now transformed into: There is no alternative to state intervention to save capitalism from its inevitable tendency toward crisis.

Let us be very clear: State intervention to save capitalism from its own contradictions has nothing to do with socialism. The U.S. government is a capitalist government, staffed by political representatives of the capitalist class from the Democratic and Republican Parties. Paulson, for example, was once a top executive at Goldman Sachs. The government thinks in the same way the capitalist class does; it defends their interests, and it wears the same blinders. It was the government that deregulated the banking system, in particular under the leadership of Alan Greenspan (chair of the Federal Reserve from 1987–2006), Robert Rubin (treasury secretary under Clinton) and Lawrence Summers (treasury secretary in the last year and a half of the Clinton administration). Together, they deregulated the banks and defended the development of the unregulated debt trading system. It was the government and its policies that greased the wheels for this catastrophe. It presided over the redistribution of wealth from labor to capital, it gave enormous tax breaks to the rich, and it encouraged easy credit and debt spending. The government therefore bears as much responsibility for this crisis as the bankers do.

The response of the government to the financial meltdown until mid-October, moreover, has been totally inadequate. This crisis has been unfolding for two years now, and for months the government refused to recognize the depth of the problem, taking action that was too little, too late. There have been five different ad-hoc rescue attempts, including cutting interest rates and opening up cheap credit lines to the banks, and the takeover of Fannie Mae and Freddie Mac. Paulson then allowed Lehman Brothers to go bankrupt, a move that triggered a deeper financial panic. This was followed by the bailout of AIG, leading up to Paulson's $700 bailout plan to buy up the banks' bad assets. Now comes the sixth attempt to stabilize the financial system—the decision in mid-October to recapitalize the banks and partially nationalize them—a plan initiated by British Prime Minister Gordon Brown. This might finally be the one that unfreezes banking loans.

In their ad-hoc attempts to solve the crisis, officials took this to be a liquidity rather than an insolvency problem—a problem simply of getting money into the banking system so that the banks would loan. But the banks refused to loan to each other because they knew that other banks had assets on their books that were as bad as their own—and which might lead to defaults. This is called counterparty risk: banks are afraid that the other banks are on the verge of bankruptcy and so won't give them loans. This aversion to risk reached a crescendo when Lehman Brothers was allowed to go bankrupt in mid-September. This is what led to the credit meltdown of late September into mid-October that roiled markets all over the world.

The other problem with Washington policy makers is that they refused to put any floor under the housing crisis. When Bear Stearns went bankrupt last March, the New York Times ran an editorial and liberal economist Paul Krugman wrote a column arguing that while the government is right to defend the banking system, it cannot save the housing market because the housing market is overinflated. That has been the government policy at all points—and it is why it refused to do anything about foreclosures. However, it is the deflation of housing asset prices that has thrown mortgage-backed securities and other loans into crisis, and is why the banks are becoming insolvent. The government has tried to save the holders of the bad debt while allowing the cause of the bad debt problem to get worse.

For months the government refused to recapitalize the banks. Instead, they said to the banks: we will take some bad assets off your books at inflated prices to give you some money. This is the worst possible way in which to try and restore lending. Banks can loan up to ten times the amount they are capitalized, whereas taking bad debt off their books does not have the same effect. The truth was that nobody understood what Paulson's plan was and how it would work, and he could never explain it. British Prime Minister Brown denounced it as worthless. Paulson only decided to adopt the partial (and temporary) nationalization plan after Britain adopted it, and then Europe followed suit.

Paulson therefore bears responsibility for the depth of this crisis. In a normal situation he would be forced to walk the plank. However, there is a total political vacuum in this country. The Bush administration did nothing; the Republicans in Congress are living in the nineteenth century; and the Democrats are afraid to do anything that might hurt their chances in the election—so they all do nothing. It has been Paulson and Fed chairman Ben Bernanke who have been filling the vacuum; and it has been Paulson who has been carrying out economic policy.

Bernanke now claims that he was always for the recapitalization of the banks. Paulson and Bush vetoed it, however, on the grounds that it represented a partial nationalization; they did not want the government having stock in the banks. Paulson told the Senate Banking Committee: "There were some that said we should just go and stick capital in the banks, put preferred stocks... But we said, the right way to do this is not going around and using guarantees or injecting capital, and there's been various proposals to do that, but to use market mechanisms." Today Paulson is singing a different tune.

Paulson's version of the partial nationalization plan involves giving the banks cash without exercising control over how they spend it. Banks will have a relatively free hand to do with it what they please because the state is going to purchase non-voting shares. What we're looking at, in the words of Multinational Monitor writer Robert Weissman, is public ownership without public control. Paulson's new plan sets up minimal rules that require participating financial firms merely to discourage "unnecessary and excessive risks that threaten the value of the financial institution." In essence, the same banks whose unregulated, profligate investing led us to this impasse are being entrusted again to "self-regulate." What's to stop them from using state funds, even as they continue to hemorrhage hundreds of billions of dollars, to pay off shareholders and executives rather than using them to restart lending? As Weissman notes, "The banks are not

obligated to lend with the money they are getting. The banks are not obligated to renegotiate mortgage terms with borrowers—even though a staggering one in six homeowners owe more than the value of their homes."
If more evidence is needed of the reluctance of the state to exercise too much control over the banks, the insurance giant AIG, after the government took an 80 percent controlling stake in the company, is being permitted to spend millions lobbying Congress to ease some provisions in a new federal law establishing strict oversight of mortgage originators.

So the government, at all points, has operated with the same blinders as the richest capitalists. It has been obvious for well over a year that we have been in an enormous financial crisis, the worst since the 1930s. Yet until now, the government has reacted on an ad-hoc, knee-jerk basis, allowing the problem to get bigger and bigger.

The Limits Of State Intervention
This is an international crisis, and yet there is no international government that can impose a coordinated response. There's no government that's going to protect all the banks internationally. Each state is attempting to save its own banks. Things have now come to such a juncture, however, that everyone is forced to act, and the scale of the crisis has forced them all to finally act in a similar way. Estimates are that the U.S. has so far committed $4 to $6 trillion in tax dollars to bailout efforts, and Europe has committed $2.3 trillion. But this isn't so much cooperation as it is an attempt by each state to keep pace with its national rivals. Everyone understands to some extent what happened in the 1930s—that the recession became a world depression when the international banking system collapsed and states imposed beggar-thy-neighbor policies that further contracted world trade and deepened the world depression. Yet at the same time there are limits to what states can do because they also compete with each other. Each one only controls a small patch of an integrated world economy. State intervention can therefore mitigate the effects of the crisis, but it cannot prevent the recession.

Until now, the only state that could have coordinated international action was the United States. But it failed to do so. Its plans were inadequate, and no one took them seriously internationally. Now, there is a consensus that only massive recapitalization and state guarantee of loans between banks can unlock the financial system. The British government is going a step further by guaranteeing not only bank deposits, but also all interbank loans. However, in the U.S., Paulson is refusing to do this. He is still trying to protect the shadow banking system.

At the same time, what coordination there is seems to be taking place between the older developed nations, without including BRIC [Brazil, Russia, India, and China] or other developing countries. Some of the richer countries will find it relatively easier to withstand the strain, whereas many of the developing countries (other than China) will find it more difficult. As Lee Sustar writes in *Socialist Worker*, "Once the banks are effectively nationalized, the health of the financial system will depend on the fiscal situation in each country." Smaller, more heavily indebted states, for example in Eastern Europe and Latin America, will have far less room to maneuver and may well face 1930s-style depression conditions.

If the bailouts restore lending, as they may have done by the time this article appears, it will not mean that the crisis is over. For even though banks may start making loans again, they will be doing so with far less capital, since they're still dealing with the losses from mortgage-backed securities. Lehman Brothers went down over the decline of commercial real estate, and AIG required an $85 billion bailout in mid-September (later expanded to $122 billion) to cover its credit-default swaps, and there will be other shoes to drop. There will be more bank losses related to auto loans, business and construction loans, and merger and acquisition loans. The entire credit structure was as bad in other areas as it was in housing. Many poor-quality loans, made without documentation or down payments, were extended to private equity firms and hedge funds. These loans are going to come due, and the banks are not going to be able to roll them over with new credit. As a result, all sorts of junk bonds and leveraged buyout deals are also going to go bankrupt.

The entire banking system is being de-leveraged. Banks will no longer be allowed to make loans thirty or forty times the value of their capital. Instead, they will be held to a leverage ratio of ten. That means tight credit. Just as the asset inflation and credit bubble extended the boom, and contributed to the creation of an enormous amount of fictitious capital, the destruction of that fictitious capital, and the destruction of real capital, will prolong the slowdown.

The Impact Of The Crisis On The Position Of The U.S. In The World System
The United States—economically, militarily, and ideologically—is in decline. There is no longer a "Washington Consensus"—the dominance of the United States economically and ideologically in the world system. The U.S. is no longer in a position to dictate what the rest of the world must do. That world—a world in which the U.S. could dominate the world trading system and set its rules; in which it could dominate the world financially through its banks, which were the most powerful in the world—is gone.

Militarily, the U.S. remains unchallenged; but the crisis puts greater economic strain on its ability to maintain this dominance. It is still militarily bogged down in Iraq and Afghanistan, in a losing situation in the Middle East that is costing it enormous amounts of money and is putting a great strain on the military. The U.S. does not have the wherewithal now to go after North Korea, or Syria, or other members of the so-called Axis of Evil. It cannot respond as it would like, except with hot air, to Russia's reassertion of control over Georgia. What we are witnessing is the simultaneous collapse of the Washington Consensus and the Bush Doctrine, i.e., of the twin pillars of American economic and military policy.

The U.S. ruling class will have to reexamine its policies and options. They are not being examined in the pre-election period. Instead, we are getting platitudes. This is true of both John McCain and Barack Obama and their respective political parties, because they want to avoid making any difficult decisions in the midst of this election. Nevertheless, everything is going to have to be reexamined.

However, it is difficult to discuss how things will play out, because this economic crisis has just begun, and we do not yet know its impact on other countries. For example, the Russians felt emboldened to deal with American encroachments on what they considered to be their area of control, the former Soviet Union in Central Asia and the Caucasus, as a result of the enormous economic rise of Russia that resulted from the oil and commodities boom. The boom led Russia to hold more than $500 billion dollars in U.S. currency reserves, the third largest in the world after China and Japan. It thought it had the money to modernize its military. All that was true just a few months ago. The collapse of oil prices, however, has produced an enormous credit crunch in Russia, whose stock market is now one of the weakest in the world. In October 2008, it shut down three times in two weeks as a result of the banking crisis. So, whereas one could talk about a resurgent Russia some months ago, it is difficult now to discuss it in the same way.

Similarly, the German finance minister, Peer Steinbruck, claimed at the end of September that the U.S. will no longer be the world's financial superpower, and that there will now be a financially multipolar world. The following week, when the French proposed a joint bailout plan similar to Paulson's plan, Germany refused to participate, which triggered a credit crunch in Europe. The Germans argued that the crisis was an American problem, not a German problem. The truth of the matter is that the banking system in Germany may be the weakest, because they had even greater leverage than the American banks. They have been carrying hugely overinflated assets. The fact that Germany finally pledged $679 billion to recapitalize its banks in mid-October is proof enough of the seriousness of its banking crisis.

The position of the dollar is another question mark. Three months ago, the American dollar was collapsing; more recently, there has been an enormous dollar rally as the crisis has spread internationally. So the question is not just the effect of the crisis on the U.S., but also the impact of the crisis on each country, and how it positions them in relation to the others.

We know there is going to be an enormous shift in the balance of forces internationally. We know that the United States had an exaggerated view of what its power was. This was what was behind the huffing and puffing of the neocons and the trumpeting of the Bush Doctrine—that the U.S. had the ability not just to preemptively invade, but to occupy countries at will. All that is now out the window. So there's going to have to be an enormous rebalancing on the basis of the real relation of forces in the world. But it is impossible to say too much about how that will look at the beginning of this crisis because we are not just talking about the United States, but about how the crisis affects the rest of the world.

Very clearly, however, there are going to be a large number of nationalist and protectionist conflicts. Even before this recession began, the Doha round of world trade talks had collapsed, due to the resistance of developing countries, led by China and India, against efforts of the G-8 countries to force greater openings in developing markets without offering any reciprocal concessions. Various countries are going to do whatever is necessary to protect themselves against their competitors. We don't know how it's going to play out. But we do know that just as there is going to be an attempt made to get the working class to pay for the crisis, which will create the possibility of greater resistance and class struggle, there will also be the attempt to get other nations to pay the price, and therefore for struggles between nations. Beyond those generalizations, it's too early to say more. We will know much better in the coming months.

The U.S. in the late 1980s and 1990s improved its competitive position in the world economy and attempted to assert its role as the sole superpower. Though it secured better rates of growth than its competitors in Japan and Europe over the past twenty-five years, it fell behind the growth rates of emerging nations like China, and in order to sustain its own economy it fell into debt. The result is that in the last decade, the United States has lost its competitive position on the world market. Now it will have to restructure, which will involve attempting to raise the rate of exploitation—increasing productivity while lowering wages and benefits even further. We've already seen it in the auto industry, where wages have already been cut in half in many cases. The United States will become a cheap labor country compared to its competitors. Auto wages in this country are probably about a third of what they are in Germany. The minimum wage is half of what it is in Britain, France, Germany, and Ireland. The contradictions of neoliberalism have increased the immiseration and the poverty of the American working class. And to get out of the crisis they are going to attack workers' living standards even further.

Questions Raised By The Crisis

The economic instability of this period is leading to political and ideological instability. Working-class consciousness is going to shift in response. Until now, people thought of this recession mainly in terms of the decline of the housing market, and then in the last year in the rise of food and gasoline prices. Now their pensions are being destroyed; that is, the savings of the American working class are being wiped out by the decline of housing prices, pension funds, and so on. People's incomes are declining, and layoffs are mounting. Everyone knows we are in a crisis, and no one has confidence in the banking system or the government. Some people will be swept up by Obabamania, just for the hope of any change, because there is no faith in existing institutions or in the politicians. It would be hard to find another figure, aside from Obama, in which there are illusions. It isn't that ordinary people were gung ho about the market—they accepted it, but they didn't embrace it. Now they are seeing its total failure, and that government intervention is necessary.

The state must intervene. That's what the banks all say, and that's what the capitalist class says, aside from increasingly marginal conservatives. There has been an enormous shift in terms of what was the prevailing free market ideology that the media and the universities all upheld. They promoted the idea that government intervention is bad, markets are good, and that unrestrained globalization was the answer. All of that is collapsing in front of our eyes.

What is going to replace it? The immediate replacement will be traditional liberalism. The Democrats are going to sweep the elections. They are going to come up with an alternative economic plan. There will be programs for stimulating the economy through more unemployment benefits, more infrastructural spending. Overall, there will be a call for more shared sacrifice. The billionaires cannot make that call—you need the liberals and the Democrats to make that appeal. Until now, it has been the Bush administration that is held responsible for the war and for the economic disaster—the enemy has been the right wing. Now you're going to have liberalism in power, and whatever it does not accomplish—in terms of easing layoffs, extending unemployment benefits, and stopping foreclosures—will reshape U.S. politics.

The economic crisis does not mean that there are openings for only the Left. The Right will also grow. In Austria, the far Right emerged with 30 percent of the vote. In Italy, neofascists are in the coalition government introducing racist laws against Roma people (gypsies). In South Africa, there was a pogrom against refugees from other African countries. There will be a lot of nasty political moves by the Right, which will become a bigger danger. It won't be the traditional Right, but new right formations that will organize around anti-immigrant racism, protectionism, and other forms of right-wing populism.

On the other hand, there's an enormous opening for a Left that has been marginalized for decades. The disaster of the free market makes it easier for us to argue about the failure of capitalism and the need for an alternative based on human needs. The free market, which supposedly triumphed in 1989 and brought us the "end of history," has led to nothing but misery and the ruin of millions of people, who are mired in poverty, hunger, unemployment, and ill health, but thanks to the free-market mania of the past decades, face a shredded safety net that doesn't begin to address these problems.

People will also be forced to ask: what does government intervention mean when this is a government not of the workers, not of the masses of people, but a government that represents the interests of the owners, the bankers, and the industrialists? The state is being used for state capitalist purposes, in order to reorganize capital, even to curb some of its excesses. But its aim is to keep capitalism and its social relations going—relations in which labor is dominated and exploited for the profits of a few. Part of the restructuring will involve, as we've said, an even harsher attack on working-class living standards. At the same time, nationalization opens up space for us to argue against wholesale privatization, for the defense of public schools against privatization, and even to argue for nationalized health care. But we have to be clear that state capitalist nationalization—that is, the intervention of the state in order to prop up the bankers and the industrialists at our expense and without any democratic control over the process—is no great improvement over what went before. Liberals will accept that kind of state intervention. We must demand the kind of state intervention that will come only with mass pressure and control from below—intervention to improve health care, education, unemployment benefits, to prevent foreclosures, and so on.

The Left has to operate on two levels. First, a Left has to be built, or rather rebuilt, in this country that is prepared to fight on every front in defense of working-class interests, whether it is against layoffs, against foreclosures, or against cuts in health care and social services. Second, the Left must be prepared to take part in any struggles to defend the interests of the working class, as well as creating a political and ideological alternative to the free market and its defenders, conservative or liberal. The Left must utilize the crisis to conduct an ideological offensive against capitalism and to argue for a socialist alternative.

T o x i c   C a p i t a l i s m

Michel Husson

The crisis that we are witnessing today is shaking the very foundations of neo-liberal capitalism. It is unfolding at an accelerating speed, and nobody is capable of saying where it will lead.

This section does not try to follow its unfolding step by step, because it would be likely to be outdated by the time it was published. It seeks rather to suggest some keys to interpret this crisis and to demonstrate what is at stake on the social level.

The Mechanics Of The Financial Crisis

The complexity of the financial crisis makes us a bit dizzy, but it is nevertheless possible to identify its principal mechanisms [1] [2]. The starting point is the existence of a considerable mass of "free" capital in search of maximum profitability. Periodically, this capital discovers a new seam and unleashes a dynamic which feeds on "self-fulfilling prophecies": by rushing to cash in on what seems most profitable, the capitalists in fact raise the cost and thus confirm the optimism that started the rush. The warnings of those who explain why the Stock Exchange or the mortgage market cannot go sky-high are made to seem ridiculous, since the system works.

Graph 1 points out these principal episodes: the Stock Exchange crash of 1987, followed by another in 1990 preceding the First Gulf War. From the middle of the year 1995 there began the period known as the "new economy" which was accompanied by a delirious rise of the Stock Exchange. The crises in Southeast Asia and Russia - and the bankruptcy of Long Term credit Management (LTCM) in the United States - only temporarily deflated the bubble in 1998, and it was at the start of the year 2000 that it burst violently.

The headlong forward flight started again two years later and finally led to the subprime crisis in July 2007.

For the bubble to be able to take off, it is not enough to have available capital; it is also necessary for the system of regulation not to put up any obstacles. And regulations were circumvented by decisions of a political nature and by the implementation of sophisticated financial innovations and increasingly opaque practices. We can take the example of the leverage effect, which makes it possible to multiply enormously the sum of which a financial institution initially disposes. Derivative products make possible complicated operations of purchase and forward sale. The banks can get rid of their doubtful debts by placing them with others in a kind of lucky bag which can then be sold in the form of a security (whence comes the term of securitization). The risk attached to the various debts starts to circulate and no longer forms part of the institution's balance sheet, thus escaping the prudent rules which require debts to be limited to a certain proportion of the institution's own equity.

The subprime crisis erupted in a relatively narrow economic sector, the one dealing with loans granted to poor households and guaranteed by the house that they were buying. These contracts were real swindles, since the banks knew very well that they would not be repaid. But securitization made it possible to get rid of them. The fall in the real estate market coincided with the first bankruptcies of households: the sale of the houses with which these rotten loans were guaranteed was no longer possible, or was possible at a price which no longer covered the initial loan. The housing crisis started a chain reaction: one after the other the banks discovered their losses and were gradually unable to obtain new funding sources to cover these losses. In order to prevent a series of bankruptcies, central banks and governments injected money or "nationalized" part of the banks.

From The Virtual To The Real

This briefly summarized scenario raises several questions. The most fundamental one is that of the passage from the virtual economy to the real economy. Every financial crisis, such as the one that is currently unfolding, must in fact be interpreted as a call to order by the law of value.

Financial assets have a "value". If I have a million shares whose price is 100 euros, my wealth is 100 million euros. If the price of my shares doubles, my wealth doubles, and if it falls by half, I lose 50 million euros. But these figures only measure the virtual value of my financial fortune. Profits (or losses) become real only at the point where I seek to get rid of my shares in order to obtain cash for the purpose of buying something real, for example a house. The stock exchange capitalisation, i.e. the total value of the shares, does not in itself mean anything. The financial markets are mainly secondary markets, where people sell, for example, shares in Vivendi in order to buy shares in France Telecom. According to supply and demand, the price of these shares can fluctuate, but these transactions are also virtual in the sense that the price at which these exchanges are carried out is relatively symbolic. These prices, of a particular kind, could be multiplied by a thousand, as if they were expressed in a special currency, disconnected from real currencies. So we could imagine an economy where everyone would be a billionaire in shares, on condition of not seeking to sell them. To use expressions which are really quite eloquent, we would have a real economy progressing at a measured pace, and a financial sphere inflating at incredible speed.

But a lasting divergence between the two is not possible, because there exist "nodes of conversion" between the financial sphere and the real sphere. An economy which grows at 2 or 3 per cent cannot provide a universal profit of 15 per cent, as the defenders of equities claim. As long as the incomes drawn from financial assets are re-invested, the fortunes increase independently of any material link with the real sphere and the variation can potentially become infinite. But if part of these drawing rights which are constituted by financial assets seek to be transferred to the real sphere, in other words to be exchanged against goods, this transfer must comply with the law of value, or more prosaically, with the law of supply and demand. Let us in fact imagine that this new purchasing power does not find a counterpart on the production side, nor does it succeed in becoming a substitute for demand emanating from wages: the adjustment then takes place through rising prices, which amounts to devaluing incomes, including financial revenues. This is what in fact explains the great sensitivity of shareholders to inflation, since the real income derived from their fortunes depends on it. But if such a devalorization occurs, it has repercussions on the evaluation of fortunes and the price of shares must then fall, in order to correspond to the real income which they provide.

Financial assets represent the right to a share of the surplus value that is produced. As long as this right is not exercised, it remains virtual. But as soon as anyone exercises it, they discover that it is subject to the law of value, which means, quiet simply, that you cannot distribute more real wealth than is produced. From an objective point of view, prices on the Stock Exchange should thus represent the anticipated profits of companies, from which financial revenues can be paid. But they have completely taken off and now maintain nothing more than a distant relationship with the profitability of capital based on the exploitation of human labour. Never, in the entire history of capitalism, has this phenomenon attained such scope, and it was not possible for it to last forever.

The Economic Basis Of Financialisation
Financial bubbles are not based solely on the covetous illusions of speculators. They are nourished by the permanent creation of free capital. The first source is the tendential growth of non-accumulated profit, which results itself from a double movement: on the one hand, a generalized decline in wages [3] and on the other hand the stagnation, even a decline, in the rate of accumulation, in spite of the re-establishment of the rate of profit. Graph

2 shows that the rate of profit and the rate of accumulation evolved in parallel until the beginning of the 1980s, then started to diverge considerably. The gray zone makes it possible to measure the increase in the non-accumulated fraction of surplus value.

This new and unprecedented configuration poses a priori a problem of realization: if the share of wages drops and if investment stagnates, who will buy what is produced? In other words, what are the reproduction schemas that are compatible with this new model? There is only one possible answer: consumption resulting from non-wage incomes must compensate for the stagnation of wage consumption. And this indeed what is happening, as graph 3 shows.

In a stylized way, we can summarize as follows how things have evolved: in the United States, the share of wages remains relatively constant but household consumption increases much more quickly than GDP. In Europe, it is the share of consumption in the GDP which remains fairly constant, in spite of the marked decrease in the share of wages. In both cases, the gap widens between the share of wages and the share of consumption (gray zones), so as to compensate for the difference between profit and accumulation. Finance is what is used to effect this compensation, and to do so it follows it three main routes. The first is the consumption of shareholders: part of the non-accumulated surplus value is distributed to the holders of financial revenues, who consume it. This is an important point: reproduction is possible only if the consumption of shareholders comes to support the consumption of wage-earners, in order to provide sufficient outlets, and the increase in inequalities is thus consubstantial with this model.

The second intervention of finance consists in introducing a certain confusion between wages and unearned income: an increasing part of the income of wage-earners takes the form of financial remunerations which can be analyzed as a distribution of surplus value rather than as real wages. Lastly, and this is especially true of the United States, finance makes possible an enormous increase in the debt of households, whose consumption increases, not because of rising wages, but by a decrease in the rate of saving [4].

Finance is thus not a parasite on a healthy body. It feeds off uninvested profit but, in time, it acquires a degree of autonomy which reinforces this mechanism. Free capital circulates in search of maximum profitability (the famous 15 per cent norm) and it succeeds, at least temporarily, in obtaining it in certain sectors. The banks themselves collect an increasing share of profits. This competition for maximum profitability raises the norm of profitability and rarefies a little more the places for investment that are considered to be profitable, thus releasing new free capital which will in its turn go in search of financial hyper-profitability. This vicious circle is based once again on a distribution of income that is unfavourable to workers and to the recognition of their social needs.

Transmission To The Real Economy

In 1987, the stock exchange crash led the majority of economists to envisage a brutal deceleration of the world economy. It was the opposite that happened: as from 1988, the developed countries experienced a very dynamic cycle of growth. The stock exchange crisis had thus not been transmitted to the real economy and, on the contrary, it had served to purge it and make it possible to start afresh. It is after all a traditional function of crises to clean up the accounts and eliminate lame ducks. A few years later, a large-scale estate and mortgage crisis struck Japan, which was at that time being presented as the rising power out to conquer world markets. There then began a decade of almost zero growth, from which the Japanese economy had great difficulty in escaping.

Finance is thus more or less autonomous according to the place and the time and today we have to address the question of whether the financial crisis will be communicated to the real economy. A first thesis consists of saying that the current deceleration is not explained mainly by the financial crisis, but by other factors: the rise in the prices of oil and raw materials, inadequate monetary and budgetary policies in Europe, competition from the emergent countries, etc. According to this thesis, the financial crisis concerns above all the United States and will have relatively little effect on the world economic situation. The demand of the emergent countries will be there to take over from the United States, according to the so-called decoupling thesis. The intervention of the central banks and governments will make it possible to avoid a sequence similar to that of the great crisis of 1929 and to spread out over time the losses of the banks. In short, the financial sphere and the economic sphere will be relatively compartmentalized.

This analysis is based on undeniable realities but does not draw from them the conclusions which go against its relative optimism. It is true that the crisis combines several dimensions, and in particular the rise in the prices of oil and raw materials. But these various aspects are part of the same system and bring us back, fundamentally, to a common origin, which is the current organization of the world economy. You do not understand anything about the present crisis if you think that it can be divided into watertight compartments. This simultaneity of several dimensions will on the contrary reinforce the transmission of the financial crisis to the real economy. It will follow six principal channels, whose relative importance can vary from one country to another:

- The contraction of credit (credit crunch) plays a big role in the diffusion of the financial crisis, since the banks which are put in difficulty by their losses are not succeeding in being refinanced. But these restrictions also concern household consumption and investment by companies. This effect will be particularly marked in countries like the United States or the United Kingdom where household consumption is fuelled by debt.

- The fall in prices on the Stock Exchange devalues the financial and real estate holdings of households (see graph 1) and pushes them to consume less. This is the "wealth effect".

- Generalized uncertainty - the "loss of confidence" - influences how people behave in regard to consumption and investment.

- The housing crisis as such contributes to the general economic deceleration.

- The considerable sums assigned to the various rescue plans will necessitate a reduction in public spending or an increase in taxes.

- Lastly, the deceleration is transmitted to the whole of the world economy through trade and investment.

All these mechanisms are currently at work and they combine with other dimensions of the crisis (oil, etc.) to extend its effects well beyond the financial sphere. There is thus no watertight bulkhead between finance and the real economy, because finance is a key component of neo-liberal capitalism.

Where Is The Crisis Going?
It would be premature (and presumptuous) today to try and predict where this crisis is taking us, but its scale makes going back to normal improbable. One thing is sure, in any case: the very foundations of the United States model will be called into question by the financial crisis. This model rests on a double deficit, an external trade deficit and a deficit of domestic saving. In both cases, finance plays a crucial role in the management of these imbalances: on the domestic level, it is finance which made possible the growth of debt, in particular on the mortgage market; externally, its function is to ensure the equilibrium of the balance of payments. But if finance

deflates, the foundations of this model of growth disappear: household debt is henceforth blocked, and the entries of foreign capital are no longer guaranteed. Consequently, the financial crisis will result in a durable deceleration of growth in the United States, which will be transmitted to the rest of the world.

But at the same time, it is not easy to see what it could be replaced by. The real alternative would be to go back to a form of "Fordism" based on rising wages parallel to rising productivity, a less uneven distribution of income and a rebalancing of foreign trade. Such a model is possible in the abstract but supposes a brutal inversion of social relations which is for the moment out of reach. If Obama is elected, as seems probable today, we cannot count on him to carry out a "Rooseveltian": programme: he lacks the political will, but also the means, since the rescue plan will durably weigh down the budget.

The concrete modalities of the way out of the American model will have repercussions on the rest of the world economy. The first unknown factor relates to the exchange value of the dollar, which should continue to fall, because it is a means for the United States of giving a shot in the arm to its exports and reducing its trade deficit, but also because of the loss of quality of the US national debt. But that amounts to exporting the recession towards Europe, which is globally sensitive to an overvalued exchange rate of the euro. This fall of the dollar, or even its maintenance at its present rate of exchange, raises another question: will capital continue to flow towards the United States? The emergent and oil-producing countries are likely at a certain point to be discouraged from exporting it because of insufficient profitability or increasing risks. From another angle, they have no interest in acting to weaken the dollar, since the value of their holdings already placed in dollars would also be devalued. Another factor must be also taken into account: if the economy of the United States slows down durably, an important outlet for the exports of the emergent countries will dry up and to push them to recentre their growth on the internal market. It is difficult to balance these different factors, which will not evolve at the same speed, but we can nevertheless make two prognostics:

1. The time necessary to get out the crisis is proportional to the enormity of the sums devoted to the rescue of the financial sector. The most probable trajectory is a Japanese-style scenario, where several years will be necessary to absorb the amounts of money that have been swallowed up, which are in another league from what we have seen during preceding financial failures. If no alternative measure is imposed, capitalism will find itself, at least in the developed countries, in a situation of slow

growth and social regression. The real economic recession is already with us, and its objective determining factors, for example the crisis of the car industry, are taking over from the financial storm.

2. The way out of the crisis will be marked by an intense struggle of the major economic actors, each seeking to dump the consequences of the crisis on others. On the social terrain, that implies increased pressure of capital against wages and social spending. On the international level, the commercial and economic war between great powers will take place on a larger scale and will generate a tendency towards the fractioning of the world economy, all the more so in that, as the German Minister for Finance, Peter Steinbrück, said: "The United States will lose its status as the superpower of the world financial system".

European Dogmas Put To The Test

During the crisis, competition continues. The cacophony of declarations and government decisions partly reflects this dilemma: on the one hand, everyone has understood that the crisis calls for global solutions; but, at the same time, everyone seeks to draw advantage from the situation, or at least save the essential. This is obviously true for individual capitals and the discussion over the modalities of the Paulson plan also dealt with this question: is it necessary to save all the financial institutions or only the "lame ducks"? But it is especially true on the level of the famous world government, and everyone has been able to observe the return in force of national interests.

The capitals deployed on the world market may find it very beneficial to return to port and shelter under the umbrella of their national state. But we cannot speak about "the return of the state" because the state always, in the last resort, provides a guarantee for the interests of the bourgeoisie. Once again, the theses on the "Empire" demonstrate their limits: globalization did not remove competition between capitals and inter-capitalist rivalry, nor did it lead to the formation of a world capitalist government. In Europe, the difficulties of coordination are explained by the unequal degree of exposure to the effects of the crisis and express the inexistence of a true European capital. As long as it was a question of injecting liquidities, the European Central Bank could intervene, certainly in response to events. But as soon as it was a question of expenditure to be integrated into the budget, we saw that the European Union was "constitutionally" deprived of the means of facing such a crisis. The gap is widening between France, which would like there to be a rescue plan on a European scale, and Germany and Ireland which prefer a policy of every country for itself. These divergences will no doubt be temporarily overcome if the crisis develops. It is nonetheless true that this crisis will durably call into question the very principles of European neo-liberal construction. Furthermore, it will underline the structural weaknesses of the European economy: "pessimism is necessary" even in the medium term.[5].

Effects On The Workers

Everything is happening today as if the crisis were a kind of natural cataclysm which struck everyone in the same way, and French Prime Minister Fillon did not fail to call for national unity. The climate of panic is instrumentalised so that every one of us is put in the skin of a speculator. Banking bankruptcies are presented as a threat which also menaces the most modest depositors. All this is obviously not some kind of plot, but it contributes to try and obscure what is at stake socially, which we can summarize by posing the real question: who will pay for the damage?

As far as the rich are concerned, it is the workers who must now be put in the front line, not so much as savers, but as workers or pensioners. The crisis has already ruined millions of households in the United States, but it carries very serious consequences, first of all for pensioners in countries where pension funds are the most developed, as in the United States and the United Kingdom. In these two countries, the system was already on the verge of bankruptcy and the real value of pensions will obviously slump with the fall in the Stock Exchange. This is a lesson to be learnt: it is definitely a very bad idea to gamble your pension on the Stock Exchange and any rescue protection plan should take into account this aspect of things, which is of course absent from the Paulson plan.

Workers are doubly in the firing line: directly, because companies will try to compensate for their financial losses by freezing wages even more strictly, using the argument of the risks of inflation and oil prices, and taking advantage of the general climate of uncertainty. They will also suffer the indirect effects of the financial crisis on the real economy, which will bring a string of bankruptcies and lay-offs. The destruction of jobs has already started in the United States and in France. They will be also the first victims of the cuts in welfare spending that are intended to compensate for the cost of the rescue plans.

The Eradication Of Finance And A Social Shield

The crisis is a glaring confirmation of the criticisms addressed to financialised capitalism from an anti-capitalist of and/or global justice point of view. All the economists who praised the benefits of finance are today making big speeches about the need to regulate it. In France, Sarkozy cannot find words hard enough to denounce the excesses of capitalism, whereas had put in his programme the development of mortgage lending. So the ideological landscape is changing extremely quickly and we have to take strength from the rout of the advocates of neo-liberalism.

But for all that, the crisis does not spontaneously create a climate that is favourable to alternatives. All the recycled neo-liberals have turned the lukewarm water tap full on and they are multiplying their own ideological rescue plans based on transparency, prudential ratios, separation of investment and deposit banks, reintegration of securitization into the balance sheets, limitation on the remunerations of the top executives, a credit rating agency, reform of accounting norms, etc.

It is a question, as one of them has put it, "of saving capitalism from the capitalists".[6] These proposals destabilize the social-liberal left, because basically that is their own programme. But it is a thoroughly minimum program which is even likely to divert attention from the real issues. Some of the measures that are being proposed must be supported, such as the prohibition of tax havens, but it would be naive to have confidence in the financial authorities and governments to implement them. They have to be part of a wider project which aims at eradicating finance and which puts the social question in the foreground. Once again, the ultimate source of financialisation is the refusal to satisfy the social needs of the majority of the population. Consequently, you cannot burst the financial bubble once and for all without turning off the taps which supply it.

This orientation can be developed differently according to the countries. In Europe, it could combine two axes. The first is the nationalization of the banks. But that is exactly what they are doing, people will object. The argument can be turned around: that precisely proves that it is possible! And the nationalizations that we are seeing are only socializing the losses, and their function is to save privatized finance. Real nationalization must be carried out without any conditions and it must concern the whole of the system, because all the financiers are responsible for the crisis, whether or not they have lost money because of it. Otherwise, it is just providing state aid for the reorganization of the banking sector.

The second axis could be called a social shield, in reference to the tax shield which, in France, protects the rich from taxation. It really is a question of protecting workers from the repercussions of the crisis, because nobody can decently argue that they have any responsibility for it. At the same time, we have to think of measures which can provide the foundations for a different distribution of revenues and which is based on an elementary argument of social justice. It should be forbidden for companies to continue to pay their shareholders enormous masses of dividends, at the same time as they continue to lay off, further extend precarious work and freeze wages. In the case of France, the net dividends paid out by companies accounted for 12.4 per cent of the overall wage bill in 2007, as against 4.4 per cent 1982.

The crisis is thus the occasion to launch a counter-transfer of dividends towards wages. Rather than freezing wages, it is time to freeze dividends at their current level and transfer them to a mutual fund intended for other uses, under the control of the workers.

These sums could be used, in proportions to be discussed democratically, for the maintenance of the income of the unemployed (the prohibition on dividends would thus finance the banning of lay-offs) and for the financing of Social Security, social budgets and public services. Another measure would consist of imposing the maintenance of the purchasing power of workers by withdrawing, in corresponding proportions, government aid to companies which refuse to maintain it. Such measures are the only ones which can make pay those who are responsible for the crisis pay for it, and this would lay the foundations of a better sharing out of wealth. The sum potentially concerned is 90 billion euros: that is 5 per cent of France's Gross Domestic Product (GDP), in other words exactly the same proportion as the 700 billion dollars envisaged by the Paulson plan in the United States.

NOTES

[1] For a detailed account, see Les Echos, "La crise financiere mondial au jour le jour", http://tinyurl.com/toxico2 or Jacques Sapir, "Sept jours qui ont ebranle la finance", http://tinyurl.com/toxico1.

[2] For a synthetic presentation, see Michel Aglietta, "10 cles pour comprendre la crise", Le Nouvel Observateur, September 25, 2008, http://tinyurl.com/toxico3.

[3] See Michel Husson, "La hausse tendancielle du taux d'exploitation", Inprecor n°534-535, January-February 2008, http://hussonet.free.fr/parvainp.pdf.

[4] See Michel Husson, "Etats-Unis: la fin d'un modele", La Breche n°3, 2008, http://hussonet.free.fr/usbrech3.pdf .

[5] Patrick Artus, "Peut-on etre tres pessimiste sur la situation economique, a moyen terme, de la zone euro? ", http://gesd.free.fr/flas8420.pdf.

[6] Luigi Zingales, "Why Paulson is Wrong", September 2008, http://gesd.free.fr/zingales.pdf.

"The Climatic Crisis Will Combine With The Crisis Of Capital..."

François Chesnais

The point of view that I will defend is that the crisis which started in August 2007 represented a real break which put an end to a long phase of expansion of the world economy. This break heralds the beginning of a process of crisis whose characteristics in terms of the number of intermingled factors are comparable with those of the crisis of 1929, although this one takes place in a very different context and these factors are necessarily different.

It is important to recall initially that the crisis of 1929 took place as a process: a long process which started in 1929 with the crash of Wall Street, but whose climax took place much later, in 1933, and that the crisis was followed by a long phase of recession which led to the Second World War. I say this to stress that, in my opinion, we are witnessing the first stages, really the very first stages, the beginning of a process of an analogous breadth and temporality, even if the analogies stop there. What is happening right now on the financial markets of New York, London and the other great stock exchange centres is only one dimension - and almost certainly not the most important one - of a process which must be interpreted as a historical caesura.

We are confronted with the form of crisis which Marx said marked the historical limits of capitalism, where all of the contradictions. To say that is not to defend any version of the theory of "the final crisis" of capitalism or anything similar. What is in question, in my opinion, is understanding that we are confronted with a situation where the historical limits of capitalist production are apparent. What is it necessary to understand by that? Without wishing to sound like a Marxist preacher, I will read you a passage from Capital:

"The real barrier of capitalist production is capital itself. It is that capital and its self-expansion appear as the starting and the closing point, the motive and the purpose of production; that production is only production for capital and not vice versa, the means of production are not mere means for a constant expansion of the living process of the society of producers. The limits within which the preservation and self-expansion of the value of capital resting on the expropriation and pauperisation of the great mass of producers can alone move — these limits come continually into conflict with the methods of production employed by capital for its purposes, which drive towards unlimited extension of production, towards production as an end in itself, towards unconditional development of the social productivity of labour. The means — unconditional development of the productive forces of society — comes continually into conflict with the limited purpose, the self-expansion of the existing capital. The capitalist mode of production is, for this reason, a historical means of developing the material forces of production and creating an appropriate world-market and is, at the same time, a continual conflict between this its historical task and its own corresponding relations of social production. "[1]

Two Dimensions Which Give The Crisis Its Novelty

There are certainly some terms which we would not use today any more, like that of "historical task". On the other hand I think that the crisis that we will see in the years to come will unfold precisely on the basis of this world market, which Marx intuited and which now exists in all its abundance. This is one of the points where we dealing with a world situation different from 1929. Countries like China or India, which were then still semi-colonial countries, do not have this character any more today. Their specific features (the expression of combined and unequal development) require an attentive analysis. But these are countries which now participate fully in a single world economy, a world economy unified on a scale unknown until this stage of history.

The crisis which has started thus has as its context a world which is unique in a different sense that was not the case in 1929. It is a first point. Here is a second. In my opinion, in this new historical stage, the crisis will develop in such manner that the brutal reality of the world climatic crisis of which we are seeing the first demonstrations will be combined with the crisis of capital as such. We enter a phase which is really that of the crisis of humanity, in its complex relations. That includes wars. But even by excluding the outbreak of a war of great breadth, a world war, which could at present only be a nuclear war, we are faced with a new type of crisis, the combination of this economic crisis which started in a situation where nature, treated without regard and brutalised by humanity within the framework of capitalism, reacts in a brutal way. It is something which is almost excluded from our discussions, but which will impose itself as a central phenomenon.

For example, very recently, I learned from reading a book by a French sociologist, Franck Poupeau [2] that the Andean glaciers which are the source of the water supplies of La Paz and El Alto (Bolivia), are more than 80% exhausted and that it is estimated that in about fifteen years La Paz and El Alto will not have any more water... It is something that we, who claim to be revolutionary Marxists, have never dealt with. We never discuss facts of this nature and this breadth. However this fact can substantially modify the class struggle in Bolivia, as we know it: for example, the movement of the capital to Sucre, so controversial, imposes itself as a "natural" phenomenon, because La Paz will lack water. We enter a period where facts of this type will interfere in the class struggle. The problem is that in revolutionary circles hardly anybody speaks about that; we continue to discuss things whose importance is negligible at the present time, completely petty questions in comparison with the challenges which we must face.

Three Means Of Overcoming Capital's "Immanent Barriers"
To continue on the question of the limits of capitalism, I would like to return to a quotation from Marx, which precedes that already given: "Capitalist production seeks continually to overcome these immanent barriers, but overcomes them only by means which again place these barriers in its way and on a more formidable scale. " [3]. There is a lightning rod which can be useful in analysis and discussion. The means implemented by the bourgeoisie ranged behind the United States to overcome the inherent limits of capital during the past thirty years were primarily three.

Firstly, there was the whole process of liberalization of finances, trade and the investment, i.e. the process of destruction of the political relations which emerged on the basis of the crisis of 1929 and of the Thirties, after the Second World War, the Chinese revolution and the wars of national liberation. All these relations, which did not in Western Europe or Latin America affect the existence of the capital but which represented at the same time forms of partial control over it, were destroyed.

The second means employed to overcome these inherent limits of the capital was the recourse, on an unprecedented scale, to the creation of fictitious capital and of forms of credit which, in the countries in the centre of the system, enlarged an insufficient demand.

The third means, most important historically for capital, was rehabilitation as full components of the world capitalist system of the Soviet Union and its "satellites", and especially China, more important still because marked by a controlled modification of the relations of property and production.
It is within the framework of the contradictory effects of these three processes that it is possible to grasp the breadth and novelty of the crisis that has opened.

Liberalization, World Market, Competition...
Let us initially look at the contradictory effects of the liberalization and

deregulation undertaken on a worldwide scale in the space created by the integration into capitalism of the old Soviet "camp" after the collapse of the USSR, as well as that of China. The process of liberalization involved the dismantling of the elements of regulation built within the international framework at the end of the Second World War, leading to a capitalism about completely deprived of mechanisms of regulation. Capitalism was not only deregulated, but the world market was created really and fully, transforming into reality what was for Marx largely an intuition and an anticipation. It is useful to specify the concept of world market. The term "market" indicates a space of valorisation, released from restrictions for the operations of capital, which makes it possible for the latter to produce and realise surplus value by taking this space as basis for the mechanisms of truly international centralization and concentration. This open, non homogeneous space, but with a Draconian reduction of the obstacles to the mobility of capital enabling it to organize the cycle of valorisation on the planetary scale. It is accompanied by a situation making it possible to put all the workers of all countries in competition with each other. Thus it is founded on the fact that the industrial reserve army is truly global and that it is capital as a whole which governs, in the forms studied by Marx, the flows of integration or rejection of the workers in the process of accumulation.

Such then is the general framework of a process of "production for production" under conditions where the possibility for humanity and the masses of the world to accede to this production is very limited. This is why the positive outcome of the cycle of valorisation of the capital, for capital as a whole and each capital in particular, becomes increasingly difficult to attain. And it is from this fact that "the blind laws of competition" play an unceasingly larger role and become more determinant on the world market. The central banks and the governments can try to agree among themselves and to collaborate to overcome the crisis, but I do not think that it is possible to introduce co-operation into a world space which has become the scene of a terrible competition between capitals. And now competition between capitals goes well beyond the relationship between the capital of the older and most developed parts of the world system. It includes the least developed sectors from the capitalist point of view. Because in particular forms including the most parasitic, in the world market a process of centralization of capital apart from the traditional framework of the imperialist centres has taken place: in relation to them, but under conditions which also introduce something completely new within the world framework.

Industrial groups capable of integrating themselves in their own right as partners in world oligopolies have developed in given points of the system during the last fifteen years and in particular during the most recent stage. In India and China genuinely powerful capitalist economic groups were formed. On the financial level, as expression of the oil revenue and the parasitism which is specific to it, sovereign wealth funds became important points of centralization of capital-money. They are not simple satellites of the United States. They have their strategies and their own dynamics which modify in many respects the configuration of geopolitical relations of the key points where the life of capital is decided and will be decided.

Consequently another dimension of which we must take account is that this crisis marks the end of the stage during which the United States could act as a world power without adversaries. In my opinion, we have left the phase that Mészáros analyzed in his book of 2001 [4]. The United States will be put to the test: in a very short lapse of time their world relations have been modified and the United States will have to renegotiate them and reorganize them by basing themselves on the fact that they must share power. And that, of course, it is something which never occurred in a peaceful way in the history of capital... So, the first element is that one of the means chosen by capital to overcome its limits has become a new source of tensions, conflicts and contradictions, so that it a new historical stage has been opened through this crisis.

Uncontrolled Creation Of Fictitious Capital

The second means employed by the capital of the central economies to overcome its limits was the generalized recourse to the creation of completely artificial forms of the enlargement of solvent demand. That, added to the other forms of creation of fictitious capital, generated the conditions of the current financial crisis. In an article that comrades of Herramienta had the kindness to translate into Castilian and to publish [5], I examined rather lengthily the question of fictitious capital, its accumulation and the new processes which characterized it. For Marx, fictitious capital is the accumulation of securities which are "the shadow" of investments already made. In the form of bonds and shares, they appear in the eyes of their holders as capital. They are not capital for the system taken as a whole, but they are for their holders and, under the "normal" economic conditions, at the end of the process of valorisation of capital, they ensure them dividends and interests.

But their fictitious character appears in crisis situations. When crises of overproduction occur, with the bankruptcies of companies and so on, this capital can disappear suddenly. You read in the newspapers that this or that quantity of capital "has disappeared" during a stock market slump? These amounts did not exist as capital properly so-called, despite the fact that, for the holders of these shares, these titles represented a right to dividends and interests, a right to receive a fraction of the profits.

Of course, one of the major problems today is that, in many countries, pensions systems are based on fictitious capital, in the form of claims to a share of profits which can disappear in times of crisis. Each stage of the liberalization and the financial globalization of the years 1980 and 1990 reinforced the accumulation of fictitious capital, in particular in the hands of investment funds, pension funds and financial funds. And the great novelty which appeared in the early to mid 1990s and throughout this century is that, in particular in the United States and in Great Britain, an extraordinary push took place for the creation of fictitious capital in the form of credit. Credit to companies, but also and especially loans to households, consumer credits and mortgages. Thus we witnessed a qualitative jump in the mass of fictitious capital created, causing sharper forms of vulnerability and brittleness, even in relation to minor shocks, including completely foreseeable episodes.

For example, on the basis of former experience, which was very well studied, we knew that the property boom would necessarily end for well known endogenous reasons. While it is relatively comprehensible that on the stock market the illusion exists that there are no limits to the rise of shares, the whole of preceding history shows this is not true of the property sector: when we are talking about buildings and houses it is inevitable that the boom finishes at a given time. But the degree of dependence of the continuation of the growth and success of financial speculations was so strong, that this normal and foreseeable event was transformed into an element leading to an enormous crisis. Because I should add to what I have already said that during the two last years of the boom, loans were granted to households which did not have the least capacity to repay them. And moreover, all this combined with the new financial "techniques" - which I have tried to explain in the article mentioned above in Herramienta [6] - allowing the banks to sell designated synthetic securities in such a manner that nobody could know exactly what they had bought. This is what explained the devastating character of the contagion of the "subprime" effect which started in 2007 and the fact in particular that the "toxic effects" strongly poisoned the relations of the banks among themselves.

Now we are witnessing the "unravelling" of this process. It is necessary to erase an accumulation of "assets" which are fictitious to the nth degree, resulting from debt ratios of 30 times on average of the effective capital holdings of banks (which itself include debts, deemed "recoverable" at this time), This "unravelling" favours the concentration of financial capital of course. When Bank of America buys Merrill Lynch, it represents a classic process of concentration. The leap in the crisis that we saw on September 17 was caused by the decision of the Treasury and the Federal Reserve not to prevent the bankruptcy of Lehmann bank. On September 18 they had to change position and massively aid the AIG insurance group. The process of nationalization of debts implies a new creation of the fictitious capital. The Federal Reserve of the United States is increasing the mass of fictitious capital to maintain the illusion of the value of institutional centralizations of fictitious capital (banks and investment funds) which were about to break down, with the prospect of being obliged at a given time to strongly increase fiscal pressure, which in fact the Federal government cannot do because that means the contraction of the domestic market and the acceleration of the crisis. We are thus witnessing a headlong rush which does not solve anything.

Within the framework of this process we also see the rise in power of the sovereign wealth funds, whose effect is to modify the inter-capitalist distribution in the financial field in favour of the pensions sectors which accumulate this type of fund. And it is one more factor of disturbance in this process.

We should recall, to end on this second dimension, that it is its external deficit of 7-8% of GDP which gives the United States the characteristic of being the strategic centre of the capital valorisation cycles, which is decisive at the time of the realization of surplus value. That is true not only for capital under US control, but for the process of valorisation of capital in its totality. Now, faced with a quasi inevitable economic recession, the great question arises of whether China will be able to become the place which will guarantee this moment of realization of surplus value instead of the United States. The extent of the intervention by the Federal Reserve and the Treasury explains why the contraction of activity in the United States and the fall in its imports has until now been rather slow and limited. The question is how long they will be able to hold with the creation of more and more liquidities as the single instrument of economic policy. Is it possible that there are no limits to the creation of fictitious capital in the form of liquidities to maintain the value of the fictitious capital which already exists? That seems me to be a very hazardous assumption and very much doubted among the US economists themselves.

Over Accumulation In China?
To end, we will look at the third way in which capital has sought to exceed its inherent limits. It is the most important of all and raises the most interesting questions. I refer to the extension, in particular towards China, of the entire system of social relations of production of capitalism. It is some-

thing which Marx mentioned at one time as a possibility, but which has become reality only in recent years. And which was carried out under conditions which multiply the factors of crisis.

The accumulation of the capital in China was founded on internal processes, but also on the basis of something which is documented perfectly, but little commented on: the transfer of a great part of the production of sector II of the economy - the sector of consumer goods - from the United States to China. That has much to do with the increase in US deficits (both trade and budget deficits), which could be reversed only by a vast "reindustrialisation" of the United States.

That means that new relations have been established between the United States and China. They are not relations between an imperialist power and a semi-colonial country. The United States has created relations of a new type and they now face difficulty in recognising this and assuming the consequences. Basing itself on its trade surplus, China has accumulated hundreds of millions of dollars, which it immediately lent to the United States. An illustration of the consequences is the nationalization of the two companies named Fannie Mae and Freddy Mac: the Bank of China held 15% of these companies and informed the US government that it would not accept their devalorisation. These are international relations of a completely new type.

But, what will happen if the crisis spreads in the form of a significant fall in exports with effects on production, and crisis in the banking structure and the Shanghai Stock Exchange in China? In my already mentioned article [7] there is only one page on this question right at the end, but in a certain manner, it is the most decisive question for the next stage of the crisis.

In China, there has been an internal process of competition between capital, combined with a process of rivalry between sectors of the Chinese political apparatus and competition between them to attract foreign companies. This has resulted, in addition to destruction of nature on a great scale, in a process of creation of immense capacities of production: in China an over accumulation of capital has been concentrated which, at a given time, will become insupportable. In Europe the acceleration of the relocation of productive capacities and jobs, to transfer them to this singular paradise of the capitalist world that is China today, was notorious among the big industrial groups. My assumption is that this transfer of capital to China has led to a change in the previous movement of accumulation and caused a new rise in the organic composition of capital. Accumulation is intense in means of production and very wasteful of raw materials, the other component of constant capital. The massive creation of productive capacities in sector I (means of production) has been the motor of growth in China, but the final market allowing this production to flow and realise value and surplus value has been the world market. By worsening it the recession highlights this over accumulation of capital. Michel Aglietta, who has studied it specifically [8], affirms that there is really an over accumulation, that there was an accelerated process of creation of productive capacities in China, a process which will pose problems of the realization of all this production when the external market contracts, which it is starting to do today. China plays a really decisive part, because even small variations in its economy determine the economic situation of many other countries of the world. It is enough if Chinese demand for investment goods falls a little for Germany to lose exports and enter recession. These "small oscillations" in China have very strong repercussions elsewhere, as should be obvious in the case of Argentina.

Continuing To Reflect And Discuss
I return to what I said at the beginning. Even if they are comparable, the phases of this crisis are distinct from that of 1929, because the crisis of overproduction of the United States occurred then from the first moments. Afterwards, it deepened, but it was clear from the beginning that it amounted to a crisis of overproduction. Today, on the contrary, the policies implemented by the big central capitalist countries are delaying this moment, but they cannot do much more than that.

Simultaneously, and as happened also in the case of the crisis of 1929 and the 1930s, even if under different conditions and forms, the crisis combines with capitalism's necessity for a total reorganisation of its economic relations of force at the world level, marking the moment where the US will see that its military supremacy is only an element, and a subordinate element, in renegotiating their relations with China and the other parts of the world. Unless of course they embark on a military adventure with unforeseeable consequences. For the moment the internal political conditions intern do not allow it in any way, but it cannot be excluded if the recession leads to a long depression and revolutionary movements.

For all these reasons, I conclude that we are dealing with much more than one financial crisis, even if we are for the moment at this stage. Even if I have had to concentrate this evening on the attempt to unpick the threads of fictitious capital and to help to understand why it is so difficult to dismantle this capital, we are facing an infinitely broader crisis.

By taking account of the questions and various observations which were made to me since I arrived in Buenos Aires and here even this evening, I have the impression that many think that I am drawing a catastrophist picture of the current moment of capitalism. I indeed think that we are facing a risk of catastrophe, not a catastrophe of capitalism, not a "final crisis", but a catastrophe of humanity. If we take the climatic crisis seriously, probably there is already something of that. I share the views of Mészáros, for example [9], but there are not many of us who attach the same importance to it, that from this point of view we are facing an imminent danger. What is tragic is that for the moment this directly affects only peoples whose existence is not taken into account: what can happen in Haiti seems not to have any historical importance, what happens in Bangladesh has no weight outside of the affected area, nor what occurred in Burma, because the control of the military junta prevents this being known. It is the same thing in China: we discuss the indices of the growth but not other ecological catastrophes, because the repressive apparatus controls information on that subject.

And the worst thing is that this view that "the ecological crisis is not as serious as is claimed", which is constantly projected by the media, is very deeply internalized, including by a number of left intellectuals. I had started to work and write on this subject, but with the beginning of the financial crisis I was to some extent forced to return to concerning myself with finances, although that does not satisfy me so much, because the essential seems to me to be located at another level.

In conclusion: the fact that all this happens after such a long phase, without parallel in the history of capitalism, of fifty years of uninterrupted accumulation (except for a small break in 1974-1975) and also that the capitalist leadership circles, and in particular the central banks, have learned from the crisis of 1929, all meant that the development of the crisis was slow. Since September 2007, the discourse of the leadership circles repeats unceasingly that "the worst is behind us", whereas what is certain is that "the worst" is in front of us.

This is why I insist on the risk there is of minimizing the gravity of the situation. And I suggest that, in our analysis and our manner of approaching these things, we must integrate the possibility, at least the possibility, that inadvertently we could have internalized the discourse that at the end of the day "nothing is happening".

October 2008

NOTES

[1] Karl Marx, "Capital":www.marxists.org/archive/marx/works/1894-c3/ch15.htm
[2] Franck Poupeau, "Carnets boliviens 1999-2007, Un goût de poussière", Éditions Aux lieux d'être, Paris 2008
[3] Karl Marx, "Capital", op. cit.
[4] István Mészáros, "Socialism or Barbarism : From the "American Century" to the Crossroads", Monthly Review Press, 2001
[5] "El fin de un ciclo. Alcance y rumbo de la crisis financier", "Herramienta" number 37, March 2008. This article first appeared in French, see François Chesnais, "Fin d'un cycle, sur la portée et le cheminement de la crise financière", Carré rouge-La brèche number 1, December 2007-January 2008
[6] Ibid [7] Ibid.
[8] See Michel Aglietta and Yves Landry, "La Chine vers la superpuissance", Économica, Paris 2007
[9] István Mészáros, "The sole viable economy", Monthly Review Press, 2007

Ecology And The Transition From Capitalism To Socialism

John Bellamy Foster

The transition from capitalism to socialism is the most difficult problem of socialist theory and practice. To add to this the question of ecology might therefore be seen as unnecessarily complicating an already intractable issue. I shall argue here, however, that the human relation to nature lies at the heart of the transition to socialism. An ecological perspective is pivotal to our understanding of capitalism's limits, the failures of the early socialist experiments, and the overall struggle for egalitarian and sustainable human development.

My argument has three parts. First, it is crucial to understand the intimate connection between classical Marxism and ecological analysis. Far from being an anomaly for socialism, as we are often led to believe, ecology was an essential component of the socialist project from its inception—notwithstanding the numerous later shortcomings of Soviet-type societies in this respect. Second, the global ecological crisis that now confronts us is deeply rooted in the "world-alienating" logic of capital accumulation, traceable to the historical origins of capitalism as a system. Third, the transition from capitalism to socialism is a struggle for sustainable human development in which societies on the periphery of the capitalist world system have been leading the way.

Classical Marxism And Ecology

Research carried out over the last two decades has demonstrated that there was a powerful ecological perspective in classical Marxism. Just as a transformation of the human relation to the earth was, in Marx's view, an essential presupposition for the transition from feudalism to capitalism, so the rational regulation of the metabolic relation to nature was understood as an essential presupposition for the transition from capitalism to socialism.[1] Marx and Engels wrote extensively about ecological problems arising from capitalism and class society in general, and the need to transcend these under socialism. This included discussions of the nineteenth-century soil crisis, which led Marx to develop his theory of metabolic rift between nature and society. Basing his analysis on the work of the German chemist Justus von Liebig, he pointed to the fact that soil nutrients (nitrogen, phosphorus and potassium) were removed from the soil and shipped hundreds and thousands of miles to the cities where they ended up polluting the water and the air and contributing to the poor health of the workers. This break in the necessary metabolic cycle between nature and society demanded for

Marx nothing less than the "restoration" of ecological sustainability for the sake of "successive generations". [2]

In line with this, Marx and Engels raised the main ecological problems of human society: the division of town and country, soil depletion, industrial pollution, urban maldevelopment, the decline in health and crippling of workers, bad nutrition, toxicity, enclosures, rural poverty and isolation, deforestation, human-generated floods, desertification, water shortages, regional climate change, the exhaustion of natural resources (including coal), conservation of energy, entropy, the need to recycle the waste products of industry, the interconnection between species and their environments, historically conditioned problems of overpopulation, the causes of famine, and the issue of the rational employment of science and technology.

This ecological understanding arose from a deep materialist conception of nature that was an essential part of Marx's underlying vision. "Man", he wrote, "*lives* from nature, i.e. nature is his *body*, and he must maintain a continuing dialogue with it if he is not to die. To say that man's physical and mental life is linked to nature simply means that nature is linked to itself, for man is a part of nature".[3] Not only did Marx declare in direct opposition to capitalism that no individual owned the earth, he also argued that no nation or people owned the earth; that it belonged to successive generations and should be cared for in accordance with the principle of good household management. [4]

Other early Marxists followed suit, although not always consistently, in incorporating ecological concerns into their analyses and embodying a general materialist and dialectical conception of nature. William Morris, August Bebel, Karl Kautsky, Rosa Luxemburg and Nikolai Bukharin all drew on ecological insights from Marx. The Ukrainian socialist Sergei Podolinsky's early attempt at developing an ecological economics was inspired to a considerable extent by the work of Marx and Engels. Lenin stressed the importance of recycling soil nutrients and supported both conservation and pioneering experiments in community ecology (the study of the interaction of populations within a specific natural environment). This led to the development in the Soviet Union in the 1920s and early 1930s of probably the most advanced conception of ecological energetics or trophic dynamics (the basis of modern ecosystem analysis) in the world at the time. The same revolutionary-scientific climate produced V. I. Vernadsky's theory of the biosphere, A. I. Oparin's theory of the origin of life and N. I. Vavilov's discovery of the world centres of germplasm (the genetic sources of the world's crop plants). In the West, and in Britain in particular, leading scientists influenced by Marxism in the 1930s, such as J. B. S. Haldane, J. D. Bernal, Hyman Levy, Lancelot Hogben and Joseph Needham, pioneered in exploring the dialectics of nature. It is even possible to argue that ecological science had its genesis almost entirely in the work of thinkers on the left (socialist, social democratic and anarchist). [5]

Obviously not all major figures or all developments in the socialist tradition can be seen as ecological. Soviet Marxism succumbed to an extreme version of the productivism that characterised early twentieth-century modernity in general, leading to its own version of ecocide. With the rise of the Stalinist system the pioneering ecological developments in the Soviet Union were largely crushed (and some of the early ecologically oriented Marxists such as Bukharin and Vavilov were killed). Simultaneously, a deep antipathy to natural science emerging out of an extreme negation of positivism led to the abandonment of attempts to theorise the dialectics of nature in Western Marxism, seriously weakening its link to ecology—though the question of the domination of nature was raised by the Frankfurt School as part of its critique of science. If today socialism and ecology are once again understood as dialectically interconnected, it is due both to the evolution of the ecological contradictions of capitalism and the development of socialism's own self-critique.

Capitalism's World Alienation
The key to understanding capitalism's relation to the environment is to examine its historical beginnings, i.e., the transition from feudalism to capitalism. This transition was enormously complex, occurring over centuries, and obviously cannot be fully addressed here. I shall focus on just a few factors. The bourgeoisie arose within the interstices of the feudal economy. As its name suggests, the bourgeoisie had its point of origin as a class primarily in the urban centres and mercantile trade. What was necessary, however, in order for bourgeois society to emerge fully *as a system*, was the revolutionary transformation of the feudal mode of production and its replacement by capitalist relations of production. Since feudalism was predominantly an agrarian system, this meant of course transformation of agrarian relations, i.e., the relation of workers to the land as a means of production.

Capitalism therefore required for its development a new relation to nature, one which severed the direct connection of labour to the means of production, i.e., the earth, along with the dissolution of all customary rights in relation to the commons. The *locus classicus* of the industrial revolution was Britain, where the removal of the workers from the land by means of expropriation took the form of the enclosure movement from the fifteenth to the eighteenth centuries. Under colonialism and imperialism an even more brutal transformation occurred on the outskirts or the external areas of the capitalist world economy. There all preexisting human productive relations to nature were torn asunder in what Marx called the "extirpation, enslavement and entombment in mines of the indigenous population"—the most violent expropriation in all of human history. [6]

The result was proletarianisation within the centre of the system as masses of workers were thrown out of work and moved to the city. There they were met by the capital being amassed through organised robbery, giving rise to what Marx called "modern industry". Simultaneously, various forms of servitude and what we now call precarious work were imposed on the periphery, where social reproduction was always secondary to the most rapacious imperialist exploitation. The surplus forcibly extracted from the periphery fed industrialisation at the centre of the world economy. [7]

What made this new system work was the incessant accumulation of capital in one cycle after another, with each new phase of accumulation taking the last as its starting point. This meant ever more divided, more alienated human beings, together with a more globally destructive metabolism between humanity and nature. As Joseph Needham observed, the "conquest of Nature" under capitalism turned into "the conquest of man"; the "technological instruments utilised in the dominance of Nature" produced "a qualitative transformation in the mechanisms of social domination". [8] There is no doubt that this dialectic of domination and destruction is now spiraling out of control on a planetary scale. Economically, overall inequality between the centre and periphery nations of the world system is increasing together with the intensification of class inequality within each capitalist state. Ecologically, the world's climate and the life-support systems of the entire earth are being transformed by a process of runaway global warming.[9]

In addressing this planetary environmental problem it is useful to turn to Hannah Arendt's concept of "world alienation", introduced fifty years ago in *The Human Condition*. "World alienation" for Arendt began with the "alienation from the earth" at the time of Columbus, Galileo, and Luther. Galileo trained his telescope on the heavens, thereby converting human beings into creatures of the cosmos, no longer simply earthly beings. Science seised on cosmic principles in order to obtain the "Archimedean point" with which to move the world, but at the cost of immeasurable world alienation. Human beings no longer apprehended the world immediately through the direct evidence of their five senses. The original unity of the human relation to the world exemplified by the Greek polis was lost.

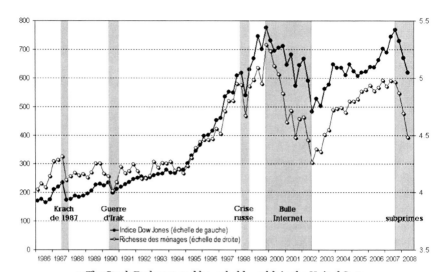

1: The Stock Exchange and household wealth in the United States
The Dow Jones index at current prices (base: 100 in 1960)
Net wealth of households as a multiple of their current income Sources and data for the
graphs: http://hussonet.free.fr/toxicap.xls

Arendt noted that Marx was acutely aware of this world alienation from his earliest writings, pointing out that the world was "denatured" as all natural objects—the wood of the wood-user and the wood-seller—were converted into private property and the universal commodity form. Original or primitive accumulation, the alienation of human beings from the land, as Marx described it, became a crucial manifestation of world alienation. However, Marx, in Arendt's view, chose to stress human self-alienation rooted in labour rather than world alienation. In contrast, "world alienation, and not [primarily] self-alienation as Marx thought", she concluded, "has been the hallmark of the modern age".

"The process of wealth accumulation, as we know it", Arendt went on to observe, depended on expanding world alienation. It "is possible only if the world and the very worldliness of man are sacrificed". This process of the accumulation of wealth in the modern age "enormously increased human power of destruction" so "that we are able to destroy all organic life on earth and shall probably be able one day to destroy even the earth itself". Indeed, "Under modern conditions", she explained, "not destruction but conservation spells ruin because the very durability of conserved objects is the greatest impediment to the turnover process, whose constant gain in speed is the only constancy left wherever it has taken hold".[10]

Arendt had no final answers to the dire problem she raised. Despite tying world alienation to a system of destruction rooted in wealth accumulation, she identified it with the development of science, technology, and modernity rather than capitalism as such. World alienation in her view was the triumph of *homo faber* and *animal labourans*. In this tragic conception, her readers were called upon to look back to the lost unity of the Greek polis, rather than, as in Marx, toward a new society based on the restoration at a higher level of the human metabolism with nature. In the end world alienation for Arendt was a Greek tragedy raised to the level of the planet.

There is no doubt that the concrete manifestations of this world alienation are evident everywhere today. The latest scientific data indicate that global emissions of carbon dioxide from fossil fuels experienced a "sharp acceleration…in the early 2000s" with the growth rate reaching levels "greater than for the most fossil-fuel intensive of the Intergovernmental Panel on Climate Change emissions scenarios developed in the late 1990s". Further, "the mean global atmospheric CO2 concentration" has been increasing "at a progressively faster rate each decade". The most rapid acceleration in emissions has been in a handful of emergent industrialising countries such as China, but "no region" in the world is currently "decarbonising its energy supply". All ecosystems on earth are in decline, water shortages are on the rise, and energy resources are becoming more than ever the subject of global monopolies enforced by war.

The "man-made fingerprint of global warming" has been detected "on 10 different aspects of Earth's environment: surface temperatures, humidity, water vapor over the oceans, barometric pressure, total precipitation, wildfires, change in species of plants and animals, water run-off, temperatures in the upper atmosphere, and heat content in the world's oceans". The cost now descending on the world if it doesn't radically change course is a *regression* of civilisation and life itself beyond comprehension: an economy and ecology of destruction that will finally reach its limits.[11]

Socialism And Sustainable Human Development

How are we to meet this challenge, arguably the greatest that human civilisation has ever faced? A genuine answer to the ecological question, transcending Arendt's tragic understanding of world alienation, requires a revolutionary conception of sustainable human development—one that addresses both human self-estrangement (the alienation of labour) and world alienation (the alienation of nature). It was Ernesto "Che" Guevara who most famously argued in his "Man and Socialism in Cuba" that the crucial issue in the building of socialism was not economic development but human development. This needs to be extended by recognising, in line with Marx, that the real question is one of sustainable human development, explicitly addressing the human metabolism with nature through human labour .[12]

Too often the transition to socialism has been approached mechanistically as the mere expansion of the means of production, rather than in terms of the development of human social relations and needs. In the system that emerged in the Soviet Union the indispensable tool of planning was misdirected to production for production's sake, losing sight of genuine human needs, and eventually gave rise to a new class structure. The detailed division of labour, introduced by capitalism, was retained under this system and extended in the interest of higher productivity. In this type of society, as Che critically observed, "the period of the building of socialism...is characterised by the extinction of the individual for the sake of the state".[13]

The revolutionary character of Latin American socialism today derives its strength from an acute recognition of the negative (as well as some positive) lessons of the Soviet experience, partly through an understanding of the problem raised by Che: the need to develop socialist humanity. Further, the

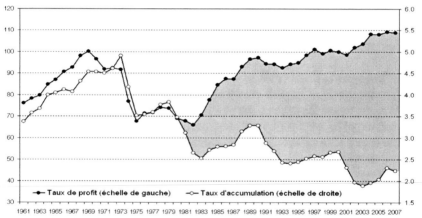

2: Rate of profit and rate of accumulation: The United States + European Union + Japan
* Rate of accumulation = rate of growth rate of the net volume of capital * Rate of profit = profit/capital (base: 100 in 2000)

Sources and data of the graphs: http://hussonet.free.fr/toxicap.xls

Bolivarian vision proclaimed by Hugo Chávez has its own deep roots of inspiration drawing on an older pre-Marxian socialism. Thus it was Simon Bolívar's teacher Simón Rodríguez who wrote in 1847: "The division of labour in the production of goods only serves to brutalise the workforce. If to produce cheap and excellent nail scissors, we have to reduce the workers to machines, we would do better to cut our finger nails with our teeth." Indeed, what we most admire today with regard to Bolívar's own principles is his uncompromising insistence that equality is "the law of laws". [14]

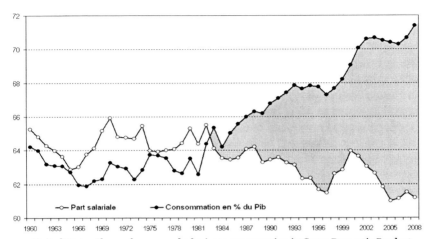

3: United States Share of wages and of private consumption in Gross Domestic Product (GDP)
Source of data and graphics: http://hussonet.free.fr/toxicap.xls

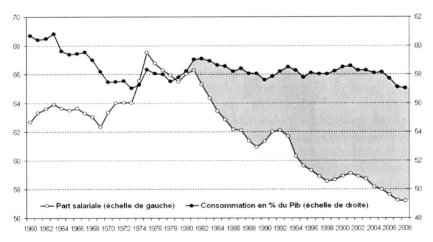

4. European Union Share of wages and of private consumption in Gross Domestic Product (GDP)
Source of data and graphics: http://hussonet.free.fr/toxicap.xls

The same commitment to the egalitarian, universal development of humanity was fundamental to Marx. The evolution of the society of associated producers was to be synonymous with the positive transcendence of human alienation. The goal was a many-sided human development. Just as "all history is nothing but a continuous transformation of human nature", so "the *cultivation* of the five senses is the work of all previous history". Socialism thus appears as the "complete emancipation of the senses", of human sensuous capacities and their wide-ranging development. "Communism, as fully developed naturalism", Marx wrote, "equals humanism, and as fully developed humanism equals naturalism". [15]

The contrast between this revolutionary, humanistic-naturalistic vision and today's dominant mechanical-exploitative reality could not be starker. We find ourselves in a period of imperialist development that is potentially the most dangerous in all of history.[16] There are two ways in which life on the planet as we know it can be destroyed—either instantaneously through global nuclear holocaust, or in a matter of a few generations by climate change and other manifestations of environmental destruction. Nuclear weapons continue to proliferate in an atmosphere of global insecurity promoted by the world's greatest power. War is currently being waged in the Middle East over geopolitical control of the world's oil at the same time that carbon emissions from fossil fuels and other forms of industrial production are generating global warming. Biofuels offered up today as a major alternative to pending world oil shortages are destined only to enlarge world hunger.[17] Water resources are being monopolised by global corporations. Human needs are everywhere being denied: either in the form of extreme deprivation for a majority of the population of the world, or, in the richer countries, in the form of the most intensive self-estrangement conceivable, extending beyond production to a managed consumption, enforcing lifelong dependence on alienating wage labour. More and more life is debased in a welter of artificial wants dissociated from genuine needs.

All of this is altering the ways in which we think about the transition from capitalism to socialism. Socialism has always been understood as a society aimed at reversing the relations of exploitation of capitalism and removing the manifold social evils to which these relations have given rise. This requires the abolition of private property in the means of production, a high degree of equality in all things, replacement of the blind forces of the market by planning by the associated producers in accordance with genuine social needs, and the elimination to whatever extent possible of invidious distinctions associated with the division of town and country, mental and manual labour, race divisions, gender divisions, etc. Yet, the root problem of socialism goes much deeper. The transition to socialism is possible only through a revolutionising practice that *revolutionises human beings themselves*.[18] The only way to accomplish this is by altering our human metabolism with nature, along with our human-social relations, transcending both the alienation of nature and of humanity. Marx, like Hegel, was fond of quoting Terence's famous statement "Nothing human is alien to me".

Now it is clear that we must deepen and extend this to: *Nothing of this earth is alien to me.*[19]

Mainstream environmentalists seek to solve ecological problems almost exclusively through three mechanical strategies: (1) technological bullets, (2) extending the market to all aspects of nature, and (3) creating what are intended as mere islands of preservation in a world of almost universal exploitation and destruction of natural habitats. In contrast, a minority of critical human ecologists have come to understand the need to change our fundamental social relations. Some of the best, most concerned ecologists, searching for concrete models of change, have thus come to focus on those states (or regions) that are both ecological and socialistic (in the sense of relying to a considerable extent on social planning rather than market forces) in orientation. Thus Cuba, Curitiba and Porto Alegre in Brazil, and Kerala in India, are singled out as the leading lights of ecological transformation by some of the most committed environmentalists, such as Bill McKibben, best known as the author of *The End of Nature*.[20] More recently Venezuela has been using its surplus from oil to transform its society in the direction of sustainable human development, thereby laying the foundation for a greening of its production. Although there are contradictions to what has been called Venezuelan "petro socialism", the fact that an oil-generated surplus is being dedicated to genuine social transformation rather than feeding into the proverbial "curse of oil" makes Venezuela unique.[21]

Of course there are powerful environmental movements within the centre of the system as well to which we might look for hope. But severed from strong socialist movements and a revolutionary situation they have been constrained much more by a perceived need to adapt to the dominant accumulation system, thereby drastically undermining the ecological struggle. Hence, revolutionary strategies and movements with regard to ecology and society are world-historical forces at present largely in the periphery, in the weak links and breakaways from the capitalist system.

I can only point to a few essential aspects of this radical process of ecological change as manifested in areas of the global South. In Cuba the goal of human development that Che advanced is taking on a new form through what is widely regarded as "the greening of Cuba". This is evident in the emergence of the most revolutionary experiment in agroecology on earth, and the related changes in health, science, and education. As McKibben states, "Cubans have created what may be the world's largest working model of a semisustainable agriculture, one that relies far less than the rest of the world does on oil, on chemicals, on shipping vast quantities of food back and forth... Cuba has thousands of *organopónicos*—urban gardens—

more than two hundred in the Havana area alone." Indeed, according to the World Wildlife Fund's *Living Planet Report*, "Cuba alone" in the entire world has achieved a high level of human development, with a human development index greater than 0.8, while also having a per capita ecological footprint below the world's average.[22]

This ecological transformation is deeply rooted in the Cuban revolution rather than, as frequently said, simply a forced response in the Special Period following the fall of the Soviet Union. Already in the 1970s Carlos Rafael Rodriguez, one of the founders of Cuban ecology, had introduced arguments for "integral development, laying the groundwork"—as ecologist Richard Levins points out—for "harmonious development of the economy and social relations with nature". This was followed by the gradual flowering of ecological thought in Cuba in the 1980s. The Special Period, Levins explains, simply allowed the "ecologists by conviction" who had emerged through the internal development of Cuban science and society to recruit the "ecologists by necessity", turning many of them too into ecologists by conviction.[23]

Venezuela under Chávez has not only advanced revolutionary new social relations with the growth of Bolivarian circles, community councils, and increased worker control of factories, but has introduced some crucial initiatives with regard to what István Mészáros has called a new "socialist time accountancy" in the production and exchange of goods. In the new Bolivarian Alternative for the Americas (ALBA), the emphasis is on *communal exchange*, the exchange of activities rather than exchange values.[24] Instead of allowing the market to establish the priorities of the entire economy, planning is being introduced to redistribute resources and capacities to those most in need and to the majority of the populace. The goal here is to address the most pressing individual and collective requirements of the society related in particular to physiological needs and hence raising directly the question of the human relation to nature. This is the absolute precondition of the creation of a sustainable society. In the countryside preliminary attempts have also been made to green Venezuelan agriculture.[25]

In Bolivia the rise of a socialist current (though embattled at present) embedded in the needs of indigenous peoples and the control of basic resources such as water and hydrocarbons offers hope of another kind of development. The cities of Curitiba and Porto Alegre in Brazil point to the possibility of more radical forms of management of urban space and transportation. Curitiba, in McKibbens's words, "is as much an example for the sprawling, decaying cities of the first world as for the crowded, booming cities of the Third World". Kerala in India has taught us that a poor state or region, if animated by genuine socialist planning, can go a long way toward unleashing human potentials in education, health care, and basic environmental conditions. In Kerala, McKibben observes, "the Left has embarked on a series of 'new democratic initiatives' that come as close as anything on the planet to actually incarnating 'sustainable development.'"[26]

To be sure, these are mainly islands of hope at present. They constitute fragile new experiments in social relations and in the human metabolism with nature. They are still subject to the class and imperial war imposed from above by the larger system. The planet as a whole remains firmly in the grip of capital and its world alienation. Everywhere we see manifestations of a metabolic rift, now extended to the biospheric level.

It follows that there is little real prospect for the needed global ecological revolution unless these attempts to revolutionize social relations in the struggle for a just and sustainable society, now emerging in the periphery, are somehow mirrored in movements for ecological and social revolution in the advanced capitalist world. It is only through fundamental change at the centre of the system, from which the pressure on the planet principally emanates, that there is any genuine possibility of avoiding ultimate ecological destruction.

For some this may seem to be an impossible goal. Nevertheless, it is important to recognize that there is now an ecology as well as a political economy of revolutionary change. The emergence in our time of sustainable human development in various revolutionary interstices within the global periphery could mark the beginning of a universal revolt against both world alienation and human self-estrangement. Such a revolt if consistent could have only one objective: the creation of a society of associated producers rationally regulating their metabolic relation to nature, and doing so not only in accordance with their own needs but also those of future generations and life as a whole. Today the transition to socialism and the transition to an ecological society are one.

Notes

[1.]Karl Marx, *Capital*, vol. 3 (New York: Vintage, 1981), 959.

[2.] Karl Marx, *Capital*, vol.1 (New York: Vintage, 1976), 636–39, *Capital*, vol. 3, 754, 911, 948–49

[3.] Karl Marx, *Early Writings* (New York: Vintage, 1974), 328. Documentation of Marx and Engels's ecological concerns listed above can be found in the following works: Paul Burkett, *Marx and Nature* (New York: St. Martin's Press, 1999); John Bellamy Foster, *Marx's Ecology* (New York:

monthly Review Press, 2000); and Paul Burkett and John Bellamy Foster, "Metabolism, Energy, and Entropy in Marx's Critique of Political Economy", *Theory & Society* 35 (2006): 109–56. On the problem of local climate change as it was raised by Engels and Marx in their time (speculations on temperature changes due to deforestation) see Engels's notes on Fraas in Marx and Engels, *MEGA IV*, 31 (Amsterdam: Akadamie Verlag, 1999), 512–15.

[4.] Marx, *Capital*, vol. 3, 911.

[5.] On ecological insights of socialists after Marx see Foster, *Marx's Ecology*, 236–54. On early Soviet ecology see also Douglas R. Weiner, *Models of Nature* (Bloomington: Indiana University Press, 1988). On Podolinsky seek John Bellamy Foster and Paul Burkett, "Ecological Economics and Classical Marxism", *Organisation & Environment* 17, no. 1 (March 2004): 32–60.

[6.] Karl Marx, *Grundrisse* (London: Penguin, 1973), 471–79, and *Capital*, vol. 1 (London: Penguin, 1976), 915.

[7.] On precarious work see Fatma Ülkü Selçuk, "Dressing the Wound", *Monthly Review* 57, no. 1 (May 2005): 37–44.

[8.] Joseph Needham, *Moulds of Understanding* (London: George Allen & Unwin, 1976), 301.

[9.] Branko Milanovic, *Worlds Apart* (Princeton: Princeton University Press, 2005); John Bellamy Foster, "The Imperialist World System", Monthly Review, vol. 59, no. 1 (May 2007): 1–16.

[10.] Hannah Arendt, *The Human Condition* (Chicago: University of Chicago Press, 1958), 248–73; Karl Marx & Frederick Engels, *Collected Works* (New York: International Publishers, 1975), vol. 1, 224–63.

[11.] Michael R. Raupach, et al., "Global & Regional Drivers of Accelerating CO_2 Emissions", *Proceedings of the National Academy of Sciences* 104, no. 24 (June 12, 2007): 10289, 10288; Associated Press, "Global Warming: It's the Humidity", Oct 10, 2007.

[12.] See Paul Burkett's "Marx's Vision of Sustainable Human Development", *Monthly Review* 57, no. 5 (Oct 2005): 34–62.

[13.] Ernesto "Che" Guevara, "Man & Socialism in Cuba". Che was referring to bourgeois criticisms of socialist transition but it was clear that he saw this problem as an actual contradiction of early socialist experiments that had to be transcended. See also Michael Löwy, *The Marxism of Che Guevara* (New York: Monthly Review Press, 1973), 59–73.

[14.] Rodríguez quoted in Richard Gott, *In the Shadow of the Liberator* (London: Verso, 2000), 116; Simón Bolívar, "Message to the Congress of Bolivia", May 25, 1826, *Selected Works* (New York: The Colonial Press, 1951), vol. 2, 603.

[15.] Karl Marx, *The Poverty of Philosophy* (New York: International Publishers, 1963), 146, & *Early Writings* (New York: Vintage, 1974), 348, 353.

[16.] István Mészáros, *Socialism or Barbarism* (New York: Monthly Review Press, 2002), 23.

[17.] A powerful critique of biofuel production has been authored by Fidel Castro Ruiz in a series of reflections over the past years. See http://www.monthlyreview.org/castro/index.php.

[18.] See Paul M. Sweezy, "The Transition to Socialism", in Sweezy & Charles Bettelheim, *On the Transition to Socialism* (New York: Monthly Review Press, 1971), 112, 115; Michael Lebowitz, *Build it Now* (New York: Monthly Review Press, 2006), 13–14.

[19.] G. W. F. Hegel, *Introductory Lectures on Aesthetics* (London: Penguin, 1993), 51; Karl Marx, "Confessions", in Teodor Shanin, *Late Marx & the Russian Road* (New York: Monthly Review Press, 1983), 140.

[20.] See Bill McKibben, *Hope, Human & Wild* (Minneapolis: Milkweed Editions, 1995), & *Deep Economy* (New York: Henry Holt, 2007).

[21.] Michael A. Lebowitz, "An Alternative Worth Struggling For", *Monthly Review* 60, no. 5 (October 2008): 20–21.

[22.] McKibben, *Deep Economy*, 73. See also Richard Levins, "How Cuba is Going Ecological", in Richard Lewontin & Richard Levins, *Biology Under the Influence* (New York: Monthly Review Press, 2007), 343–64; Rebecca Clausen, "Healing the Rift: Metabolic Restoration in Cuban Agriculture", *Monthly Review* 59, no. 1 (May 2007): 40–52; World Wildlife Fund, *Living Planet Report 2006*, http://assets.panda.org/downloads/living_planet_report.pdf, 19; Peter M. Rosset, "Cuba: A Successful Case Study of Sustainable Agriculture", in Fred Magdoff, John Bellamy Foster, & Frederick H. Buttel, eds., *Hungry for Profit* (New York: Monthly Review Press, 1999), 203–14.

[23.] Levins, "How Cuba is Going Ecological", 355–56 in Lewontin & Levins, *Biology Under the Influence*, 367.

[24.] Lebowitz, *Build it Now*, 107–09; On the theory of communal exchange that influenced Chávez see István Mészáros, *Beyond Capital* (New York: Monthly Review Press, 1995), 758–60. On "socialist time accountancy" see Mészáros's *Crisis & Burden of Historical Time* (New York: Monthly Review Press, 2008)

[25.] David Raby, "The Greening of Venezuela", *Monthly Review* 56, no. 5 (Nov 2004): 49–52.

[26.] McKibben, *Hope*, 62, 154.

Basic Theories of Karl Marx

Ernest Mandel

1. Life and Work

Karl Marx was born on 5 May 1818, the son of the lawyer Heinrich Marx and Henriette Pressburg. His father was descended from an old family of Jewish rabbis, but was himself a liberal admirer of the Enlightenment and not religious. He converted to Protestantism a few years before Karl was born to escape restrictions still imposed upon Jews in Prussia. His mother was of Dutch-Jewish origin.

Karl Marx studied at the Friedrich-Wilhelm Gymnasium in Trier, and at the universities of Bonn and Berlin. His doctoral thesis, Differenz der demokritischen und epikurischen Naturphilosophie, was accepted at the University of Jena on 15 April 1841. In 1843 he married Jenny von Westphalen, daughter of Baron von Westphalen, a high Prussian government official.

Marx's university studies covered many fields, but centred around philosophy and religion. He frequented the circle of the more radical followers of the great philosopher Hegel, befriended one of their main representatives, Bruno Bauer, and was especially influenced by the publication in 1841 of Ludwig Feuerbach's Das Wesen des Christentums (The Nature of Christianity). He had intended to teach philosophy at the university, but that quickly proved to be unrealistic. He then turned towards journalism, both to propagandise his ideas and to gain a livelihood. He became editor of the Rheinische Zeitung, a liberal newspaper of Cologne, in May 1842. His interest turned more and more to political and social questions, which he treated in an increasing radical way. The paper was banned by the Prussian authorities a year later.

Karl Marx then planned to publish a magazine called Die Deutsch-Französische Jahrbücher in Paris, in order to escape Prussian censorship and to be more closely linked and identified with the real struggles for political and social emancipation which, at that time, were centred around France. He emigrated to Paris with his wife and met there his lifelong friend Friedrich Engels.

Marx had become critical of Hegel's philosophical political system, a criticism which would lead to his first major work, Zur Kritik des Hegelschen Rechtsphilosophie (1843, A Critique of Hegel's Philosophy of Right). Intensively studying history and political economy during his stay in Paris, he became strongly influenced by socialist and working-class circles in the French capital. With his 'Paris Manuscripts' (Oekonomisch-philosophische Manuskripte, 1844), he definitely became a communist, i.e. a proponent of collective ownership of the means of production.

He was expelled from France at the beginning of 1845 through pressure from the Prussian embassy and migrated to Brussels. His definite turn towards historical materialism (see below) would occur with his manuscript Die Deutsche Ideologue (1845-6) culminating in the eleven Theses on Feuerbach, written together with Engels but never published during his lifetime.

This led also to a polemical break with the most influential French socialist of that period, Proudhon, expressed in the only book Marx would write in French, Misère de la Philosophie (1846).
Simultaneously he became more and more involved in practical socialist politics, and started to work with the Communist League, which asked Engels and himself to draft their declaration of principle, This is the origin of the Communist Manifesto (1848, Manifest der Kommunistischen Partei).

As soon as the revolution of 1848 broke out, he was in turn expelled from Belgium and went first to France, then, from April 1848 on, to Cologne. His political activity during the German revolution of 1848 centred around the publication of the daily paper Die Neue Rheinische Zeitung, which enjoyed wide popular support. After the victory of the Prussian counter-revolution, the paper was banned in May 1849 and Marx was expelled from Prussia. He never succeeded in recovering his citizenship.

Marx emigrated to London, where he would stay, with short interruptions, till the end of his life. For fifteen years, his time would be mainly taken up with economic studies, which would lead to the publication first of Zur Kritik der Politischen Oekonomie (1859) and later of Das Kapital, Vol. I (1867).

He spent long hours at the British Museum, studying the writings of all the major economists, as well as the government Blue Books, Hansard and many other contemporary sources on social and economic conditions in Britain and the world. His readings also covered technology, ethnology and anthropology, besides political economy and economic history; many notebooks were filled with excerpts from the books he read.

But while the activity was mainly studious, he never completely abandoned practical politics. He first hoped that the Communist League would be kept alive, thanks to a revival of revolution. When this did not occur, he progressively dropped out of emigré politics, but not without writing a scathing indictment of French counter-revolution in Der 18. Brumaire des Louis Bonaparte (1852), which was in a certain sense the balance sheet of his political activity and an analysis of the late 1848-52 cycle of revolution and counter-revolution. He would befriend British trade-union leaders and gradually attempt to draw them towards international working class interests and politics. These efforts culminated in the creation of the International Working Men's Association (1864) - the so-called First International - in which Marx and Engels would play a leading role, politically as well as organisationally.

It was not only his political interest and revolutionary passion that prevented Marx from becoming an economist pure and simple. It was also the pressure of material necessity. Contrary to his hopes, he never succeeded in earning enough money from his scientific writings to sustain himself and his growing family. He had to turn to journalism to make a living, He had initial, be it modest, success in this field, when he became European correspondent of the New York Daily Tribune in the summer of 1851. But he never had a regular income from that collaboration, and it ended after ten years.

So the years of his London exile were mainly years of great material deprivation and moral suffering. Marx suffered greatly from the fact that he could not provide a minimum of normal living conditions for his wife and children, whom he loved deeply. Bad lodgings in cholera-stricken Soho, insufficient food and medical care, led to a chronic deterioration of his wife's and his own health and to the death of several of their children; that of his oldest son Edgar in 1855 struck him an especially heavy blow. Of his seven children only three daughters survived, Jenny, Laura and Eleanor (Tussy). All three were very gifted and would play a significant role in the international labour movement, Eleanor in Britain, Jenny and Laura in France (where they married the socialist leaders Longuet and Lafargue).

During this long period of material misery, Marx survived thanks to the financial and moral support of his friend Friedrich Engels, whose devotion to him stands as an exceptional example of friendship in the history of science and politics. Things started to improve when Marx came into his mother's inheritance; when the first independent working-class parties (followers of Lassalle on the one hand, of Marx and Engels on the other) developed in Germany, creating a broader market for his writings; when the IWMA became influential in several European countries, and when Engels' financial conditions improved to the point where he would sustain the Marx family on a more regular basis.

The period 1865- 71 was one in which Marx's concentration on economic studies and on the drafting of Das Kapital was interrupted more and more by current political commitments to the IWMA, culminating in his impassioned defence of the Paris Commune (Der Bürgerkrieg in Frankreich, 1871). But the satisfaction of being able to participate a second time in a real revolution - be it only vicariously - was troubled by the deep divisions inside the IMWA, which led to the split with the anarchists grouped around Michael Bakunin.

Marx did not succeed in finishing a final version of Das Kapital vols II and III, which were published posthumously, after extensive editing, by Engels. It remains controversial whether he intended to add two more volumes to these, according to an initial plan. More than 25 years after the death of Marx, Karl Kautsky edited what is often called vol. IV of Das Kapital, his extensive critique of other economists: Theorien über den Mehrwert (Theories of Surplus Value).

Marx's final years were increasingly marked by bad health, in spite of slightly improved living conditions. Bad health was probably the main reason why the final version of vols II and III of Capital could not be finished. Although he wrote a strong critique of the Programme which was adopted by the unification congress (1878) of German social democracy (Kritik des Gothaer Programms), he was heartened by the creation of that united working-class party in his native land, by the spread of socialist organisations throughout Europe, and by the growing influence of his ideas in the socialist movement. His wife fell ill in 1880 and died the next year. This came as a deadly blow to Karl Marx, who did not survive her for long. He himself died in London on 14 March 1883.

2. Historical Materialism

Outside his specific economic theories, Marx's main contribution to the social sciences has been his theory of historical materialism. Its starting point is anthropological. Human beings cannot survive without social organisation.

Social organisation is based upon social labour and social communication. Social labour always occurs within a given framework of specific, historically determined, social relations of production. These social relations of production determine in the last analysis all other social relations, including those of social communication. It is social existence which determines social consciousness and not the other way around.

Historical materialism posits that relations of production which become stabilised and reproduce themselves are structures which can no longer be changed gradually, piecemeal. They are modes of production. To use Hegel's dialectical language, which was largely adopted (and adapted) by Marx: they can only change qualitatively through a complete social upheaval, a social revolution or counter-revolution. Quantitative changes can occur within modes of production, but they do not modify the basic structure. In each mode of production, a given set of relations of production constitutes the basis (infrastructure) on which is erected a complex superstructure, encompassing the state and the law (except in a classless society), ideology, religion, philosophy, the arts, morality, etc.

Relations of production are the sum total of social relations which human beings establish among themselves in the production of their material lives. They are therefore not limited to what actually happens at the point of production. Humankind could not survive, i.e. produce, if there did not exist specific forms of circulation of goods, e.g. between producing units (circulation of tools and raw materials) and between production units and consumers. A priori allocation of goods determines other relations of production than does allocation of goods through the market. Partial commodity production (what Marx calls 'simple commodity production' or 'petty commodity production' - 'einfache Waren-produktion') also implies other relations of production than does generalised commodity production.

Except in the case of classless societies, modes of production, centred around prevailing relations of production, are embodied in specific class relations which, in the last analysis, over-determine relations between individuals.

Historical materialism does not deny the individual's free will, his attempts to make choices concerning his existence according to his individual passions, his interests as he understands them, his convictions, his moral options etc. What historical materialism does state is: (1) that these choices are strongly predetermined by the social framework (education, prevailing ideology and moral 'values', variants of behaviour limited by material conditions etc.); (2) that the outcome of the collision of millions of different passions, interests and options is essentially a phenomenon of social logic and not of individual psychology. Here, class interests are predominant.

There is no example in history of a ruling class not trying to defend its class rule, or of an exploited class not trying to limit (and occasionally eliminate) the exploitation it suffers. So outside classless society, the class struggle is a permanent feature of human society. In fact, one of the key theses of historical materialism is that 'the history of humankind is the history of class struggles' (Marx, Communist Manifesto, 1848).

The immediate object of class struggle is economic and material. It is a struggle for the division of the social product between the direct producers (the productive, exploited class) and those who appropriate what Marx calls the social surplus product, the residuum of the social product once the producers and their offspring are fed (in the large sense of the word; i.e. the sum total of the consumer goods consumed by that class) and the initial stock of tools and raw materials is reproduced (including the restoration of the initial fertility of the soil). The ruling class functions as a ruling class essentially through the appropriation of the social surplus product. By getting possession of the social surplus product, it acquires the means to foster and maintain most of the superstructural activities mentioned above; and by doing so, it can largely determine their function - to maintain and reproduce the given social structure, the given mode of production - and their contents.

We say 'largely determine' and not 'completely determine'. First, there is an 'immanent dialectical', i.e. an autonomous movement, of each specific superstructural sphere of activity. Each generation of scientists, artists, philosophers, theologians, lawyers and politicians finds a given corpus of ideas, forms, rules, techniques, ways of thinking, to which it is initiated through education and current practice, etc. It is not forced to simply continue and reproduce these elements. It can transform them, modify them, change their interconnections, even negate them. Again: historical materialism does not deny that there is a specific history of science, a history of art, a history of philosophy, a history of political and moral ideas, a history of religion etc., which all follow their own logic. It tries to explain why a certain number of scientific, artistic, philosophical, ideological, juridical changes or even revolutions occur at a given time and in given countries, quite different from other ones which occurred some centuries earlier elsewhere. The nexus of these 'revolutions' with given historical periods is a nexus of class interests.

Second, each social formation (i.e. a given country in a given epoch) while being characterised by predominant relations of production (i.e. a given mode of production at a certain phase of its development) includes different relations of production which are largely remnants of the past, but also sometimes nuclei of future modes of production. Thus there exists not only the ruling class and the exploited class characteristic of that prevailing mode of production (capitalists and wage earners under capitalism). There also exist remnants of social classes which were predominant when other relations of production prevailed and which, while having lost their hegemony, still manage to survive in the interstices of the new society. This is, for example, the case with petty commodity producers (peasants, handicraftsmen, small merchants), semi-feudal landowners, and even slave-owners, in many already predominantly capitalist social formations throughout the 19th and part of the 20th centuries. Each of these social classes has its own ideology, its own religious and moral values, which are intertwined with the ideology of the hegemonic ruling class, without becoming completely absorbed by that ideology.

Third, even after a given ruling class (e.g. the feudal or semi-feudal nobility) has disappeared as a ruling class, its ideology can survive through sheer force of social inertia and routine (custom). The survival of traditional ancien régime catholic ideology in France during a large part of the 19th century, in spite of the sweeping social, political and ideological changes ushered in by the French revolution, is an illustration of that rule.

Finally, Marx's statement that the ruling ideology of each epoch is the ideology of the ruling class - another basic tenet of historical materialism - does not express more than it actually says. It implies that other ideologies can exist side by side with that ruling ideology without being hegemonic. To cite the most important of these occurrences: exploited and (or) oppressed social classes can develop their own ideology, which will start to challenge the prevailing hegemonic one. In fact, an ideological class struggle accompanies and sometimes even precedes the political class struggle properly speaking. Religious and philosophical struggles preceding the classical bourgeois revolutions; the first socialist critiques of bourgeois society preceding the constitution of the first working-class parties and revolutions, are examples of that type.

The class struggle has been up to now the great motor of history. Human beings make their own history. No mode of production can be replaced by another one without deliberate actions by large social forces, i.e. without social revolution (or counter-revolution). Whether these revolutions or counter- revolutions actually lead to the long-term implementation of deliberate projects of social reorganization is another matter altogether. Very often, their outcome is to a large extent different from the intention of the main actors.

Human beings act consciously, but they can act with false consciousness. They do not necessarily understand why they want to realise certain social and (or) political plans, why they want to maintain or to change economic or juridical institutions; and especially, they rarely understand in a scientific sense the laws of social change, the material and social preconditions for successfully conserving or changing such institutions. Indeed, Marx claims that only with the discovery of the main tenets of historical materialism have we made a significant step forward towards understanding these laws, without claiming to be able to predict 'all' future developments of society.

Social change, social revolutions and counter-revolutions are furthermore occurring within determined material constraints. The level of development of the productive forces - essentially tools and human skills, including their effects upon the fertility of the soil - limits the possibilities of institutional change. Slave labour has shown itself to be largely incompatible with the factory system based upon contemporary machines. Socialism would not be durably built upon the basis of the wooden plough and the potter's wheel.

A social revolution generally widens the scope for the development of the productive forces and leads to social progress in most fields of human activity in a momentous way. Likewise, an epoch of deep social crisis is ushered in when there is a growing conflict between the prevailing mode of production (i.e. the existing social order) on the one hand, and the further development of the productive forces on the other. Such a social crisis will then manifest itself on all major fields and social activity: politics, ideology, morals and law, as well as in the realm of the economic life properly speaking.

Historical materialism thereby provides a measuring stick for human progress: the growth of the productive forces, measurable through the growth of the average productivity of labour, and the number, longevity and skill of the human species. This measuring stick in no way abstracts from the natural preconditions for human survival and human growth (in the broadest sense of the concept). Nor does it abstract from the conditional and partial character of such progress, in terms of social organisation and individual alienation.

In the last analysis, the division of society into antagonistic social classes rejects, from the point of view of historical materialism, an inevitable limitation of human freedom. For Marx and Engels, the real measuring rod of human freedom, i.e. of human wealth, is not 'productive labour'; this only creates the material pre-condition for that freedom. The real measuring rod is leisure time, not in the sense of 'time for doing nothing' but in the sense of time freed from the iron necessity to produce and reproduce material livelihood, and therefore disposable for all-round and free development of the individual talents, wishes, capacities, potentialities, of each human being.

As long as society is too poor, as long as goods and services satisfying basic needs are too scarce, only part of society can be freed from the necessity to devote most of its life to 'work for a livelihood' (i.e. of forced labour, in the anthropological/sociological sense of the word, that is in relation to desires, aspirations and talents, not to a juridical status of bonded labour). That is essentially what represents the freedom of the ruling classes and their hangers-on, who are 'being paid to think', to create, to invent, to administer, because they have become free from the obligation to bake their own bread, weave their own clothes and build their own houses.

Once the productive forces are developed far enough to guarantee all human beings satisfaction of their basic needs by 'productive labour' limited to a minor fraction of lifetime (the half work-day or less), then the material need of the division of society in classes disappears. Then, there remains no objective basis for part of society to monopolise administration, access to information, knowledge, intellectual labour. For that reason, historical materialism explains both the reasons why class societies and class struggles arose in history, and why they will disappear in the future in a classless society of democratically self-administering associated producers. Historical materialism therefore contains an attempt at explaining the origin, the functions and the future withering away of the state as a specific institution, as well as an attempt to explain politics and political activity in general, as an expression of social conflicts centred around different social interests (mainly, but not only, those of different social classes; important fractions of classes, as well as non-class social groupings, also come into play).

For Marx and Engels, the state is not existent with human society as such, or with 'organised society' or even with 'civilised society' in the abstract, neither is it the result of any voluntarily concluded 'social contract' between individuals. The state is the sum total of apparatuses, i.e. special groups of people separate and apart from the rest (majority) of society, that appropriate to themselves functions of a repressive or integrative nature which were initially exercised by all citizens. This process of alienation occurs in conjunction with the emergence of social classes. The state is an instrument for fostering, conserving and reproducing a given class structure, and not a neutral arbiter between antagonistic class interests.

The emergence of a classless society is therefore closely intertwined, for adherents to historical materialism, with the process of withering away of the state, i.e. of gradual devolution to the whole of society (self-management, self-administration) of all specific functions today exercised by special apparatuses, i.e. of the dissolution of these apparatuses. Marx and Engels visualised the dictatorship of the proletariat, the last form of the state and of political class rule, as an instrument for assuring the transition from class society to classless society. It should itself be a state of a special kind, organising its own gradual disappearance.

We said above that, from the point of view of historical materialism, the immediate object of class struggle is the division of the social product between different social classes. Even the political class struggle in the final analysis serves that main purpose; but it also covers a much broader field of social conflicts. As all state activities have some bearing upon the relative stability of a given social formation, and the class rule to which it is submitted, the class struggle can extend to all fields of politics from foreign policy to educational problems and religious conflicts. This has of course to be proven through painstaking analysis, and not proclaimed as an axiom or a revealed truth. When conducted successfully, such exercises in class analysis and class definition of political, social and even literary struggles becomes impressive works of historical explanation, as for example Marx's Class Struggles in France 1848-50, Engels' The German Peasant War, Franz Mehring's Die Lesssing-Legende, Trotsky's History of the Russian Revolution, etc.

**3. *Marx's Economic Theory - General approach and influence*
A general appraisal of Marx's method of economic analysis is
called for prior to an outline of his main economic theories (theses and hypotheses). Marx is distinct from most important economists of the 19th and 20th centuries in that he does not
consider himself at all an 'economist' pure and simple.**

The idea that 'economic science' as a special science completely separate
from sociology, history, anthropology etc. cannot exist, underlies most of
his economic analysis. Indeed, historical materialism is an attempt at uni-
fying all social sciences, if not all sciences about humankind, into a single
'science of society'. For sure, within the framework of this general 'science
of society', economic phenomena could and should be submitted to analysis
as specific phenomena. So economic theory, economical science, has a definite autonomy after all; but it is only a partial and relative one.

Probably the best formula for characterising Marx's economic theory would
be to call it an endeavour to explain the social economy. This would be true
in a double sense. For Marx, there are no eternal economic laws, valid in
every epoch of human prehistory and history. Each mode of production has
its own specific economic laws, which lose their relevance once the general
social framework has fundamentally changed. For Marx likewise, there are
no economic laws separate and apart from specific relations between
human beings, in the primary (but not only, as already summarised) social
relations of production. All attempts to reduce economic problems to purely
material, objective ones, to relations between things, or between things and
human beings, would be considered by Marx as manifestations of mystifi-
cation, of false consciousness, expressing itself through the attempted relocation of human relations. Behind relations between things, economic
science should try to discover the specific relations between human beings
which they hide. Real economic science has therefore also a demystifying
function compared to vulgar 'economics', which takes a certain number of
'things' for granted without asking the questions: Are they really only what
they appear to be? From where do they originate? What explains these appearances? What lies behind them? Where do they lead? How could they
(will they) disappear? Problemblindheit, the refusal to see that facts are
generally more problematic than they appear at first sight, is certainly not
a reproach one could address to Marx's economic thought.

Marx's economic analysis is therefore characterised by a strong ground current of historical relativism, with a strong recourse to the genetical and evolutionary method of thinking (that is why the parallel with Darwin has often
been made, sometimes in an excessive way). The formula 'genetic struc-

turalism' has also been used in relation to Marx's general approach to economic analysis. Be that as it may, one could state that Marx's economic theory is essentially geared to the discovery of specific 'laws of motion' for successive modes of production. While his theoretical effort has been mainly centred around the discovery of these laws of motion for capitalist society, his work contains indications of such laws - different ones, to be sure - for pre-capitalist and post-capitalist social formations too.

The main link between Marx's sociology and anthropology on the one hand, and his economic analysis on the other, lies in the key role of social labour as the basic anthropological feature underlying all forms of social organisation. Social labour can be organised in quite different forms, thereby giving rise to quite different economic phenomena ('facts'). Basically different forms of social labour organisation lead to basically different sets of economic institutions and dynamics, following basically different logics (obeying basically different 'laws of motion').

All human societies must assure the satisfaction of a certain number of basic needs, in order to survive and reproduce themselves. This leads to the necessity of establishing some sort of equilibrium between social recognised needs, i.e. current consumption and current production. But this abstract banality does not tell us anything about the concrete way in which social labour is organised in order to achieve that goal.

Society can recognise all individual labour as immediately social labour. Indeed, it does so in innumerable primitive tribal and village communities, as it does in the contemporary kibbutz. Directly social labour can be organised in a despotic or in a democratic way, through custom and superstition as well as through an attempt at applying advanced science to economic organisation; but it will always be immediately recognised social labour, inasmuch as it is based upon a priori assignment of the producers to their specific work (again: irrespective of the form this assignation takes, whether it is voluntary or compulsory, despotic or simply through custom etc.)

But when social decision-taking about work assignation (and resource allocation closely tied to it) is fragmented into different units operating independently from each other - as a result of private control (property) of the means of production, in the economic and not necessarily the juridical sense of the word - then social labour in turn is fragmented into private labours which are not automatically recognised as socially necessary ones (whose expenditure is not automatically compensated by society). Then the private producers have to exchange parts or all of their products in order to satisfy some or all of their basic needs. Then these products become commodities, The economy becomes a (partial or generalised) market economy.

Only by measuring the results of the sale of his products can the producer (or owner) ascertain what part of his private labour expenditure has been recognized (compensated) as social labour, and what part has not.

Even if we operate with such simple analytical tools as 'directly social labour', 'private labour', 'socially recognised social labour', we have to make quite an effort at abstracting from immediately apparent phenomena in order to understand their relevance for economic analysis. This is true for all scientific analysis, in natural as well as in social sciences. Marx's economic analysis, as presented in his main books, has not been extremely popular reading; but then, there are not yet so many scientists in these circumstances. This has nothing to do with any innate obscurity of the author, but rather with the nature of scientific analysis as such.

The relatively limited number of readers of Marx's economic writings (the first English paperback edition of Das Kapital appeared only in 1974!) is clearly tied to Marx's scientific rigour, his effort at a systematic and all-sided analysis of the phenomena of the capitalist economy.

But while his economic analysis lacked popularity, his political and historical projections became more and more influential. With the rise of independent working-class mass parties, an increasing number of these proclaimed themselves as being guided or influenced by Marx, at least in the epoch of the Second and the Third Internationals, roughly the half century from 1890 till 1940. Beginning with the Russian revolution of 1917, a growing number of governments and of states claimed to base their policies and constitutions on concepts developed by Marx. (Whether this was legitimate or not is another question.) But the fact itself testifies to Marx's great influence on contemporary social and political developments, evolutionary and revolutionary alike.

Likewise, his diffused influence on social science, including academic economic theory, goes far beyond general acceptance or even substantial knowledge of his main writings. Some key ideas of historical materialism and of economic analysis which permeate his work - e.g. that economic interests to a large extent influence, if not determine, political struggles; that historic evolution is linked to important changes in material conditions; that economic crises ('the business cycle') are unavoidable under conditions of capitalist market economy - have become near-platitudes. It is sufficient to notice how major economists and historians strongly denied their validity throughout the 19th century and at least until the 1920s, to understand how deep has been Marx's influence on contemporary social science in general.

4. Marx's Labour Theory of Value

As an economist, Marx is generally situated in the continuity of the great classical school of Adam Smith and Ricardo. He obviously owes a lot to Ricardo, and conducts a running dialogue with that master in most of his mature economic writings.

Marx inherited the labour theory of value from the classical school. Here the continuity is even more pronounced; but there is also a radical break, For Ricardo, labour is essentially a numeraire, which enables a common computation of labour and capital as basic elements of production costs. For Marx, labour is value. Value is nothing but that fragment of the total labour potential existing in a given society in a certain period (e.g. a year or a month) which is used for the output of a given commodity, at the average social productivity of labour existing then and there, divided by the total number of these commodities produced. and expressed in hours (or minutes), days, weeks, months of labour.

Value is therefore essentially a social, objective and historically relative category, It is social because it is determined by the overall result of the fluctuating efforts of each individual producer (under capitalism: of each individual firm or factory). It is objective because it is given, once the production of a given commodity is finished, and is thus independent from personal (or collective) valuations of customers on the market place; and it is historically relative because it changes with each important change (progress or regression) of the average productivity of labour in a given branch of output, including in agriculture and transportation.

This does not imply that Marx's concept of value is in any way completely detached from consumption. It only means that the feedback of consumers' behaviour and wishes upon value is always mediated through changes in the allocation of labour inputs in production, labour being seen as subdivided into living labour and dead (dated) labour, i.e. tools and raw materials. The market emits signals to which the producing units react. Value changes after these reactions, not before them. Market price changes can of course occur prior to changes in value. In fact, changes in market prices are among the key signals which can lead to changes in labour allocation between different branches of production, i.e. to changes in labour quantities necessary to produce given commodities. But then, for Marx, values determine prices only basically and in the medium-term sense of the word. This determination only appears clearly as an explication of medium and long-term price movements. In the shorter run, prices fluctuate around values as axes. Marx never intended to negate the operation of market laws, of the law of supply and demand, in determining these short-term fluctuations.

The 'law of value' is but Marx's version of Adam Smith's 'invisible hand'. In a society dominated by private labour, private producers and private ownership of productive inputs, it is this 'law of value', an objective economic law operating behind the backs of all people, all 'agents' involved in production and consumption, which, in the final analysis, regulates the economy, determines what is produced and how it is produced (and therefore also what can be consumed). The 'law of value' regulates the exchange between commodities, according to the quantities of socially necessary abstract labour they embody (the quantity of such labour spent in their production). Through regulating the exchange between commodities, the 'law of value' also regulates, after some interval, the distribution of society's labour potential and of society's non-living productive resources between different branches of production. Again, the analogy with Smith's 'invisible hand' is striking.

Marx's critique of the 'invisible hand' concept does not dwell essentially on the analysis of how a market economy actually operates. It would above all insist that this operation is not eternal, not immanent in 'human nature', but created by specific historical circumstances, a product of a special way of social organisation, and due to disappear at some stage of historical evolution as it appeared during a previous stage. And it would also stress that this 'invisible hand' leads neither to the maximum of economic growth nor to the optimum of human wellbeing for the greatest number of individuals, i.e. it would stress the heavy economic and social price humankind had to pay, and is still currently paying, for the undeniable progress the market economy produced at a given stage of historical evolution.

The formula 'quantities of abstract human labour' refers to labour seen strictly as a fraction of the total labour potential of a given society at a given time, say a labour potential of 2 billion hours a year (1 million potential producers, each supposedly capable of working 2000 hours a year). It therefore implies making an abstraction of the specific trade or occupation of a given male or female producer, the product of a day's work of a weaver not being worth less or more than that of a peasant, a miner, a housebuilder, a milliner or a seamstress. At the basis of that concept of 'abstract human labour' lies a social condition, a specific set of social relations of production, in which small independent producers are essentially equal. Without that equality, social division of labour, and therefore satisfaction of basic consumers' needs, would be seriously endangered under that specific organisational set-up of the economy. Such an equality between small commodity owners and producers is later transformed into an equality between owners of capital under the capitalist mode of production.

But the concept of the homogeneity of productive human labour, underlying that of 'abstract human labour' as the essence of value, does not imply a negation of the difference between skilled and unskilled labour. Again: a negation of that difference would lead to the breakdown of the necessary division of labour, as would any basic heterogeneity of labour inputs in different branches of output. It would then not pay to acquire skills: most of them would disappear. So Marx's labour theory of value, in an internally coherent way, leads to the conclusion that one hour of skilled labour represents more value than one hour of unskilled labour, say represents the equivalent of 1.5 hours of unskilled labour. The difference would result from the imputation of the labour it costs to acquire the given skill, While an unskilled labourer would have a labour potential of 120,000 hours during his adult life, a skilled labourer would only have a labour potential of 80,000 hours, 40,000 being used for acquiring, maintaining and developing his skill. Only if one hour of skilled labour embodies the same value of 1.5 hours of unskilled labour, will the equality of all 'economic agents' be maintained under these circumstances, i.e. will it 'pay' economically to acquire a skill.

Marx himself never extensively dwelled on this solution of the so-called reduction problem. This remains indeed one of the most obscure parts of his general economic theory. It has led to some, generally rather mild, controversy. Much more heat has been generated by another facet of Marx's labour theory of value, the so-called transformation problem. Indeed, from Böhm-Bawerk writing a century ago till the recent contributions of Sraffa (1960) and Steedman (1977), the way Marx dealt with the transformation of values into 'prices of production' in Capital Vol. III has been considered by many of his critics as the main problem of his 'system', as well as being a reason to reject the labour theory of value out of hand.

The problem arises out of the obvious modification in the functioning of a market economy when capitalist commodity production substitutes Itself for simple commodity production. In simple commodity production, with generally stable technology and stable (or easily reproducible) tools, living labour is the only variable of the quantity and subdivision of social production. The mobility of labour is the only dynamic factor in the economy. As Engels pointed out in his Addendum to Capital Vol. III (Marx, g, pp, 1034-7), in such an economy, commodities would be exchanged at prices which would be immediately proportional to values, to the labour inputs they embody.

But under the capitalist mode of production, this is no longer the case. Economic decision-taking is not in the hands of the direct producers. It is in the hands of the capitalist entrepreneurs in the wider sense of the word (bankers - distributors of credit - playing a key role in that decision-taking, besides entrepreneurs in the productive sector properly speaking). Investment decisions, i.e. decisions for creating, expanding, reducing or closing enterprises, determine economic life. It is the mobility of capital and not the mobility of labour which becomes the motive force of the economy. Mobility of labour becomes essentially an epiphenomenon of the mobility of capital.

Capitalist production is production for profit. Mobility of capital is determined by existing or expected profit differentials. Capital leaves branches (countries, regions) with lower profits (or profit expectations) and flows towards branches (countries, regions) with higher ones. These movements lead to an equalisation of the rate of profit between different branches of production. But approximately equal returns on all invested capital (at least under conditions of prevailing 'free competition') coexist with unequal proportions of inputs of labour in these different branches. So there is a disparity between the direct value of a commodity and its 'price of production', that 'price of production' being defined by Marx as the sum of production costs (costs of fixed capital and raw materials plus wages) and the average rate of profit multiplied with the capital spent in the given production.

The so-called 'transformation problem' relates to the question of whether a relation can nevertheless be established between value and these 'prices of production', what is the degree of coherence (or incoherence) of the relation with the 'law of value' (the labour theory of value in general), and what is the correct quantitative way to express that relation, if it exists.

We shall leave aside here the last aspect of the problem, to which extensive analysis has recently been devoted (Mandel and Freeman, 1984). From Marx's point of view, there is no incoherence between the formation of 'prices of production' and the labour theory of value. Nor is it true that he came upon that alleged difficulty when he started to prepare Capital Vol.III, i.e. to deal with capitalist competition, as several critics have argued (see e.g. Joan Robinson, 1942). In fact, his solution of the transformation problem is already present in the Grundrisse, before he even started to draft Capital Vol. I.

The sum total of value produced in a given country during a given span of time (e.g. one year) is determined by the sum total of labour-inputs. Competition and movements of capital cannot change that quantity, The sum total of values equals the sum total of 'prices of production'. The only effect of capital competition and capital mobility is to redistribute that given sum - and this through a redistribution of surplus value (see below) - between different capitals, to the benefit of some and at the expense of others.

Now the redistribution does not occur in a haphazard or arbitrary way. Essentially value (surplus-value) is transferred from technically less advanced branches to technologically more advanced branches. And here the concept of 'quantities of socially necessary labour' comes into its own, under the conditions of constant revolutions of productive technology that characterise the capital mode of production. Branches with lower than average technology (organic composition of capital, see below) can be considered as wasting socially necessary labour. Part of the labour spent in production in their realm is therefore not compensated by society. Branches with higher than average technology (organic composition of capital) can be considered to be economising social labour; their labour inputs can therefore be considered as more intensive than average, embodying more value. In this way, the transfer of value (surplus-value) between different branches, far from being in contradiction with the law of value, is precisely the way it operates and should operate under conditions of 'capitalist equality', given the pressure of rapid technological change.

As to the logical inconsistency often supposedly to be found in Marx's method of solving the 'transformation problem' - first advanced by von Bortkiewicz (1907) - it is based upon a misunderstanding in our opinion. It is alleged that in his 'transformation schemas' (or tables) Marx calculates inputs in 'values' and outputs in 'prices of production', thereby omitting the feedback effect of the latter on the former. But that feedback eject is unrealistic and unnecessary, once one recognises that inputs are essentially data. Movements of capital posterior to the purchase of machinery or raw materials, including the ups and dawns of prices of finished products produced with these raw materials, cannot lead to a change in prices and therefore of profits of the said machinery and raw materials, on sales which have already occurred. What critics present as an inconsistency between 'values' and 'prices of production' is simply a recognition of two different time-frameworks (cycles) in which the equalisation of the rate of profit has been achieved, a first one for inputs, and a second, later one for outputs.

5. *Marx's Theory of Rent*

The labour theory of value defines value as the socially necessary quantity of labour determined by the average productivity of labour of each given sector of production. But these values are not mathematically fixed data. They are simply the expression of a process going on in real life, under capitalist commodity production. So this average is only ascertained in the course of a certain time-span.

There is a lot of logical argument and empirical evidence to advance the hypothesis that the normal time-span for essentially modifying the value of commodities is the business cycle, from one crises of over-production (recession) to the next one.

Before technological progress and (or) better (more 'rational') labour organisation etc. determines a more than marginal change (in general: decline) in the value of a commodity, and the crisis eliminates less efficient firms, there will be a coexistence of firms with various 'individual values' of a given commodity in a given branch of output, even assuming a single market price. So, in his step-for-step approach towards explaining the immediate phenomena (facts of economic life) like prices and profits, by their essence, Marx introduces at this point of his analysis a new mediating concept, that of market value. The market value of a commodity is the 'individual value' of the firm, or a group of firms, in a given branch of production, around which the market price will fluctuate. That 'market value' is not necessarily the mathematical (weighted) average of labour expenditure of all firms of that branch. It can be below, equal or above that average, for a certain period (generally less than the duration of the business cycle, at least under 'free competition'), according to whether social demand is saturated, just covered or to an important extent not covered by current output plus existing stocks. In these three cases respectively, the more (most) efficient firms, the firms of average efficiency, or even firms with labour productivity below average, will determine the market value of that given commodity.

This implies that the more efficient firms enjoy surplus profits (profits over and above the average profit) in case 2 and 3 and that a certain number of firms work at less than average profit in all three cases, but especially in case 1.

The mobility of capital, i.e. normal capitalist competition, generally eliminates such situations after a certain lapse of time. But when that mobility of capital is impeded for long periods by either unavoidable scarcity (natural conditions that are not renewable or non-substitutable, like land and mineral deposits) or through the operation of institutional obstacles (private property of land and mineral resources forbidding access to available capital, except in exchange for payments over and above average profit), these surplus profits can be frozen and maintained for decades. They thus become rents, of which ground rent and mineral rent are the most obvious examples in Marx's time, extensively analysed in Capital Vol.III.

Marx's theory of rent is the most difficult part of his economic theory, the one which has witnessed fewer comments and developments, by followers and critics alike, than other major parts of his 'system'. But it is not obscure. And in contrast to Ricardo's or Rodbertus's theories of rent, it represents a straight-forward application of the labour theory of value. It does not imply any emergence of 'supplementary' value (surplus value, profits) in the market, in the process of circulation of commodities, which is anathema to Marx and to all consistent upholders of the labour theory of value. Nor does it in any way suggest that land or mineral deposits 'create' value. It simply means that in agriculture and mining less productive labour (as in the general case analysed above) determines the market value of food or minerals, and that therefore more efficient farms and mines enjoy surplus profits which Marx calls differential (land and mining) rent. It also means that as long as productivity of labour in agriculture is generally below the average of the economy as a whole (or more correctly: that the organic composition of capital, the expenditure in machinery and raw materials as against wages, is inferior in agriculture to that in industry and transportation), the sum total of surplus-value produced in agriculture will accrue to landowners + capitalist farmers taken together, and will not enter the general process of (re)distribution of profit throughout the economy as a whole.

This creates the basis for a supplementary form of rent, over and above differential rent, rent which Marx calls absolute land rent. This is, incidentally, the basis for a long-term separation of capitalist landowners from entrepreneurs in farming or animal husbandry, distinct from feudal or semi-feudal landowners or great landowners under conditions of predominantly petty commodity production, or in the Asiatic mode of production, with free peasants.

The validity of Marx's theory of land and mining rents has been confirmed by historical evidence, especially in the 20th century. Not only has history substantiated Marx's prediction that, in spite of the obstacle of land and mining rent, mechanisation would end up by penetrating food and raw materials production too, as it has for a long time dominated industry and transportation, thereby causing a growing decline of differential rent (this has occurred increasingly in agriculture in the last 25-50 years, first in

North America, and then in Western Europe and even elsewhere). It has also demonstrated that once the structural scarcity of food disappears, the institutional obstacle (private property) loses most of its efficiency as a brake upon the mobility of capital. Therefore the participation of surplus-value produced in agriculture in the general process of profit equalisation throughout the economy cannot be prevented any more. Thereby absolute rent tends to wither away and, with it, the separation of land ownership from entrepreneurial farming and animal husbandry. It is true that farmers can then fall under the sway of the banks, but they do so as private owners of their land which becomes mortgaged, not as share-croppers or entrepreneurs renting land from separate owners.

On the other hand, the reappearance of structural scarcity in the realm of energy enabled the OPEC countries to multiply the price of oil by ten in the 1970s, i.e. to have it determined by the oilfields where production costs are the highest, thereby assuring the owners of the cheapest oil wells in Arabia, Iran, Libya, etc. huge differential minerals rents.

Marx's theory of land and mineral rent can be easily extended into a general theory of rent, applicable to all fields of production where formidable difficulties of entry limit mobility of capital for extended periods of time. It thereby becomes the basis of a marxist theory of monopoly and monopoly surplus profits, i.e. in the form of cartel rents (Hilferding, 1910) or of technological rent (Mandel, 1972). Lenin's and Bukharin's theories of surplus profit are based upon analogous but not identical reasoning (Bukharin, 1914, 1926; Lenin, 1917).

But in all these cases of general application of the marxist theory of rent, the same caution should apply as Marx applied to his theory of land rent. By its very nature, capitalism, based upon private property, i.e. 'many capitals' - that is competition - cannot tolerate any 'eternal' monopoly, a 'permanent' surplus profit deducted from the sum total of profits which is divided among the capitalist class as a whole. Technological innovations, substitution of new products for old ones including the fields of raw materials and of food, will in the long run reduce or eliminate all monopoly situations, especially if the profit differential is large enough to justify huge research and investment outlays.

6. Marx's Theory of Money

In the same way as his theory of rent, Marx's theory of money is a straightforward application of the labour theory of value. As value is but the embodiment of socially necessary labour, commodities exchange with each other in proportion to the labour quanta they contain. This is true for the exchange of iron against wheat, as it is true for the exchange of iron against gold or silver.

Marx's theory of money is therefore in the first place a commodity theory of money. A given commodity can play the role of universal medium of exchange, as well as fulfil all the other functions of money, precisely because it is a commodity, i.e. because it is itself the product of socially necessary labour. This applies to the precious metals in the same way it applies to all the various commodities which, throughout history, have played the role of money.

It follows that strong upheavals in the 'intrinsic' value of the money-commodity will cause strong upheavals in the general price level. In Marx's theory of money, (market) prices are nothing but the expression of the value of commodities in the value of the money commodity chosen as a monetary standard. If £1 sterling = 1/10 ounce of gold, the formula 'the price of 10 quarters of wheat is f 1' means that 10 quarters of wheat have been produced in the same socially necessary labour times as 1/10 ounce of gold. A strong decrease in the average productivity of labour in gold mining (as a result for example of a depletion of the richer gold veins) will lead to a general depression of the average price level, all other things remaining equal. Likewise, a sudden and radical increase in the average productivity of labour in gold mining, through the discovery of new rich gold fields (California after 1848; the Rand in South Africa in the 1890s) or through the application of new revolutionary technology, will lead to a general increase in the price level of all other commodities.

Leaving aside short-term oscillations, the general price level will move in medium and long-term periods according to the relation between the fluctuations of the productivity of labour in agriculture and industry on the one hand, and the fluctuations of the productivity of labour in gold mining (if gold is the money-commodity), on the other.

Basing himself on that commodity theory of money, Marx therefore criticized as inconsistent Ricardo's quantity theory. But for exactly the same reason of a consistent application of the labour theory of value, the quantity of money in circulation enters Marx's economic analysis when he deals with the phenomenon of paper money.

As gold has an intrinsic value, like all other commodities, there can be no 'gold inflation ', as little as there can be a 'steel inflation'. An abstraction made of short-term price fluctuations caused by fluctuations between supply and demand, a persistent decline of the value of gold (exactly as for all other commodities) can only be the result of a persistent increase in the average productivity of labour in gold mining and not of an 'excess' of circulation in gold. If the demand for gold falls consistently, this can only indirectly trigger a decline in the value of gold through causing the closure of the least productive old mines. But in the case of the money-commodity, such overproduction can hardly occur, given the special function of gold of serving as a universal reserve fund, nationally and internationally. It will always therefore find a buyer, be it not, of course, always at the same 'prices' (in Marx's economic theory, the concept of the 'price of gold' is meaningless. As the price of a commodity is precisely its expression in the value of gold, the 'price of gold' would be the expression of the value of gold in the value of gold).

Paper money, banks notes, are a money sign representing a given quantity of the money-commodity. Starting from the above-mentioned example, a banknote of £1 represents 1/10 ounce of gold. This is an objective 'fact of life', which no government or monetary authority can arbitrarily alter. It follows that any emission of paper money in excess of that given proportion will automatically lead to an increase in the general price level, always other things remaining equal. If £1 suddenly represents only 1/20 ounce of gold, because paper money circulation has doubled without a significant increase in the total labour time spent in the economy, then the price level will tend to double too. The value of 1/10 ounce of gold remains equal to the value of 10 quarters of wheat. But as 1/10 ounce of gold is now represented by £2 in paper banknotes instead of being represented by £1, the price of wheat will move from £1 to £2 for 10 quarters (from two shillings to four shillings a quarter before the introduction of the decimal system).

This does not mean that in the case of paper money, Marx himself has become an advocate of a quantity theory of money. While there are obvious analogies between his theory of paper money and the quantity theory, the main difference is the rejection by Marx of any mechanical automatism between the quantity of paper money emitted on the one hand, and the general dynamic of the economy (including on the price level) on the other.

In Marx's explanation of the movement of the capitalist economy in its totality, the formula ceteris paribus is meaningless. Excessive (or insufficient) emission of paper money never occurs in a vacuum. It always occurs at a given stage of the business cycle, and in a given phase of the longer-term historical evolution of capitalism. It is thereby always combined with given ups and downs of the rate of profit, of productivity of labour, of output, of market conditions (overproduction or insufficient production). Only in connection with these other fluctuations can the effect of paper money 'inflation' or 'deflation' be judged, including the effect on the general price level. The key variables are in the field of production. The key synthetic resultant is in the field of profit. Price moments are generally epiphenomena as much as they are signals. To untwine the tangle, more is necessary than a simple analysis of the fluctuations of the quantity of money.

Only in the case of extreme runaway inflation of paper money would this be otherwise; and even in that border case, relative price movements (different degrees of price increases for different commodities) would still confirm that, in the last analysis, the law of values rules, and not the arbitrary decision of the Central Banks or any other authority controlling or emitting paper money.

7. Marx's Theory of Surplus Value

Marx himself considered his theory of surplus-value his most important contribution to the progress of economic analysis (Marx, letter to Engels of 24 August 1867). It is through this theory that the wide scope of his sociological and historical thought enables him simultaneously to place the capitalist mode of production in his historical context, and to find the root of its inner economic contradictions and its laws of motion in the specific relations of production on which it is based.

As said before, Marx's theory of classes is based on the recognition that in each class society, part of society (the ruling class) appropriates the social surplus product. But that surplus product can take three essentially different forms (or a combination of them). It can take the form of straightforward unpaid surplus labour, as in the slave mode of production, early feudalism or some sectors of the Asiatic mode of production (unpaid corvée labour for the Empire). It can take the form of goods appropriated by the ruling class in the form of use-values pure and simple (the products of surplus labour), as under feudalism when feudal rent is paid in a certain amount of produce (produce rent) or in its more modern remnants, such as sharecropping. And it can take a money form, like money-rent in the final phases of feudalism, and capitalist profits. Surplus-value is essentially just that: the money form of the social surplus product or, what amounts to the same, the money product of surplus labour. It has therefore a common root with all other forms of surplus product: unpaid labour.

This means that Marx's theory of surplus-value is basically a deduction (or residual) theory of the ruling classes' income. The whole social product (the net national income) is produced in the course of the process of production, exactly as the whole crop is harvested by the peasants. What happens on the market (or through appropriation of the produce) is a distribution (or redistribution) of what already has been created. The surplus product, and therefore also its money form, surplus-value, is the residual of that new (net) social product (income) which remains after the producing classes have received their compensation (under capitalism: their wages). This 'deduction' theory of the ruling classes' income is thus ipso factor an exploitation theory. Not in the ethical sense of the word - although Marx and Engels obviously manifested a lot of understandable moral indignation at the fate of all the exploited throughout history, and especially at the fate of the modern proletariat - but in the economic one. The income of the ruling classes can always be reduced in the final analysis to the product of unpaid labour: that is the heart of Marx's theory of exploitation.

That is also the reason why Marx attached so much importance to treating surplus-value as a general category, over and above profits (themselves subdivided into industrial profits, bank profits, commercial profits etc.), interest and rent, which are all part of the total surplus product produced by wage labour. It is this general category which explains both the existence (the common interest) of the ruling class (all those who live off surplus value), and the origins of the class struggle under capitalism.

Marx likewise laid bare the economic mechanism through which surplus-value originates. At the basis of that economic mechanism is a huge social upheaval which started in Western Europe in the 15th century and slowly spread over the rest of the continent and all other continents (in many so-called underdeveloped countries, it is still going on to this day).

Through many concomitant economic (including technical), social, political and cultural transformations, the mass of the direct producers, essentially peasants and handicraftsmen, are separated from their means of production and cut off from free access to the land. They are therefore unable to produce their livelihood on their own account. In order to keep themselves and their families alive, they have to hire out their arms, their muscles and their brains, to the owners of the means of production (including land). If and when these owners have enough money capital at their disposal to buy raw materials and pay wages, they can start to organise production on a capitalist basis, using wage labour to transform the raw materials which they buy, with the tools they own, into finished products which they then automatically own too.

The capitalist mode of production thus presupposes that the producers' labour power has become a commodity. Like all other commodities, the commodity labour power has an exchange value and a use value. The exchange value of labour power, like the exchange value of all other commodities, is the amount of socially necessary labour embodied in it, i.e. its reproduction costs. This means concretely the value of all the consumer goods and services necessary for a labourer to work day after day, week after week, month after month, at approximately the same level of intensity, and for the members of the labouring classes to remain approximately stable in number and skill (i.e. for a certain number of working-class children to be fed, kept and schooled, so as to replace their parents when they are unable to work any more, or die). But the use value of the commodity labour power is precisely its capacity to create new value, including its potential to create more value than its own reproduction costs. Surplus-value is but that difference between the total new value created by the commodity labour power, and its own value, its own reproduction costs. The whole marxian theory of surplus-value is therefore based upon that subtle distinction between 'labour power' and 'labour' (or value). But there is nothing 'metaphysical' about this distinction. It is simply an explanation (demystification) of a process which occurs daily in millions of cases.

The capitalist does not buy the worker's 'labour'. If he did that there would be obvious theft, for the worker's wage is obviously smaller than the total value he adds to that of the raw materials in the course of the process of production. No: the capitalist buys 'labour power', and often (not always of course) he buys it at its justum pretium, at its real value. So he feels unjustly accused when he is said to have caused a 'dishonest' operation. The worker is victim not of vulgar theft but of a social set-up which condemns him first to transform his productive capacity into a commodity, then to sell that labour power on a specific market (the labour market) characterised by institutional inequality, and finally to content himself with the market price he can get for that commodity, irrespective of whether the new value he creates during the process of production exceeds that market price (his wage) by a small amount, a large amount, or an enormous amount.

The labour power the capitalist has bought 'adds value' to that of the used-up raw materials and tools (machinery, buildings etc.). If, and until that point of time, this added value is inferior or equal to the workers' wages, surplus-value cannot originate. But in that case, the capitalist has obviously no interest in hiring wage labour. He only hires it because that wage labour has the quality (the use value) to add to the raw materials' value more than its own value (i.e. its own wages). This 'additional added value' (the difference between total 'value added' and wages) is precisely surplus-value. Its emergence from the process of production is the precondition for the capitalists' hiring workers, for the existence of the capitalist mode of production.

The institutional inequality existing on the labour market (masked for liberal economists, sociologists and moral philosophers alike by juridical equality) arises from the very fact that the capitalist mode of production is based upon generalised commodity production, generalised market economy. This implies that a propertyless labourer, who owns no capital, who has no reserves of larger sums of money but who has to buy his food and clothes, pay his rent and even elementary public transportation for journeying between home and workplace, in a continuous way in exchange of money, is under the economic compulsion to sell the only commodity he possesses, to wit his labour power, also on a continuous basis. He cannot withdraw from the labour market until the wages go up. He cannot wait.

But the capitalist, who has money reserves, can temporarily withdraw from the labour market. He can lay his workers off, can even close or sell his enterprise and wait a couple of years before starting again in business. The institutional differences makes price determination of the labour market a game with loaded dice, heavily biased against the working class. One just has to imagine a social set-up in which each citizen would be guaranteed an annual minimum income by the community, irrespective of whether he is employed or not, to understand that 'wage determination' under these circumstances would be quite different from what it is under capitalism. In such a set-up the individual would really have the economic choice whether to sell his labour power to another person (or a firm) or not. Under capitalism, he has no choice. His is forced by economic compulsion to go through that sale, practically at any price.

The economic function and importance of trade unions for the wage-earners also clearly arises from that elementary analysis. For it is precisely the workers' 'combination' and their assembling a collective resistance fund (what was called by the first French unions caisses de résistance, 'reserve deposits') which enables them, for example through a strike, to withdraw the supply of labour power temporarily from the market so as to stop a downward trend of wages or induce a wage increase. There is nothing 'unjust' in such a temporary withdrawal of the supply of labour power, as there are constant withdrawals of demand for labour power by the capitalists, sometimes on a huge scale never equalled by strikes. Through the functioning of strong labour unions, the working class tries to correct, albeit partially and modestly, the institutional inequality on the labour market of which it is a victim, without ever being able to neutralise it durably or completely.

It cannot neutralise it durably because in the very way in which capitalism functions there is a powerful built-in corrective in favour of capital: the inevitable emergence of an industrial reserve army of labour. There are three key sources for that reserve army: the mass of precapitalist producers and self-employed (independent peasants, handicraftsmen, trades-people, professional people, small and medium-sized capitalists); the mass of housewives (and to a lesser extent, children); the mass of the wage-earners themselves, who potentially can be thrown out of employment.

The first two sources have to be visualised not only in each capitalist country seen separately but on a world scale, through the operations of international migration. They are still unlimited to a great extent, although the number of wage-earners the world over (including agricultural wage labourers) has already passed the one billion mark. As the third source, while it is obviously not unlimited (if wage labour would disappear altogether, if all wage labourers would be fired, surplus-value production would disappear too; that is why 'total robotism' is impossible under capitalism), its reserves are enormous, precisely in tandem with the enormous growth of the absolute number of wage earners.

The fluctuations of the industrial reserve army are determined both by the business cycle and by long-term trends of capital accumulation. Rapidly increasing capital accumulation attracts wage labour on a massive scale, including through international migration. Likewise, deceleration, stagnation or even decline of capital accumulation inflates the reserve army of labour. There is thus an upper limit to wage increases, when profits (realised profits and expected profits) are 'excessively' reduced in the eyes of the capitalists, which triggers off such decelerated, stagnating or declining capital accumulation, thereby decreasing employment and wages, till a 'reasonable' level of profits is restored. This process does not correspond to any 'natural economic law' (or necessity), nor does it correspond to any 'immanent justice'. It just expresses the inner logic of the capitalist mode of production, which is geared to profit. Other forms of economic organisation could function, have functioned and are functioning on the basis of other logics, which do not lead to periodic massive unemployment. On the contrary, a socialist would say - and Marx certainly thought so - that the capitalist system is an 'unjust', or better stated 'alienating', 'inhuman' social system, precisely because it cannot function without periodically reducing employment and the satisfaction of elementary needs for tens of millions of human beings.

Marx's theory of surplus-value is therefore closely intertwined with a theory of wages which is far away from Malthus's, Ricardo's or the early socialists' (like Ferdinand Lassalle's) 'iron law of wages', in which wages tend to fluctuate around the physiological minimum. That crude theory of 'absolute pauperisation' of the working class under capitalism, attributed to Marx by many authors (Popper, 1945, et a1.), is not Marx's at all, as many contemporary authors have convincingly demonstrated (see among others Rosdolsky, 1968). Such an 'iron law of wages' is essentially a demographic one, in which birth rates and the frequency of marriages determine the fluctuation of employment and unemployment and thereby the level of wages.

The logical and empirical inconsistencies of such a theory are obvious. Let it be sufficient to point out that while fluctuations in the supply of wage-labourers are considered essential, fluctuations in the demand for labour power are left out of the analysis. It is certainly a paradox that the staunch opponent of capitalism, Karl Marx, pointed out as early as in the middle of the 19th century the potential for wage increases under capitalism, even though not unlimited in time and space. Marx also stressed the fact that for each capitalist, wage increases of other capitalists' workers are considered increases of potential purchasing power, not increases in costs.

Marx distinguishes two parts in the workers' wage, two elements of reproduction costs of the commodity labour power. One is purely physiological, and can be expressed in calories and energy quanta; this is the bottom below which the wage cannot fall without destroying slowly rapidly the workers' labour capacity. The second one is historical-moral, as Marx calls it, and consists of those additional goods and services which a shift in the class relationship of forces, such as a victorious class struggle, enables the working class to incorporate into the average wage, the socially necessary (recognised) reproduction costs of the commodity labour power (e.g. holidays after the French general strike of June 1936). This part of the wage is essentially flexible. It will differ from country to country, continent to continent and from epoch to epoch, according to many variables. But it has the upper limit indicated above: the ceiling from which profits threaten to disappear, or to become insufficient in the eyes of the capitalists, who then go on an 'investment strike'.

So Marx's theory of wages is essentially an accumulation-of-capital theory of wages which sends us back to what Marx considered the first 'law of motion' of the capitalist mode of production: the compulsion for the capitalists to step up constantly the rate of capital accumulation.

8. *The Laws of Motion of the Capitalist Mode of Production*
If Marx's theory of surplus-value is his most revolutionary con-tribution to economic science, his discovery of the basic long-term 'laws of motion' (development trends) of the capitalist mode of production constitutes undoubtedly his most impres-sive scientific achievement.

No other 19th-century author has been able to foresee in such a coherent way how capitalism would function, would develop and would transform the world, as did Karl Marx. Many of the most distinguished contemporary economists, starting with Wassily Leontief (1938), and Joseph Schumpeter (1942) have recognised this.

While some of these 'laws of motion' have obviously created much contro-versy, we shall nevertheless list them in logical orders rather than according to the degree of consensus they command.

(a) The capitalist's compulsion to accumulate. Capital appears in the form of accumulated money, thrown into circulation in order to increase in value. No owner of money capital will engage in business in order to re-cuperate exactly the sum initially invested, and nothing more than that. By definition, the search for profit is at the basis of all economic opera-tions by owners of capital.

Profit (surplus-value, accretion of value) can originate outside the sphere of production in a precapitalist society. It represents then essen-tially a transfer of value (so-called primitive accumulation of capital); but under the capitalist mode of production, in which capital has pene-trated the sphere of production and dominates it, surplus-value is cur-rently produced by wage labour. It represents a constant increase in value.

Capital can only appear in the form of many capitals, given its very his-torical-social origin in private property (appropriation) of the means of production. 'Many capitals' imply unavoidable competition. Competi-tion in a capitalist mode of production is competition for selling com-modities in an anonymous market. While surplus-value is produced in the process of production, it is realised in the process of circulation, i.e. through the sale of the commodities. The capitalist wants to sell at max-imum profit. In practice, he will be satisfied if he gets the average profit, which is a percentage really existing in his consciousness (e.g. Mr Charles Wilson, the then head of the US automobile firm General Mo-tors, stated before a Congressional enquiry: we used to fix the expected sales price of our cars by adding 15% to production costs). But he can never be sure of this. He cannot even be sure that all the commodities produced will and a buyer.

Given these uncertainties, he has to strive constantly to get the better of his competitors. This can only occur through operating with more capital. This means that at least part of the surplus-value produced will not be unproductively consumed by the capitalists and their hangers-on through luxury consumption, but will be accumulated, added to the previously existing capital.

The inner logic of capitalism is therefore not only to 'work for profit', but also to 'work for capital accumulation'. 'Accumulate, accumulate; that is Moses and the Prophets', states Marx in Capital, Vol. I. Capitalists are compelled to act in that way as a result of competition. It is competition which basically fuels this terrifying snowball logic: initial value of capital -> accretion of value (surplus-value) -> accretion of capital -> more accretion of surplus-value -> more accretion of capital etc. Without competition, the fire of growth would burn out.

(b) The tendency towards constant technological revolutions. In the capitalist mode of production, accumulation of capital is in the first place accumulation of productive capital, or capital invested to produce more and more commodities. Competition is therefore above all competition between productive capitals, i.e. 'many capitals' engaged in mining, manufacturing, transportation, agriculture, telecommunications. The main weapon in competition between capitalist firms is cutting production costs. More advanced production techniques and more 'rational' labour organisation are the main means to achieve that purpose. The basic trend of capital accumulation in the capitalist mode of production is therefore a trend towards more and more sophisticated machinery. Capital growth takes the dual form of higher and higher value of capital and of constant revolutions in the techniques of production, of constant technological progress.

(c) The capitalists' unquenchable thirst for surplus-value extraction. The compulsion for capital to grow, the irresistible urge for capital accumulation, realises itself above all through a constant drive for the increase of the production of surplus-value. Capital accumulation is nothing but surplus-value capitalisation, the transformation of part of the new surplus-value into additional capital. There is no other source of additional capital than additional surplus-value produced in the process of production.

Marx distinguishes two different forms of additional surplus-value production. Absolute surplus-value accretion occurs essentially through the extension of the work day. If the worker reproduces the equivalent of his wages in 4 hours a day, an extension of the work day from 10 to 12 hours will increase surplus-value from 6 to 8 hours. Relative surplus-value accretion occurs through an increase of the productivity of labour in the wage-goods sector of the economy. Such an increase in productivity implies that the equivalent of the value of an identical basket of goods and services consumed by the worker could be produced in 2 hours instead of 4 hours of labour. If the work day remains stable at 10 hours and real wages remain stable too, surplus-value will then increase from 6 to 8 hours.

While both processes occur throughout the history of the capitalist mode of production (viz. the contemporary pressure of employers in favour of overtime!), the first one was prevalent first, the second one became prevalent since the second half of the 19th century, first in Britain, France and Belgium, then in the USA and Germany, later in the other industrialized capitalist countries, and later still in the semi-industrialised ones. Marx calls this process the real subsumption (subordination) of labour under capital, for it represents not only an economic but also a physical subordination of the wage-earner under the machine. This physical subordination can only be realized through social control. The history of the capitalist mode of production is therefore also the history of successive forms of - tighter and tighter - control of capital over the workers inside the factories (Braverman, 1974); and of attempts at realising that tightening of control in society as a whole.

The increase in the production of relative surplus-value is the goal for which capitalism tends to periodically substitute machinery for labour, i.e. to expand the industrial reserve army of labour. Likewise, it is the main tool for maintaining a modicum of social equilibrium, for when productivity of labour strongly increases, above all in the wage-good producing sectors of the economy, real wages and profits (surplus-value) can both expand simultaneously. What were previously luxury goods can even become mass-produced wage-goods.

(d) The tendency towards growing concentration and centralisation of capital. The growth of the value of capital means that each successful capitalist firm will be operating with more and more capital. Marx calls this the tendency towards growing concentration of capital. But in the competitive process, there are victors and vanquished. The victors grow. The vanquished go bankrupt or are absorbed by the victors. This process Marx calls the centralisation of capital. It results in a declining number of firms which survive in each of the key fields of production. Many small and medium-sized capitalists disappear as independent business men and women. They become in turn salary earners, employed by successful capitalism firms. Capitalism itself is the big 'expropriating' force, suppressing private property of the means of production for many, in favour of private property for few.

(e) The tendency for the 'organic composition of capital' to increase. Productive capital has a double form. It appears in the form of constant capital: buildings, machinery, raw materials, energy, It appears in the form of variable capital: capital spent on wages of productive workers. Marx calls the part of capital used in buying labour power variable, because only that part produces additional value. In the process of production, the value of constant capital is simply maintained (transferred in toto or in part into the value of the finished product). Variable capital on the contrary is the unique source of 'added value'.

Marx postulates that the basic historic trend of capital accumulation is to increase investment in constant capital at a quicker pace than investment in variable capital; the relation between the two he calls the 'organic composition of capital'. This is both a technical/physical relation (a given production technique implies the use of a given number of productive wage earners even if not in an absolutely mechanical way) and a value relation. The trend towards an increase in the 'organic composition of capital' is therefore a historical trend towards basically labour-saving technological progress.

This tendency has often been challenged by critics of Marx. Living in the age of semi-automation and 'robotism', it is hard to understand that challenge. The conceptual confusion on which this challenge is most based is an operation with the 'national wage bill', i.e. a confusion between wages in general and variable capital, which is only the wage bill of productive labour. A more correct index would be the part of the labour costs in total production costs in the manufacturing (and mining) sector. It is hard to deny that this proportion shows a downward secular trend.

(f) The tendency of the rate of profit to decline. For the workers, the basic relation they are concerned with is the rate of surplus-value, i.e. the division of 'value added' between wages and surplus-value. When this goes up, their exploitation (the unpaid labour they produce) obviously goes up. For the capitalists, however, this relationship is not meaningful. They are concerned with the relation between surplus-value and the totality of capital invested, never mind whether in the form of machinery and raw materials or in the form of wages. This relation is the rate of profit. It is a function of two variables, the organic composition of capital and the rate of surplus-value. If the value of constant capital is represented by c, the value of variable capital (wages of productive workers) by v and surplus-value by s, the rate of profit will be $s/(c + v)$. This can be rewritten as $[s/v]/[(c+v)/v]$ with the two variables emerging ($(c + v)/v$ obviously reflects c/v).

Marx postulates that the increase in the rate of surplus value has definite limits, while the increase in the organic composition of capital has practically none (automation, robotism). There will be a basic tendency for the rate of profit to decline.

This is however absolutely true only on a very long-term, i.e. essentially 'secular', basis. In other time-frameworks, the rate of profit can fluctuate under the influence of countervailing forces. Constant capital can be devalorised, through 'capital saving' technical process, and through economic crises (see below). The rate of surplus-value can be strongly increased in the short or medium terms although each strong increase makes a further increase more difficult; and capital can flow to countries (e.g. 'Third World' ones) or branches (e.g. service sectors) where the organic composition of capital is significantly lower than in the previously industrialised ones, thereby raising the average rate of profit.

Finally, the increase in the mass of surplus-value - especially through the extension of wage labour in general, i.e. the total number of workers - offsets to a large extent the depressing effects of moderate declines of the average rate of profit. Capitalism will not go out of business if the mass of surplus-value produced increases 'only' from £10 to 17 billion, while the total mass of capital has moved from £100 to 200 billion; and capital accumulation will not stop under these circumstances, nor necessarily slow down significantly. It would be sufficient to have the unproductively consumed part of surplus-value pass e.g. from £3 to £2 billion, to obtain a rate of capital accumulation of 15/200, i.e. 7.5%, even higher than the previous one of 7/100, in spite of a decline of the rate of profit from 10 to 8.5%.

(g) The inevitability of class struggle under capitalism. One of the most impressive projections by Marx was that of the inevitability of elementary class struggle under capitalism. Irrespective of the social global framework or of their own historical background, wage-earners will fight everywhere for higher real wages and a shorter work day. They will form elementary organisations for the collective instead of the individual sale of the commodity labour power, i.e., trade unions. While at the moment Marx made that projection there were less than half a million organised workers in at the most half a dozen countries in the world, today trade unions encompass hundreds of millions of wage-earners spread around the globe. There is no country, however, remote it might be, where the introduction of wage labour has not led to the appearance of worker's coalitions.

While elementary class struggle and elementary unionisation of the working class are inevitable under capitalism, higher, especially political forms of class struggle, depend on a multitude of variables which determine the rapidity with which they extend beyond smaller minorities of each 'national' working class and internationally. But there too the basic secular trend is clear. There were in 1900 innumerably more conscious socialists than in 1850, fighting not only for better wages but, to use Marx's words, for the abolition of wage labour and organising working class parties for that purpose. There are today many more than in 1900.

(h) The tendency towards growing social polarisation. From two previously enumerated trends, the trend towards growing centralisation of capital and the trend towards the growth of the mass of surplus-value, flow the trend towards growing social polarisation under capitalism. The proportion of the active population represented by wage-labour in general, i.e. by the modern proletariat (which extends far beyond productive workers in and by themselves), increases. The proportion represented by self-employed (small, medium-sized and big capitalists, as well as independent peasants, handicraftsmen, trades-people and 'free professions' working without wage-labour) decreases. In fact, in several capitalist countries the first category has already passed the 90 per cent mark, while in Marx's time it was below 50 per cent everywhere but in Britain. In most industrialised (imperialist) countries, it has reached 80-85 per cent.

This does not mean that the petty entrepreneurs have tended to disappear. 10 or 15-20 per cent out of 30 million people, not to say out of 120 million, still represents a significant social layer. While many small businesses disappear, especially in times of economic depression, as a result of severe competition, they also are constantly created, especially in the interstices between big firms, and in new sectors where they play an exploratory role. Also, the overall social results of growing proletarisation are not simultaneous with the economic process in and by itself. From the point of view of class consciousness, culture, political attitude, there can exist significant time-lags between the transformation of an independent farmer, grocer or doctor into a wage-earner, and his acceptance of socialism as an overall social solution for his own and society's ills. But again, the secular trend is towards growing homogeneity, less and less heterogeneity, of the mass of the wage-earning class, and not the other way around. It is sufficient to compare the differences in consumer patterns, attitudes towards unionisation or voting habits between manual workers, bank employees and government functionaries in say 1900 and today, to note that they have decreased and not increased.

(i) The tendency towards growing objective socialisation of labour. Capitalism starts in the form of private production on a medium-sized scale for a limited number of largely unknown customers, on an uncontrollably wide market, i.e. under conditions of near complete fragmentation of social labour and anarchy of the economic process. But as a result of growing technological progress, tremendously increased concentration of capital, the conquest of wider and wider markets throughout the world, and the very nature of the labour organisation inside large and even medium-sized capitalist factories, a powerful process of objective socialisation of labour is simultaneously set in motion. This process constantly extends the sphere of economy in which not blind market laws but conscious decisions and even large-scale co-operation prevail.

This is true especially inside mammoth firms (inside multinational corporations, such 'planning' prevails far beyond the boundaries of nation-states, even the most powerful ones!) and inside large-scale factories; but it is also increasingly true for buyer/seller relations, in the first place on an inter-firm basis, between public authorities and firms, and more often than one thinks between traders and consumers too. In all these instances, the rule of the law of value becomes more and more remote, indirect and discontinuous. Planning prevails on a short and even medium-term basis.

Certainly, the economy still remains capitalist. The rule of the law of value imposes itself brutally through the outburst of economic crises. Wars and social crises are increasingly added to these economic crises to remind society that, under capitalism, this growing objective socialisation of labour and production is indissolubly linked to private appropriation, i.e. to the profit motive as motor of economic growth. That linkage makes the system more and more crisis-ridden; but at the same time the growing socialisation of labour and production creates the objective basis for a general socialisation of the economy, i.e. represents the basis of the coming socialist order created by capitalism itself, within the framework of its own system.

(j) The inevitability of economic crises under capitalism. This is another of Marx's projections which has been strikingly confirmed by history. Marx ascertained that periodic crises of overproduction were unavoidable under capitalism. In fact, since the crisis of 1825, the first one occurring on the world market for industrial goods, to use Marx's own formula, there have been twenty-one business cycles ending (or beginning, according to the method of analysis and measurement used) with twenty-one crises of overproduction. A twenty-second is appearing on the horizon as we are writing.

Capitalist economic crises are always crises of overproduction of commodities (exchange values), as opposed to pre- and post-capitalist economic crises, which are essentially crises of underproduction of use-values. Under capitalist crises, expanded reproduction - economic growth - is brutally interrupted, not because too few commodities have been produced but, on the contrary, because a mountain of produced commodities finds no buyers. This unleashes a spiral movement of collapse of firms, firing of workers, contraction of sales (or orders) for raw materials and machinery, new redundancies, new contraction of sales of consumer goods etc. Through this contracted reproduction, prices (gold prices) collapse, production and income is reduced, capital loses value. At the end of the declining spiral, output (and stocks) has been reduced more than purchasing power. Then production can pick up again; and as the crisis has both increased the rate of surplus-value (through a decline of wages and a more 'rational' labour organisation) and decreased the value of capital, the average rate of profit increases. This stimulates investment. Employment increases, value production and national income expand, and we enter a new cycle of economic revival, prosperity, overheating and the next crisis.

No amount of capitalists' (essentially large combines' and monopolies') 'self-regulation', no amount of government intervention, has been able to suppress this cyclical movement of capitalist production. Nor can they succeed in achieving that result. This cyclical movement is inextricably linked to production for profit and private property (competition), which imply periodic over-shooting (too little or too much investment and output), precisely because each firm's attempt at maximising profit unavoidably leads to a lower rate of profit for the system as a whole. It is likewise linked to the separation of value production and value realisation.

The only way to avoid crises of overproduction is to eliminate all basic sources of disequilibrium in the economy, including the disequilibrium between productive capacity and purchasing power of the 'final consumers'. This calls for elimination of generalised commodity production, of private property and of class exploitation, i.e. for the elimination of capitalism.

9. Marx's Theory of Crises
Marx did not write a systematic treatise on capitalist crises. His major comments on the subject are spread around his major economic writings, as well as his articles for the New York Daily Tribune. The longest treatment of the subject is in his Theorien über den Mehrwert, subpart on Ricardo.

Starting from these profound but unsystematic remarks, many interpretations of the 'marxist theory of crises' have been offered by economists who consider themselves marxists. 'Monocausal' ones generally centre around 'disproportionality' (Bukharin, Hilferding, Otto Bauer) - anarchy of production as the key cause of crises - or 'underconsumption' - lack of purchasing power of the 'final consumers' as the cause of crises (Rosa Luxemburg, Sweezy). 'Non-monocausal' ones try to elaborate Marx's own dictum according to which all basic contradictions of the capitalist mode of production come into play in the process leading to a capitalist crises (Grossman, Mandel).

The question of determining whether according to Marx, a crisis of overproduction is first of all a crisis of overproduction of commodities or a crisis of overproduction of capital is really meaningless in the framework of Marx's economic analysis. The mass of commodities is but one specific form of capital, commodity capital. Under capitalism, which is generalised commodity production, no overproduction is possible which is not simultaneously overproduction of commodities and overproduction of capital (overaccumulation).

Likewise, the question to know whether the crisis 'centres' on the sphere of production or the sphere of circulation is largely meaningless. The crisis is a disturbance (interruption) of the process of enlarged reproduction; and according to Marx, the process of reproduction is precisely a (contradictory) unity of production and circulation. For capitalists, both individually (as separate firms) and as the sum total of firms it is irrelevant whether more surplus-value has actually been produced in the process of production, if that surplus-value cannot be totally realised in the process of circulation. Contrary to many economists, academic and marxist alike, Marx explicitly rejected any Say-like illusion that production more or less automatically finds is own market.

It is correct that in the last analysis, capitalist crises of overproduction result from a downslide of the average rate of profit. But this does not represent a variant of the 'monocausal' explanation of crises. It means that, under capitalism, the fluctuations of the average rate of profit are in a sense the seismograph of what happens in the system as a whole. So that formula just refers back to the sum-total of partially independent variables, whose interplay causes the fluctuations of the average rate of profit.

Capitalist growth is always disproportionate growth, i.e. growth with increasing disequilibrium, both between different departments of output (Marx basically distinguishes department I, producing means of production, and department II, producing means of consumption; other authors add a department III producing non-reproductive goods - luxury goods and arms - to that list), between different branches and between production and final consumption. In fact, 'equilibrium' under capitalism is but a conceptual hypothesis practically never attained in real life, except as a border case. The above mentioned tendency of 'overshooting' is only an illustration of that more general phenomenon. So 'average' capital accumulation leads to an over-accumulation which leads to the crisis and to a prolonged phenomenon of 'underinvestment' during the depression. Output is then consistently inferior to current demand, which spurs on capital accumulation, all the more so as each successive phase of economic revival starts with new machinery of a higher technological level (leading to a higher average productivity of labour), and to a bigger and bigger mountain of produced commodities. Indeed, the very duration of the business cycle (in average 7.5 years for the last 160 years) seemed for Marx determined by the 'moral' life-time of fixed capital, i.e. the duration of the reproduction cycle (in value terms, not in possible physical survival) of machinery.

The ups and downs of the rate of profit during the business cycle do not reflect only the gyrations of the output/disposable income relation; or of the 'organic composition of capital'. They also express the varying correlation of forces between the major contending classes of bourgeois society, in the first place the short-term fluctuations of the rate of surplus-value reflecting major victories or defeats of the working class in trying to uplift or defend its standard of living and its working conditions. Technological progress and labour organisation 'rationalisations' are capital's weapons for neutralizing the effects of these fluctuations on the average rate of profit and on the rate of capital accumulation.

In general, Marx rejected any idea that the working class (or the unions) 'cause' the crisis by 'excessive wage demands'. He would recognise that under conditions of overheating and 'full employment', real wages generally increase, but the rate of surplus-value can simultaneously increase too. It can, however, not increase in the same proportion as the organic composition of capital. Hence the decline of the average rate of profit. Hence the crisis.

But if real wages do not increase in times of boom, and as they unavoidably decrease in times of depression, the average level of wages during the cycle in its totality would be such as to cause even larger overproduction of wage goods, which would induce an even stronger collapse of investment at the height of the cycle, and in no way help to avoid the crisis.

Marx energetically rejected any idea that capitalist production, while it appears as 'production for production's sake', can really emancipate itself from dependence on 'final consumption' (as alleged e.g. by Tugan-Baranowski). While capitalist technology implies indeed a more and more 'roundabout-way-of-production', and a relative shift of resources from department II to department I (that is what the 'growing organic composition of capital' really means, after all), it can never develop the productive capacity of department I without developing in the medium and long-term the productive capacity of department II too, admittedly at a slower pace and in a lesser proportion. So any medium or long-term contraction of final consumption, or final consumers' purchasing power, increases instead of eliminates the causes of the crisis.

Marx visualised the business cycle as intimately intertwined with a credit cycle, which can acquire a relative autonomy in relation to what occurs in production properly speaking. An (over) expansion of credit can enable the capitalist system to sell temporarily more goods that the sum of real incomes created in current production plus past savings could buy. Likewise, credit (over) expansion can enable them to invest temporarily more capital than really accumulated surplus-value (plus depreciation allowances and recovered value of raw materials) would have enabled them to invest (the first part of the formula refers to net investments; the second to gross investment).

But all this is only true temporarily. In the longer run, debts must be paid; and they are not automatically paid through the results of expanded output and income made possible by credit expansion. Hence the risk of a Krach, of a credit or banking crisis, adding fuel to the mass of explosives which cause the crisis of overproduction.

Does Marx's theory of crisis imply a theory of an inevitable final collapse of capitalism through purely economic mechanisms? A controversy has raged around this issue, called the 'collapse' or 'breakdown' controversy. Marx's own remarks on the matter are supposed to be enigmatic. They are essentially contained in the famous chapter 32 of volume I of Capital entitled 'The historical tendency of capitalist accumulation', a section culminating in the battle cry: 'The expropriators are expropriated'. But the relevant paragraphs of that chapter describe in a clearly non-enigmatic way, an interplay of 'objective' and 'subjective' transformations to bring about a downfall of capitalism, and not a purely economic process. They list among the causes of the overthrow of capitalism not only economic crisis and growing centralisation of capital, but Also the growth of exploitation of the workers and their indignation and revolt n the face of that exploitation, as well as the growing level of skill, organisation and unity of the working class. Beyond these general remarks, Marx, however, does not go.

10. Marx and Engels on the Economy of Post-Capitalist Societies

Marx was disinclined to comment at length about how a socialist or communist economy would operate. He thought such comments to be essentially speculative. Nevertheless, in his major works, especially the Grundrisse and Das Kapital, there are some sparse comments on the subject.

Marx returns to them at greater length in two works he was to write in the final part of his life, his comments on the Gotha Programme of united German social-democracy, and the chapters on economics and socialism he wrote or collaborated with for Engels' Anti-Dühring (1878). Generally his comments, limited and sketchy as they are, can be summarised in the following points.

Socialism is an economic system based upon conscious planning of production by associated producers (nowhere does Marx say: by the state), made possible by the abolition of private property of the means of production. As soon as that private property is completely abolished, goods produced cease to be commodities. Value and exchange value disappear. Production becomes production for use, for the satisfaction of needs, determined by conscious choice (ex ante decisions) of the mass of the associated producers themselves. But overall economic organisation in a postcapitalist society will pass through two stages.

In the first stage, generally called 'socialism', there will be relative scarcity of a number of consumer goods (and services), making it necessary to measure exactly distribution based on the actual labour inputs of each individual (Marx nowhere refers to different quantities and qualities of labour; Engels explicitly rejects the idea that an architect, because he has more skill, should consume more than a manual labourer). Likewise, there will still be the need to use incentives for getting people to work in general. This will be based upon strict equality of access for all trades and professions to consumption. But as human needs are unequal, that formal equality masks the survival of real inequality. In a second phase, generally called 'communism', there will be plenty, i.e. output will reach a saturation point of needs covered by material goods. Under these circumstances, any form of precise measurement of consumption (distribution) will wither away. The principle of full needs satisfaction covering all different needs of different individuals will prevail. No incentive will be needed any more to induce people to work. 'Labour' will have transformed itself into meaningful manyfold activity, making possible all-round development of each individual's human personality. The division of labour between manual and intellectual labour, the separation of town and countryside, will wither away. Humankind will be organised into a free federation of producers' and consumers' communes.

The Character of Our Crisis and Our Response

Alan Thornett

One of the problems in writing about this particular crisis is that it is moving so fast that before you get to the final page new events have happened which need to be taken into account. In the past few days in completing this article the government has taken a majority shareholding in the Lloyds HBOS Group and unemployment figures for the USA show that 650,000 American workers were thrown out of work in the month of February. In Britain the banking crisis is getting worse and the CBI has just announced that they expect one in tem workers in the UK to loose their jobs during 2009.

This purpose of this text, however, is not to attempt to list every event but to look a bit deeper into a number of aspects of the crisis: its general character; the governmental responses; the turn to interventionism; the role of Obama in the USA; the role of Brown in Britain; nationalisation and what it represents, and the response of the working class in Britain to the crisis. It ends with a discussion as to how the left should respond to the crisis, its attitude to government policy, and the kind of demands it should put forward.

The origins and severity of the crisis

The origins of the crisis are arguably the most straightforward aspect of it. Two and a half decades of casino capitalism: speculation, deregulation and privatisation, under Regan and Thatcher — backed up by Blair and Brown and the rest of them — created a speculative bubble which turned into a credit and banking crisis when the US sub-prime mortgage market, where the most reckless lending regimes were located, collapsed. This brought the global financial structure to the verge of meltdown.

There has also been an ongoing debate as to the severity of the crisis — though most, on all sides, now accept that it is the biggest crisis since the 1930s (though it is not yet on the scale of those in terms of its social effects), which is rapidly moving towards a deep global recession and probably depression. Dramatically escalating bankruptcies, redundancies, unemployment, and house re-possessions, across the globe, make the point clearly enough. We are still at the early stages of the crisis, however, and it is far from clear how far it will go. What is clear is that we stand right on the verge of a major escalation of the effects of the crisis in terms of job loss and redundancy.

The context of the crisis is the unstable economic conditions brought about by the end of the post-war boom in the mid-1970s. These conditions produced a number of severe regional crises over the last 15 years, including the Mexican crisis of 1994, the Asian crisis of 1997, the Russian crisis of 1998 and the Argentine crisis of 2002. The current crisis, however, is qualitatively different and far more globally significant than any of these. And this time it started in the capitalist heartlands of the USA and in Europe.

Although it started in the capitalist heartlands its impact on developing countries has been enormous. In China manufacturing for export has been hit hard both by the fall-off of demand from the west. In Latin America the crisis is expected to increase unemployment by 3 million during 2009. (This needs expanding)

The character of the crisis

It is not just one crisis, of course. The banking crisis coincides with other major global developments which increase its severity and make it far more difficult to resolve or even mitigate. These can be identified as follows:

Firstly there is the impact of emerging countries such as China and India — particularly China since the full restoration of capitalism. The explosive growth of commodity production in China, with its vast labour force under repressive conditions, has been sucking in raw materials, in recent years, from across the globe, particularly oil and steel. This has contributed to a generalised rise in commodity prices across the globe which has hit the living standards of the poor. (In fact China is a crucial player in the situation since it has funded the credit bubble in the USA for nearly two decades by purchasing huge amounts of US treasury bonds. If China sold these bonds the dollar would collapse).

Secondly, the approach of peak oil — or, to be more precise, the beginning of the end of oil reserves which are easy to extract — is another major development and alters the basic arithmetic for oil-based economies. It was the major factor behind the invasion of Iraq, of course, and is the reason US bases are likely to remain after 'withdraw'.

Whilst the crisis has brought the price of oil and gas down the upward pressure exerted by peak oil will remain long term. The conditions of the 1990s where the price of oil fluctuated between $10 and $20 a barrel will not return. The policy of OPEC is to cut production in order to push the price back to around $70 a barrel even during the crisis. Peak oil, therefore, represents a sea change in energy costs for the future.

Thirdly, and most significant, is the ecological crisis and global warming. This is linked directly to the economic crisis of and contributes to making it a systemic crisis. This is ultimately a crisis of much greater significance than that of the economy. Global warming is expanding the deserts, melting the icecaps, drying up rivers, and destroying water reserves. It is disrupting agriculture and reducing agricultural productivity and crop yields. The impact on food prices is obvious. Bio-fuel production compounds the problem Ourby turning food into petrol (ethanol based on sugar and diesel based on vegetable oil etc) and tying up large tracks of land in the process. All this produced food riots in 37 countries during 2008.

Another effect global warming has on the economic crisis is through the impact of extreme weather events on the insurance industry and through it into the banking crisis. Katrina is a prime example. It is not difficult to see what the effects of a Katrina type event would have if it happened now with the banking system in a state of collapse. Big resources are also increasingly required in order to adapt to climate change — even with the most optimistic emission reductions.

The fourth factor is the unprecedented level of globalisation of the world economy. It is not just that the world economy is more integrated than ever before but with the collapse of the Stalinist regimes of the Soviet Union and Eastern Europe at the end of the 1980s and the full integration of China into the world economy since then capitalism now covers the whole globe. Cuba is politically significant but economically irrelevant to the global economy. This makes it a very different crisis to that of the 1930s, which was at a more primitive stage of globalisation and which had the Soviet Union outside of the system.

For all these reasons this is not a 'normal' cyclical crisis, of the capitalist system — although all the contradictions of the system, traditionally identified by Marxists, which drive such crises, exist with full force within it. This is clear in that none of the post-war economic models — Keynesianism, monetarism, or its later neoliberal form, were able to avoid periodic crisis of 'over-production'.

The duel character of the crisis also has implications for the long-term solution we propose as socialists; in other words an ecosocialist solution. We have to argue that capitalism in crisis points towards the need for an alternative society, built by and in the interests of the working class, which is at the same time ecologically sustainable.

Governmental responses

Governments around the world floundered when confronted with the scale of the crisis. None of them had remotely predicted it. Nor did the bankers or the speculators — the so-called masters of the universe. In fact many governments — with Gordon Brown to the fore —had actively promoted the myth that they had now achieved much greater control over capitalism and its contradictions, particularly since the turn of the 21st century. It was the end of boom and bust, as Gordon Brown repeatedly insisted.

The crisis began in the summer of 2007 when the US investment bank Bear Stearns revealed huge losses on the US sub-prime mortgage market — which was the weakest spot in the global bubble, the so-called toxic loans. Soon afterwards Britain experienced its first run on a bank since the 19th century with the mortgage lender Northern Rock. At first Brown tried to hold his long established New Labour neo-liberal line together and avoid intervention. But in February 2008, after weeks of agonising, he grasped the very painful nettle — and nationalised it. It was the first nationalisation in Britain for 30 years and in financial terms one of the biggest ever.

In the summer of 2008 two major US, government backed, mortgage lenders, Fannie Mae and Freddie Mac, collapsed. They were gigantic operations involved in the US mortgage market to the tune of $5.5 trillion. They were simply too big to be allowed to fail and were nationalised by US Treasury Secretary Hank Paulson along the lines of Northern Rock.

The Republican right was horrified. And a number of other major US financial institutions were already in trouble. These included Goldman Sachs, Morgan Stanley, Merrill Lynch and Lehman Brothers. Under pressure from the right Paulson resolved that interventionism had gone far enough and that when the next financial institution failed market forces should be allowed to take their course. It was a seminal decision for the Bush administration.

The next to fail, in mid-September, was Lehman Brothers. It was the fourth largest US investment bank and the one most exposed to sub-prime mortgage losses. (Merrill Lynch collapsed at the same time and was bought up by the Bank of America.) Paulson proceeded to announce that Lehman would not be saved and it promptly folded — with the famous (or infamous) pictures of the staff carrying their boxes to their cars. It was the biggest banking failure in US history at that point and it would have massive consequences. Lehman had assets of $650 billion and was at the centre of as multi-trillion derivatives system.

The shockwaves from Lehman's collapse triggered the biggest worldwide fall on the stock markets since the 1930s, and the pack of cards began to fall. If Lehman's could go to the wall anyone could go to the wall. Its other effect was to paralyse the banking system, with banks refusing to lend to other banks and credit drying up. The US mortgage industry had by now lost a staggering $2.8 trillion in sub-prime write-offs and was in a state of collapse.

Lehman triggered the collapse of AIG — the world's biggest insurance company. It insured the banks against sub-prime losses and was massively exposed. Paulson's initial reaction was to let market forces take it to the wall, but asked JP Morgan and Goldman Sachs to prepare a report on the likely effects of this on the rest of the sector. Their report, delivered almost immediately, was to the effect that the result would be global Armageddon — or in bankers' parlance a "systemic failure" of the global banking system. The scale and consequences of such an event were hard to comprehend. Paulsen didn't hesitate, however. AIG was promptly nationalised with the injection of a total of $150 billion.

Turn to interventionism
The nationalisation of AIG was a turning point in economic policy and it could hardly have been more dramatic. The hard-line monetarist, neoliberal, economic model of Milton Friedman, Ronald Regan and Margaret Thatcher, which has dominated economic policy for the last 30 years had been stopped in its tracks. And this by the actions of a right-wing Republican administration which had held market forces and market deregulation at the level of a religion. Regan's mantra had been that the state was the problem and deregulation the answer. Thatcher had held the same view. Now in place of this was a series of panic measures, designed to avoid the collapse of the banking system, which were more akin to the long discarded reformist economist John Maynard Keynes.

The move was hugely controversial. But the market forces, option — which had been the approach of the US and British governments the first years of the slump of the 1930s, in the period before the second New Deal, was seen as too dangerous to contemplate. It had resulted, at that time, in a wave of protectionism and mass unemployment (10m in the USA) which was only overcome by the Second World War and the reconstruction afterwards.
This dramatic policy change in the USA triggered a series of interventionist moves by governments around the world as they realised the depth of the crisis. This involved stuffing extremely large sums of money down the throats of the bankers in the name of "recapitalisation". In the US Paulson decided to "pump" $200bn into the credit market and the Federal Reserve

announced that it would buy up to $600bn of toxic loans. In early October the US Congress debated a proposal from Paulson to make $800 billion available to prop the mortgage system up. This was the equivalent of the total world defence spending for a year. The Republican right opposed it but it eventually went through despite them. In Britain the Bradford and Bingley was nationalised at the end of October followed by HBOS.

And along side state intervention into the banking system went Keynesian type intervention into the economies in the form of interest rate cuts, tax cuts, government spending programmes, and other fiscal stimuli, aimed at boosting the economy by spending money.

In October the head of the IMF, Dominique Strauss-Kahn, spelled out the imperative behind this. He urged governments to launch spending packages to jump-start economies in order, as he put it, try to avoid a prolonged slump and widespread social unrest. If we are not able to do this, he argued, then violent protest could break out in many countries".

All this reflects a remarkable ability, on the part of the bourgeoisie internationally, whatever the particular colour of the government, to act to defend their system of society at the expense of the working class using the best option they could see. They leave the leadership of the workers' movement a long way behind as far as defending their own class is concerned.

The G20 met in Washington in mid-December on the initiative of Brown and Sarkozy to take it a stage further. They proposed what was dubbed Bretton Woods 2. (The original Bretton Woods established the IMF and the World Bank and ended the gold standard.) They presented it as their 'master plan' to stabilise the world economy by a return to higher levels of regulation of financial services.

The main opposition to interventionism in Europe, at that stage, was German Finance Minister Peter Steinbrueck. He accused Brown of going all the way from free-market economics to "crass Keynesianism". The British Tories also nailed their colours to the market forces mast, and still do, opening up the first real policy division between them and new Labour for many years.

By the end of last year what started as a banking crisis began to hit manufacturing and retail in a big way. The giant US carmakers Chrysler and General Motors appealed to Congress for a massive bailout along the lines of those afforded to the banks. Again the Bush administration agonised and then conceded. When the Republicans blocked his aid package Bush bypassed them and authorised $24 billion to keep the two car firms going until March.

Similar interventionist moves were made across Europe most notably in cars and steel. France provided carmakers with £2.5 billion in aid. The German government began subsidising the purchase of new cars by paying for old ones to be scrapped. In Britain Peter Mandelson announced a totally inadequate £2.3 billion package of EU grants and loans for the car and steel industries. In the US GM was bankrupt again by February and was back for another $20 billion and Obama was forced to respond.

Some of these packages of aid have conflicted with EU rules, which impose a strict limitation on state-aid for industry. This is part of a much wider problem created by the crisis, however, as member states revert to their national interests and the survival of their 'own' industries rather than relating to the requirements of European integration. At the same time some of the new accession states of Eastern Europe are being hit so hard by the crisis that they could become failed states and be forced out of the euro zone, creating a major political crisis for the EU. The European banking system is in any case in a state of collapse.

New Labour in Britain
The banking crisis broke out again in full force in Britain in mid-January forcing Brown into a new round of bailouts in the financial sector. By February 2009 a trillion dollars have been handed over to the bankers worldwide and $1.5 trillion had been injected in fiscal stimuli. By the end of February RBS had turned in the biggest loss in corporate history and Lloyds was £10bn in the red thanks to toxic loans it inherited from HBOS. Citigroup, the world's biggest banking group was collapsing and the situation getting worse by the day.

New Labour is a part of the international interventionist consensus; of course (Brown would claim a leading part). They are therefore seeking to hold the banking system together whilst spending their way out of the crisis by building up debt and printing money. They have nationalised various banks with massive cash injections, they have cut interest rates to the record low 0.5%, they have cut VAT to 15%, and now they have turned to quantitative easing to the tune of a huge £75 billion over the next three months in an attempt to boost consumer spending and get the banks to lend money. This is a figure approaching the annual budget of the NHS and is clearly a last-gasp measure to prevent a slump. It is also a shot in the dark in what is completely new economic territory. And they are clocking up more debt under conditions where Britain already owes a record £2 trillion.

This severely limits their scope for fiscal stimuli and makes the problem of eventual repayment more awesome.

And they are doing all this, of course, as part of their anti-working class new labour project. It is some kind of marriage between Keynesian economics and right wing politics, and it creates huge contradictions. Whilst they are nationalising banks they are at the same time part-privatising Royal Mail. Local authorities, Labour as well as Tory, are privatising everything that is left that they can get their hands on under the impact of the crisis. Their overarching approach to the crisis, however, is interventionist Under these conditions the overall character of the Brown Government remains the same: new Labour. Brown, whilst intervening into the economy continues to support the war drive and attack public services, welfare rights, civil liberties, wages, pensions and working conditions just as he did before. Sarkozy and Merkel do the same.

The role of Obama
Far more important than what Brown does, though, from a global point of view, is the role of Obama in the USA. His election represents an important shift US politics and would have done so even without the economic crisis — assuming he could have won the election without the crisis. He will act consistently on behalf of US imperialist policy; of course, there is no doubt about that. This is already clear both from the scandalous way he allowed the blitz of Gaza to continue without comment in the run up to his inauguration and his policy of boosting the war brutal in Afghanistan.

On social policy, however, he represents a break with the bush era. And the significance of this has increased sharply with the escalation of the economic crisis. The $787 billion economic stimulus package he has launched — which was opposed almost unanimously by the Republicans — is the biggest in the world other than China and is already an international benchmark for interventionism. It is likely to become even more so as the crisis deepens.

True some of his campaign proposals for renewable energy have been watered down. And it is clearly already inadequate to the scale of the problem. But overall it is a big turn round from anything the Bush administration could have produced. And his package is linked to his $2.5 trillion budget, which reverses some of the policies of the Bush era and makes major proposals such as the reform of health care. Whether such proposals ever come to fruition is another matter of course, but we should not underestimate what Obama represents.

Brown sees his best chance at the present time in climbing aboard Obama's bandwagon. No doubt he will seek a joint proposal on tackling the crisis with Obama at the G20 meeting in London in April.

The politics of the fight back
The central political issue thrown up by the crisis is who will be made to pay for it, capital or labour. In this regard the two options that capitalist governments have been debating — market forces or interventionism — are no different. They are both designed to make the working class pay and give capitalism a new lease of life.

This does not mean, however, that the immediate impact of the two options on the working class are the same or that the opportunities that each presents for building a fight back are the same.

From this point of view socialists should welcome the 'New deal' interventionist approach in as far as it saves some industries, saves some jobs, and gives some relief to the working class in the depth of a crisis of the system. It does of course raise as many questions as it answers. We have to demand that it goes much further than Obama or Brown, or any of the others, is prepared to go. We have to demand programmes of public works which can employ and reemploy millions of workers. It can be done. If trillions of pounds can be given to the banks the same can be done for programmes of pubic works. Why not? And we have to demand that such public works are directed towards establishing a more sustainable society for the future, in order that the ecological crisis is tackled at the same time.

We should welcome this approach, as opposed to that of market forces which would send the weakest to the wall and many more millions on the dole, not only because it creates the best immediate conditions for the working class but because it creates the space in which to build a fight back. The more workers are thrown into unemployment and atomised as individuals the more difficult it will be to begin to organise. On the other hand if workers remain employed or are taken on for public infrastructure work they are in a far stronger position.

Nationalisation
The key to developing a socialist approach to this crisis is nationalisation — which takes the issue to the political level. And there is a big opportunity in this regard. The perception of nationalisation, which was discredited by Labour in the 1970s and 1980s and demonised by the Tories in the same period, has been transformed in the course of this crisis out of all recognition. It has gone from an issue discussed in socialist circles to a part of the main-

stream debate on the response to the crisis. When leading members of the US government (first the Bush regime and now Obama) discuss how much of banking and even of industry to nationalise its clear that something has changed.

This opens up a space for the left which to which it has a responsibility to respond. It gives the opportunity not only to demand that governments intervene into the crisis but that the framework for their intervention should be nationalisation. Nationalisation does not equal socialism, of course, but it does open a space in which socialist ideas and a wider socialist programme can be developed.

There are many things wrong with recent nationalisations of course. They are the nationalisation of bankrupt companies, carried out in order to socialise risk and bail out debt, and with the intention of handing them back at a later date. Many of them are not nationalisations in the formal sense but simply government majority shareholdings, which can be sold off at any time. And not only is there very little control exercised over these institutions but Brown is making it clear that he does not want to exercise control if he can possibly avoid it.

It would be a big mistake, however, in the current circumstances, for socialists to say either that such nationalisations are irrelevant or that they are unsupportable. Rather socialists should welcome the nationalisation of financial and other institutions as far as they go, whatever form they take, as better than the alternative — which is to leave it to market forces. At the same time socialists should strongly oppose any adverse conditions imposed on the workforce in the course of the takeover and vigorously demand that the initial takeover is replaced by full nationalisation under democratic control.

And the arguments for full nationalisation under democratic control are overwhelming and extremely popular. There has been a wide-ranging debate in the mainstream media about it. It has been a popular reaction. If huge sums of money are being injected into bankrupted companies it makes no sense at all to do it without full democratic control of the process and of the future development of those industries. Socialists need to put themselves at the centre of this debate. A year ago it didn't exist.

At the same time the preference given to the banks when it comes to state aid should also come to an end. Other industries have an equal need and this must be met. In many cases nationalisation is the only framework in which a solution can be found. It is the only framework which can provide any kind of answer to an industry like car manufacture which is faced with a very bleak future in its present form and which needs a serious programme to change it over to socially and environmentally useful production.

All this implies a big campaign by the labour movement and the trade unions around both the demand for nationalisation and the form it should take, which is not happening at the present time. The Peoples Charter, which is launched this week, would be a good starting point for such a campaign.

The response of the working class to the crisis

Given the scale of the crisis almost anything is possible in response. So many people are getting hurt that we are in uncharted territory. To repeat a point from above, we are still at the beginning of the crisis and are about to see a dramatic increase in unemployment worldwide as the events of the past three months come to fruition. Upheavals seem inevitable. The problem is what form will they take and will they defend the interests of the working class.

Already there has been a backlash against the effects of the crisis across Europe and beyond. France and Greece have been in the forefront but there has also been protects and action from Spain and Italy to Ireland where over a hundred thousand responded to a trade union call to demonstrate and where 300 workers are in occupation at Waterford Chrystal. There have been general strikes in Martinique and Guadeloupe and strikes and protests in Russia and Eastern Europe.

How this will play out in Britain, however it is harder to say. Some of the tabloids are predicting riots on the streets in the summer. It is one possible development. It is certainly a provocative situation. Those getting most money from the government, i.e. the bankers, are the very people most responsible for the crisis.

The situation with the unions, however, is verging on disastrous. The leaders of the major unions have nothing to say about the crisis. Nor has the TUC. They have reverted to defending their own patch — if they do anything at all. Mostly they do nothing at all — or worse, they negotiate away hard won wages and conditions in give-back deals to 'save jobs'. Every day the media carries new announcements of closures and job losses, often by the tens of thousands, and the unions are nowhere to be seen.

That trade unionists are looking for an alternative to this kind of disastrous leadership is demonstrated by the remarkable vote for Jerry Hicks in the election for General Secretary of Amicus. He came second with 39,000 votes on the basis of a radical platform which spelled out a strong and detailed response to the crisis.

There have also been some welcome protests around the privatisation of Royal Mail and the strikes by construction workers at oil refineries and power stations. The construction strikes were, in my view, confused and even problematic. But they were at least a reaction to the growing threat to jobs as the strikers perceived it. Elsewhere there is very little happening. Even in other parts of the construction and building industry the situation is absolutely dire. Swinging wage cuts are being routinely imposed, at will, on bricklayers, steel erectors carpenters and other trades right across the industry.

It is similar across a range of industries from manufacturing to retail to service industries and financial services. Previous recessions have hit the blue-collar sectors the hardest with white-collar jobs generally a safer prospect. Not so this time. Everyone is being hit from bank workers to steel workers.

There has been the scandal of the sacking of agency workers in Cowley at an hours notice with no redundancy pay. Not only did the unions refuse to defend them but it was the unions who told them that there was nothing which could be done because it was beyond everyone's control — including the management's control. Yet the unions in Cowley were built in the 1950s and 1960s out of very militant strikes against pre-emptive redundancies. After that car employers had to pay heavily to get redundancies through. Now the wheel has turned the full circle and instant dismissal is back.

Not only are people being thrown onto the dole but widespread givebacks taking place. Many unions are accepting wage cuts, longer hours, higher work rates and unpaid overtime as an attempt to save the firm.

In Birmingham workers at LDV Vans have voted to accept a 10% wage cut, a three day week and the cancellation of their bonus in a deal to 'save jobs'. At Land Rover/Jaguar workers voted to accept a package of cuts, recommended by the unions, which involved a four-day double day shift with no shift premium, a cut of one hours pay, no pay increase in 2009, and an increase in pension contributions. Staff employees are required to work three hours extra per week for no extra pay, accept full flexible working across all sites in the West Midlands, along with cuts in sick pay, holiday pay, and maternity entitlement.

What is taking place in Britain at the present time is probably the biggest attack on wages jobs and working conditions since Thatcher started it in the 1980s. If the unions fail to organise against it we could see a response which bypasses the unions, at least in its initial stages — and possibly amongst young people. Job prospects for young people are plummeting and in the summer the highest number of graduates ever will leave university without the prospect of the job. If this takes place the task will be to bring the unions on board and widen and develop the fight back.

But any fight back will also need a political expression, which makes the building of a broad political alternative to new Labour, which can articulate a response to the crisis, even more urgent. In Britain Respect is clearly the starting point for such a development along with broad initiatives such as the Peoples Charter.

At the end of the day if the working class does not defend its interests — through the unions or otherwise — capitalism will go ahead with its own solutions at the expense of working people. There is never a crisis that capitalism is incapable of resolving providing it is at liberty to impose the conditions on the working class necessary for its solution.

Bailout the people not the bankers
We say:

- Halt all further privatisations by either government or local authorities.
- Halt the attack on wages, working conditions and pension rights.
- Halt all giveback negotiations. Uphold and defend trade union agreements.
- No social dumping.
- Halt all house re-possessions for mortgage arrears. Transfer houses to local authority stock and rent them back at affordable rents.
- No attacks on public services. Defend them by taxing the rich.

For a massive, trade union backed, campaign for public ownership including:

(a) The nationalisation of all banks and financial institutions under democratic control.
(b) The nationalisation of bankrupt industries under democratic control to preserve jobs.

For a green new deal in the shape of a crash programme of public works to combat the recession, create new green collar jobs, and to build a new sustainable energy infrastructure. This to include:

(a) A crash programme to construct a sustainable, publically owned, energy infrastructure based on wind, wave, and solar power which could create a million new jobs in manufacture, construction and engineering.
(b) A crash programme to build new sustainable publically owned transport systems which could create hundreds of thousands of new jobs.
(c) The renovation and insulation of housing to conserve energy — which could also create hundreds of thousands of new jobs.
(d) A major programme of job conversion to socially useful production for industries such as car manufacture.

An extensive programme of publicly owned and financed house building to avoid another housing bubble.

Open the books of both the financial and industrial companies to public scrutiny in order to prevent the use of the crisis to force through cost-cutting and redundancies.

A full government guarantee for pension rights. Future pensions to be paid for by taxing the rich and not to be reliant on returns from shares and bonds. Current pensioners to be compensated for loss of income resulting from interest rate reductions.

Control over international financial speculation both through controls on capital movements and through taxation.

March 2009

Acknowledgements

Taking the measure of the crisis by François Sabado

This report was presented at the meeting of the Executive Bureau of the Fourth International in November 2008, and appeared in the November on the on-line edition of International Viewpoint.

The limits of green Keynesianism by Sean Thompson

This article is based on a talk given to a meeting of the Green Left in November 2008. The Green left is an ecosocialist anti-capitalist current with the Green Party

Sub-Prime Driven Recession: Coming Soon To a Neighbourhood Near You by Raphie de Santos

First published as a pamphlet by the Scottish Socialist Party in May 2008

A crash course in capitalism by Claudio Katz

This article was first published in the Argentinian review "Herramienta", number 39 of October 2008.

Capitalism's worst crisis since 1930 by Joel Geier

This article first appeared in the Nov-Dec issue of the International Socialist Review, a publication of the International Socialist Organisation in the USA.

Toxic capitalism by Michel Husson

This article first appeared in the November on-line edition of International Viewpoint.

The climatic crisis will combine with the crisis of capital... by François Chesnais
This article was first published in the Argentinian review "Herramienta", number 39 of October 2008.

Ecology and the transition from capitalism to socialism by John Bellamy Foster
This article first appeared in the November 2008 issue of Monthly Review. It is a revised version of an address delivered at the "Climate Change, Social Change" conference, Sydney, Australia, April 12, 2008, organised by Green Left Weekly.

Lenin for our time by Paul Leblanc
This article was especially written for Socialist Resistance.

Basic theories of Karl Marx by Ernest Mandel
Originally published in John Eatwell, Murray Milgate & Peter Newman (eds.), Marxian economics, London 1990.

SOCIALIST RESISTANCE
PUBLICATIONS

Socialist Resistance is engaged in a programme of publishing a new range of books. Some are reprinted, with new introductions; others are new collections of writings on issues vital to the left today.
Shown here are:
Karl Kautsky's seminal analysis of the foundations of Christianity;
collected writings on ecosocialism, edited by Jane Kelly & Sheila Malone;
Ron Ridenour's sequel to his *Cuba at the Crossroads*;
a discussion with John Holloway's argument on state power,
edited by Phil Hearse;
and a collection of writings on Israel, Palestine and the Middle East
over a 60-year period, edited by Roland Rance and Terry Conway.

These can all be ordered from Socialist Resistance
or online from Amazon (www.amazon.co.uk)

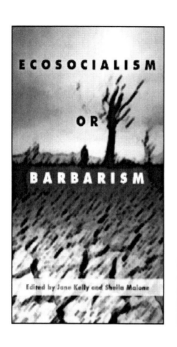

ECOSOCIALISM
OR
BARBARISM

Edited by Jane Kelly and Sheila Malone

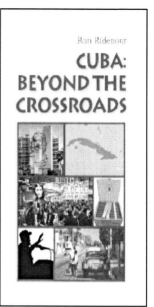

Ron Ridenour

CUBA:
BEYOND THE
CROSSROADS

TAKE THE
POWER TO
CHANGE
THE WORLD

GLOBALISATION AND THE DEBATE ON POWER

Edited with an introduction by Phil Hearse

Middle East:
war, imperialism,
and ecology
Sixty years of
resistance

PROMISED LAND
CLOSED
MILE

Edited by Roland Rance
and Terry Conway